1 MO**Ɍ**

FREE
READING

at

www.ForgottenBooks.com

By purchasing this book you are eligible for one month membership to ForgottenBooks.com, giving you unlimited access to our entire collection of over 700,000 titles via our web site and mobile apps.

To claim your free month visit:

www.forgottenbooks.com/free512325

ISBN 978-0-260-59761-8
PIBN 10512325

For support please visit www.forgottenbooks.com

" . . . . the Lord called Samuel : and he answered, Here am I.

And he ran unto Eli, and said, Here am I ; for thou calledst me. And he said, I called not, lie down again. And he went and lay down.

And the Lord called yet again, Samuel. And Samuel arose and went to Eli, and said, Here am I ; for thou didst call me. And he answered, I called not, my son ; lie down again.

Now Samuel did not yet know the Lord, neither was the word of the Lord yet revealed unto him.

And the Lord called Samuel again the third time. And he arose and went to Eli, and said, Here am I ; for thou didst call me. And Eli perceived that the Lord had called the child.

Therefore Eli said unto Samuel, Go, lie down : and it shall be, if he call thee, that thou shalt say, Speak, Lord ; for thy servant heareth. So Samuel went and lay down in his place.

And the Lord came, and stood, and called as at other times, Samuel, Samuel. Then Samuel answered, Speak ; for thy servant heareth.

And the Lord said to Samuel, Behold, I will do a thing in Israel, at which both the ears of every one that heareth it shall tingle."

First Book of Samuel.

BY HIS SON
HENRY GEORGE, JR.

THE LIFE OF
HENRY GEORGE

FIRST AND SECOND PERIODS

NEW YORK: DOUBLEDAY
PAGE & COMPANY ⸙ 1904

TO ALL WHO STRIVE FOR
THE REIGN OF JUSTICE

For it is not for knowledge to enlighten a soul that is dark of itself; nor to make a blind man to see. Her business is not to find a man eyes, but to guide, govern and direct his steps, provided he have sound feet, and straight legs to go upon. Knowledge is an excellent drug, but no drug has virtue enough to preserve itself from corruption and decay, if the vessel be tainted and impure wherein it is put to keep.

Montaigne.

First Period.
- FORMATION OF THE CHARACTER.

Second Period.
FORMULATION OF THE PHILOSOPHY.

Third Period.
PROPAGATION OF THE PHILOSOPHY.

His form and cause conjoined, preaching to stones,
Would make them capable. — *Hamlet*.

CONTENTS.

FIRST PERIOD.

CONTENTS

✿

SECOND PERIOD.

CONTENTS

CHAPTER IV.

CHAPTER V.

CHAPTER VI.

CHAPTER VII.

CHAPTER VIII.

CHAPTER IX.

CHAPTER X.

❦

THIRD PERIOD.

CHAPTER I.

CONTENTS

CONTENTS

CHAPTER XI.

CHAPTER XII.

CHAPTER XIII.

CHAPTER XIV.

Now I saw in my dream that they went on, **and** Greatheart before them.

Bunyan's " Pilgrim's Progress."

LIST OF ILLUSTRATIONS

LIST OF ILLUSTRATIONS

FIRST PERIOD

FORMATION OF THE CHARACTER

Reduced facsimile of page of original manuscript of
" Progress and Poverty," Book II, Chap. III.

CHAPTER I.

BIRTH AND EARLY TRAINING.

1839-1855.   To the 16th Year.

HENRY GEORGE was born on September 2, 1839,[1] in a little two story and attic brick house, yet standing in a good state of preservation, in Philadelphia, Pa., on Tenth Street, south of Pine, not half a mile from the old State House where the Declaration of Independence was signed.

His father's blood was English, with a tradition of Welsh; his mother's blood English and Scottish. In the main he came of middle-class stock. The only persons among his ancestors who achieved any distinction were his grandfathers; on his mother's side, John Vallance, a native of Glasgow, Scotland, who became an engraver of repute in this country in the early days of the republic and whose name may be seen on some of the commissions signed by President Washington; and on his father's side, Richard George, born in Yorkshire, England, who was one of the well-known shipmasters of Philadelphia when that city was the commercial metropolis of the new world.

Captain George married Mary Reid, of Philadelphia, and to them were born three children, the youngest of

[1] John Stuart Mill was then in his thirty-fourth year and .
Adam Smith had been forty-nine years dead.

whom, Richard Samuel Henry, in New Brunswick, New Jersey, in 1798. This Richard Samuel Henry George became the father of Henry George, the subject of the present volume. In 1873, on the day preceding his seventy-fifth natal anniversary, he wrote his son Henry a letter of reminiscences, of which the following serves to show the man and the early conditions in Philadelphia:

"I have seen all the Presidents, from Washington down to the present, Grant—that is, I cannot say I saw Washington, who died in December, 1799, but I think, although an infant, that I saw his sham funeral. . . .

"I go back to 1810, during Jefferson's long embargo. Then Front Street, Philadelphia, was what Chestnut Street is now—the fashionable thoroughfare of the city. All the principal merchants lived on Front Street and on Water Street above South. Below South lived mostly sea captains, all handy to business.

"Your grandfather had two ships, the *Medora* and *Burdo Packet,* and during the embargo and the war with England they were housed in; and from the navy yard down to the Point House, now called Greenwich, all the principal ships in port were housed in and hauled up on the mud, with noses touching the bank.

"Although times were hard, I did not feel them. I had a pleasant, happy home, let me tell you. The first thing to be done was to provide for winter. Wood was burned for cooking and heating. Your grandfather would purchase a sloop-load of wood, so that I had a good time helping to throw it down cellar. We would have enough to last all winter and late into the spring. Then there was a supply of beef to corn and two or three hogs to cut up. That was a grand time! We had a smokehouse at one corner of the yard, and when father had cut up the hogs we would have a number of hams to smoke and cure. I do not taste such now, nor ever will again. At hog time mother made all sorts of good things —scrapel, sausage and all that hog could do for man. And didn't I go in for it all with the rest of the boys,

House where Henry George was born,
east side of Tenth Street, south of Pine, Philadelphia.

for father had four 'prenticed boys and two girls in the kitchen, all in good tune and happy. We had all sorts of songs and wonderful stories, both of the sea and of the land.

"It was at this time (I am sorry I have no dates) that my father arrived at Almond Street wharf from France, to which he had gone with a flag of truce, carrying out a lot of passengers and bringing back a lot. Well, it was Sunday morning, about light, when I was waked up by mother. I asked what was the matter. She said that pop had arrived and that he had on board of the ship General Moreau and family from France;[1] and she wanted to get some fresh provisions for their breakfast. So I took on board lots of things—nice fresh milk and cream, butter, nice bread, chickens, etc.—for the general and his family. I tell you it was hard work getting on board, the crowd was so dense. On Almond Street from Second clear down to the wharf was a line of private carriages with invitations of hospitality. The boys crowded me hard, and one or two fellows I had to fight before I could pass.

"Going so often to the ship, I found I was as much noticed as the general himself. It gave me a big lift among the downtown-gang. I was made captain of a company and had to fight the Mead Alley and Catherine Street boys every Saturday afternoon. Many bricks I got on the head while leading my men (or boys) into battle. . . .

"One fight I had built me right up, and afterwards I was A No. 1 among the boys, and cock of the walk. I went on the principle of *do nothing that you are ashamed of and let no living man impose on you.*

"In my youth I could swim like a duck and skate well. And I was considered a good sailor. I could handle a boat equal to anybody. I got a good amount of praise, both on the Delaware and the Mississippi, for my sea-

---

[1] Jean Victor Moreau, the Republican French general, made famous by the extraordinary retreat through the Black Forest and the brilliant Battle of Hohenlinden, and afterwards exiled by Napoleon's jealousy.

manship. I could go aloft as quick and as handy as any seaman. Going to New Orleans, I often lent a hand on topsails, and could do as well as most of them."

R. S. H. George made this trip to New Orleans when a young man, and there engaged in the dry goods business. Returning to Philadelphia, he settled down and married Miss Louisa Lewis, by whom he had two children, one of whom died while an infant, and the other, Richard, while at boarding school in his twelfth year.[1] Within four or five years after marriage this wife died, and several years later R. S. H. George married another Philadelphia lady, Catherine Pratt Vallance. As has been said, her father was John Vallance, the engraver, born in Glasgow, Scotland. Her mother was Margaret Pratt, born in Philadelphia, but of English extraction. John Vallance died in 1823 leaving his widow, seven daughters and one son in modest means, which Henry Pratt, a wealthy merchant of Philadelphia and first cousin of the widow's father, improved by giving to each of the seven girls a small brick house. These girls received a good boarding school education, and Catherine and Mary were conducting a small private school when Catherine was married to R. S. H. George, who then had a book publishing business.

Mr. George had for several years occupied a good clerical position in the Philadelphia Custom House, and left it in 1831 to enter a book publishing partnership with Thomas Latimer, who had married Rebecca, the eldest of the Vallance girls. The business was confined to the publication and sale of Protestant Episcopal Church and Sunday School books, and for a time became the depository of the General Episcopal Sunday School Union, the Bible

---

[1] There was also an adopted child, Harriet, who, growing up, married J. H. Evans.

and Prayer Book Society and the Tract Society. After two and a half years Thomas Latimer withdrew and others were associated successively in the business, which for seventeen years Richard George carried on, the store for a time being at the north-west corner of Chestnut and Fifth Streets. A contemporary in the business was George S. Appleton, who afterwards went to New York and merged with his brother in a general book publishing and book selling business, under the firm name of D. Appleton & Co.—the same D. Appleton & Co. who, several decades later, were to be the first publishers of "Progress and Poverty."[1] By 1848 the business of the general book houses had encroached so much on denominational business that the latter became unprofitable, and Mr. George withdrew and went back to the Custom House, obtaining the position of Ascertaining Clerk, which he thereafter held for nearly fourteen years.

To the union of R. S. H. George and Catharine Pratt Vallance ten children were born, six girls—Caroline, Jane, Catharine, Chloe, Mary and Rebecca, the last two of whom died early—and four boys—Henry, Thomas, John and Morris—the second child and oldest boy being the subject of this work. Like the son by the former marriage, this boy was named after his father; but as the former bore the name of Richard, the first of the father's three Christian names—Richard Samuel Henry—the last of the names was selected for this son; and as the father desired a short name, complaining of the annoyance to himself of a long one, the simple one of Henry George was chosen.

Henry George's father was a strict churchman. He was a vestryman at St. Paul's Episcopal Church, when

---

[1] This circumstance had nothing to do with their decision to publish the book, as its author was unknown to them.

that church, under the earnest preaching of Dr. Richard Newton, was at the height of its prosperity. The congregation was of the extreme "Low Church" division and regarded "High Church" tendencies with the utmost abhorrence. Sunday was a day for austere devotions—church services morning and afternoon, and frequently in the evening. On other days there were morning and evening family prayers. Rt. Rev. Ignatius F. Horstmann, Catholic Bishop of Cleveland, O., who was a boy in the neighbourhood at the time, has said:[1] "I can recall Henry George going to church every Sunday, walking between his two elder sisters, followed by his father and mother —all of them so neat, trim and reserved."

But that there were occasional breaks in the austerity may be certain. Rev. George A. Latimer, Henry George's cousin, has said:

"Henry George was in my Sunday school class. It was the custom of Dr. Newton to have the children of the church in the main lecture room once a month in the afternoon for catechising. One Sunday the subject was that part of the catechism that declares our duty towards our neighbour, and the special topic, 'to keep my hands from picking and stealing.' Our class was on the front row. The Doctor asked the question: 'Boys, why do the grocerymen have that wire netting over the dried peaches in the barrel at the store door?' Henry George at once answered with a loud voice: 'To keep the flies out.' The Doctor's face turned as red as blood, while at the same time he said: 'Yes, to keep the hands from picking and stealing.'"

Rev. William Wilberforce Newton, son of the rector, who was in this school with Henry George, said in an

---

[1] Letter to "National Single Taxer," Aug. 31, 1898.

Henry George at about five.

From daguerreotype taken in Philadelphia.

address after the latter's death that "that school turned out some remarkable men," naming Bishop Charles R. Hall of Illinois, Bishop Wm. H. Odenheimer of New Jersey, Rev. Wm. W. Farr, Henry S. Getz, Rev. Richard N. Thomas, editor of the "American Church Sunday School Magazine," George C. Thomas, of Drexel & Co. bankers, and Treasurer of the Missionary Society of the Protestant Episcopal Church, and Rev. R. Heber Newton, William Wilberforce Newton's brother. Mr. Newton told this anecdote:

"Our class was located in that part of the church known as the basement, and as we looked out at the window, our view was obstructed by innumerable gravestones.

"My people were extremely hospitable to missionaries. One time Missionary Bishop Payne of Africa came with his wife to our house and staid six weeks. They brought with them a lot of monkeys and other beasts of the tropical clime. We used to have great times among ourselves—the boys of the neighbourhood and the monkeys and the dumb animals—playing 'firemen.' One day we were having a parade. There was no flag. So I went into the house and got a Sunday school banner with an illustration of Paul preaching at Ephesus. It was not exactly appropriate, but it answered the purpose. Henry George insisted upon carrying the banner which all the boys thought a good deal of.

"As our firemen's parade was turning the corner of the house that day, Henry George heard my father say to the missionary that if he saw anything about the house that he thought would be of service to him in Africa he was welcome to it, and the missionary replied that he thought the tool chest would come in handy. George passed the word along the line and very soon our parade was broken up and we became an army of warriors for the protection of that tool chest. But it went to Africa just the same."

At the time of his son Henry's birth, the book business enabled Mr. George to keep his family in comfort. Giving care to his children's education, he sent them as they grew old enough to Mrs. Graham's private school, on Catharine Street near Third, the family having moved from Tenth Street to the west side of Third Street, three doors north of Queen, where they remained for nearly twenty-five years. After three years at Mrs. Graham's, and when he was in his ninth year, the eldest son, Henry, was sent to a public school, Mount Vernon Grammar, where Ignatius Horstmann attended in a class above him. A year later, in 1849, he was sent to the Episcopal Academy.

This institution, flourishing to-day, was founded in revolutionary times, but seemed to decline until Bishop Alonzo Potter raised it at the end of the forties to first rank as a place of instruction in the city and State. Rev. Dr. Hare was then principal, and the institution was frequently spoken of as Hare's Academy. The Bishop's two sons, Henry C. and E. N. Potter were at the Academy then, and in the years to come were to achieve distinction, the former as the Episcopal Bishop of New York City and the other as president of two colleges successively. R. Heber Newton and William Wilberforce Newton were also fellow students. Dr. Heber Newton remembers the school as being in a most prosperous condition, "the large chapel being quite filled with boys, and the class rooms seemingly well filled, and attendance upon it was esteemed an advantage and a privilege."

But though it was a good school, young George did not stay there long. His father had now ceased to be publisher of Church books, yet he obtained for his son the reduced rate of tuition granted to clergymen's sons. This concession was regarded by the boy as something to

which he was not entitled and he believed that every boy
in the school knew of it; and perhaps it was for this
reason that from the start he did not get along well there.
At any rate, his father, yielding to his entreaties, took
him away and put him in the hands of Henry Y. Lauderbach to be prepared for High school. This short period, Henry George always recognised as the most profitable portion of his little schooling. Mr. Lauderbach had
a way of his own, drawing out and stimulating the individuality of his pupils. Thirty years afterwards he
clearly remembered Henry George as a student remarkable among boys for quickness of thought, originality and
general information. The special training under Lauderbach enabled the youth at little more than thirteen to
enter a class in the High school that was to produce some
notable men in Pennsylvania—Theodore Cramp, ship
builder; Charles W. Alexander, journalist; James Mor-
gan Hart, professor and author; Samuel L. Gracey, Methodist Episcopal clergyman; David H. Lane, a Recorder
of Philadelphia; and William Jenks Fell, Commissioner
of Deeds. This school, like the Episcopal Academy, was
an excellent one, but later in life Henry George said that
while there he was "for the most part idle and wasted
time." Perhaps it was that he had his mind's eye set
on the world outside of school! Perhaps it was that conscious that the growing family was putting a strain on
his father, whose sole income was the $800 salary of a
Custom House clerk, he felt that he should be supporting
himself. It was probably his Uncle Thomas Latimer who
at this time gave him advice of which he spoke in a
speech about thirty years later: "I remember when a boy,
I wanted to go to sea. I talked with a gentleman, who
wanted me to go into business as a boy in a store. I had
nothing, no particular facility, yet I remember his saying

to me: 'If you are honest, if you are steady, if you are industrious, you can certainly look forward to being able to retire at forty with comfort for the rest of your days.' "[1] These words may have had a strong influence on the boy's mind. At any rate, after less than five months in the High School, he induced his father to take him away, to stop his schooling altogether, and put him to work; and he never went to school afterwards. He was then less than fourteen years old.[2] He first obtained employment in the china and glass importing house of Samuel Asbury & Co., at 85 South Front Street, at $2 a week. His duties were to copy, to tie up bundles and to run errands. Afterwards he went into the office of a marine adjuster and did clerical work.

But though he had left school for good, his real education suffered no interruption. In school or out of it, he had acquired a fondness for reading. Or perhaps it was that at his birth, while the Fairies of Gain, Fashion and Pleasure passed him by, one came and sat beside his cradle and softly sang

"Mine is the world of thought, the world of dream;
   Mine all the past, and all the future mine."

First he had a grounding in the Bible; and the Puritanical familiarity with book, chapter and verse, which in the elders moulded speech, established habit, and guided the steps of life, filled the young mind with a myriad of living pictures. Then, though his father while a pub-

---

[1] Speech, " Crime of Poverty," 1885. After uttering the foregoing passage, Mr. George asked: " Who would dare in New York or in any of our great cities, to say that to a young clerk now ? "

[2] At fourteen Adam Smith was attending the University of Glasgow; while John Stuart Mill was learning Greek at three, Latin at eight, logic at twelve and political economy at thirteen,

lisher handled only religious books, and those confined to
the Episcopal Church, there were the strange tales of missionaries in foreign lands to feed the imagination. Afterwards when the father left the book business there was
still an atmosphere of reading about the home, and other
books came in the boy's way. He delighted in history,
travels and adventure, fiction and poetry. While in his
strong democratic principles and practical side, the boy
followed his father, it was in a love of poetry that he resembled his mother, who as an elderly woman could quote
verse after verse and poem after poem learned in her girl-
hood. She manifested at all times an intense fondness
for Scott, and had a taste for Shakespeare, though owing
to her austere principles, she never in her life attended
a Shakesperian play.[1]   This religious ban extended in
the boy's reading to much in the realm of romance and
adventure, such works as the "Scottish Chiefs," for instance, having to be read in the seclusion of his attic bed-
chamber.   But in the open or in the smuggled way books
were obtained, and the old Quaker Apprentice's Library
and the Franklin Institute Library furnished inexhaustible mines of reading matter.   Book after book was de-
voured with a delight that showed that now certainly the
youthful mind was not "idle" nor his "time wasted."   He

---

[1] In a speech in Liverpool many years later (Nov. 30, 1888) Henry
George said : " I was educated in a very strict faith.   My people and the
people whom I knew in my childhood, the people who went to our church
and other churches of the same kind, had a notion that the theatre was a
very bad place, and they would not go to one on any account.   There
was a celebrated fellow-citizen of mine of the name of Barnum.   Barnum
went to Philadelphia, and he recognised that prejudice, and he saw that
although there were a number of theatres running for the ungodly, a
theatre he could get the godly to go to would pay extremely well.   But
he did not start a theatre.   Oh, no ! He started a lecture room, and we
had in that lecture room theatrical representations, and it was crowded
every night in the week and there were two matinées."

absorbed information as the parched earth a summer shower, and what he thus took in he retained. To this fondness for reading he always ascribed the beginning of his real education and the commencement of his career.

And what came like enchantment to his mind and supplemented his reading were popular scientific lectures at the Franklin Institute. This institution, named after the famous townsman, Benjamin Franklin, and incorporated in 1824 for "the promotion and encouragement of manufactures and the mechanic and useful arts," in the forties and fifties took first rank in scientific learning in the city, which at the same time was without peer in this country for its public libraries, museums and private cabinets. Of the Institute, Henry George's uncle, Thomas Latimer, was a member. To him the boy was indebted for access to the lectures—lectures that revealed the wonders of the physical sciences in simple language and magic lantern pictures. Like a torch they lit up the young understanding and made a fitting attendant to that university of reading to which he was of his own volition applying himself.

This reading fed a desire that his father's stories and the tales and traditions about his grandfather had kindled in him for the sea. "One of our chief play grounds," Rev. W. W. Newton has said, "was about the wharves of the city. He had a friend who was a sea captain and I a cousin, and both of us had our minds set on a sea voyage." Mr. George encouraged in his son an active life, going to see him skate and swim. One day he saved him from drowning by putting down his cane when the boy had dived under a float. Though a strict churchman, the father could not forget his own early warlike days and was not averse to having his boy fight in just quarrels. But it was the shipping that chiefly interested fa-

From daguerreotype taken about the time that
Henry George, less than fourteen, left
school and went to work.

ther and son, and as they strolled along the river-piers together, the father talked about hull and rig, wind and weather, and the wonders of sea and foreign lands, so that the wharves had a fascination for the boy, and it was around them that with Willie Newton or Bill Horner, Col and Charley Walton and Will Jones he spent much of his play time, climbing about vessels, going swimming or sailing toy boats. And this was not all idle play, but served its purposes in later life, for the boy's powers of observation and reasoning were in constant exercise.[1]

After a while, when the boy left the crockery house and went into the marine adjuster's office, the desire for the sea increased so much that he went to his cousin, George Latimer, who was ten years older than himself, and asked him to speak in his behalf to an acquaintance of the fam-

---

[1] "When I was a boy I went down to the wharf with another boy to see the first iron steamship which had ever crossed the ocean to our port. Now, hearing of an iron steamship seemed to us then a good deal like hearing of a leaden kite or a wooden cooking stove. But, we had not been long aboard of her, before my companion said in a tone of contemptuous disgust: 'Pooh! I see how it is. She's all lined with wood; that's the reason she floats.' I could not controvert him for the moment, but I was not satisfied, and sitting down on the wharf when he left me, I set to work trying mental experiments. If it was the wood inside of her that made her float, then the more wood the higher she would float; and mentally I loaded her up with wood. But, as I was familiar with the process of making boats out of blocks of wood, I at once saw that, instead of floating higher, she would sink deeper. Then I mentally took all the wood out of her, as we dug out our wooden boats, and saw that thus lightened she would float higher still. Then, in imagination, I jammed a hole in her, and saw that the water would run in and she would sink, as did our wooded boats when ballasted with leaden keels. And thus I saw, as clearly as though I could have actually made these experiments with the steamer, that it was not the wooden lining that made her float, but her hollowness, or as I would now phrase it, her displacement of water."— Lecture on "The Study of Political Economy" at University of California, March 9, 1877.

ily, a young man named Samuel Miller who was mate
and whose father was captain of the ship *Hindoo*. No
better insight into the habits of the boy and of his constant thought of the sea can be obtained than from extracts from a short journal that he kept at the beginning
of 1855, probably at the suggestion of his uncle, Thomas
Latimer. Though then scarcely more than fifteen, and
although he had spent all his life in a town of brick houses
and perhaps had never more than seen the ocean, he noted
wind and weather with the care of a veteran sea captain.
Incidentally the journal shows the important part the
lectures at the Franklin Institute were playing:

"Jan. 7, Mon. Rose at 6. Went to store. Evening
went to lecture.

"Jan. 8, Tues. to Fri. Rainy, warm and muddy.

"Jan. 13, Sat. Went to store. Coming home stopped
in at library. Saw in 'New York Herald': 'Arrived,
Ship *Hindoo*, Miller; Canton, July 22; Angier, Sept.
28; Cape Good Hope, Nov. 6; St. Helena, ——. Was
68 to Angier. In month of August only made 200 miles
against S.W. monsoon and strong northerly currents.'
I have been expecting her for some time. Stopped at
Latimer's. Got Tom [his brother] and came home.
Little Augustine, the Chilian boy from the ship *Bow-
ditch*, came. He found his way alone. Only been here
once before, on Tuesday night. Went up to Mrs. Mc-
Donald's and got my pants. Went with Augustine to
buy a collar.

"Jan. 14, Sun. Clear and cold, wind N.W. Went
to Sunday school with Charley Walton. Mr. Newton
preached good sermon. Was coming home, corner of
Third and Catharine met Augustine. After dinner
took him up to Uncle Joe's. In evening he came again.
Took him to Trinity Church.

"Jan. 15, Mon. Wind S., moderating. Went to
store. Evening went to lecture. George Latimer said
they had received a letter from Sam Miller saying that
he would be home in a few days.

"Jan. 16, Tues. Wind N.E., clear and warm. George told me he had written to Sam Miller and told him about me.

"Jan. 17, Wed. Cloudy. Wind went around to N.W. and blew up clear. Went to lecture, last on electricity. Augustine at home.

"Jan. 18, Tues. Wind N.W., clear and cold. In evening Augustine and Charley Walton came. Went around to library and up to McDonald's for Cad [Caroline, his sister].

"Jan. 19, Fri. Told Sam that I was going to leave. He gave me $12. . . . In morning met Augustine, who said he had got place on steam tug *America*—$2 a week. Evening went to lecture.

"Jan. 20, Sat. Wind N.E. Last day at store. They expect Sam Miller home to-night.

"Jan. 21, Sun. Wind S., warm, cloudy. Sam Miller did not come home last night. They expect him home next Saturday. Went to Sunday school and Church. Augustine sat in our pew. Took him in afternoon to Sunday school. . . . It blew in the evening very strong and about one o'clock increased to perfeet hurricane, blowing as I never had heard it before from the South.

"Jan. 22, Mon. Took up a basket to the store for crockery Mr. Young said he would give me. . . . In afternoon went down to Navy Yard with Bill Horner. Evening went to lecture. Brought home a lot of crockery.

"Jan. 23, Tues. Wind N.W., clear and cool. Evening went to Thomas's book sale. Bought a lot of six books for seven cents.

"Jan. 24, Wed. Went to lecture in evening, first on climatology. Liked it very much.

"Jan. 25, Thurs. Went to store in morning. . . .

"Jan. 26, Fri. Snowed all the morning. Aunt Rebecca [Latimer] says that Sam Miller did not get George Latimer's letter. George wrote to him again yesterday. He will be here next Wednesday. . . . Cleared off with N.W. wind. In afternoon snow-balled. Went to lecture in evening, first on organic chemistry. Liked it very much.

"Jan. 27, Sat. Went skating morning and afternoon.

"Jan. 28, Sun. Augustine came in the afternoon. He is going to Cuba in Brig *Aucturus* of Union Island.

"Jan. 29, Mon. Went to navy yard and brig [*Aucturus*] in morning. Lecture in evening.

"Jan. 31, Wed. Skating in afternoon. Sam Miller did not come home. Will be home on Saturday morning.

"Feb. 1, Thurs. Skating in afternoon.

"Feb. 2, Fri. Evening went to see the panorama of Europe.

"Feb. 3, Sat. Sam Miller came home yesterday afternoon. Went to George Latimer's office to see him. He says if he goes as captain he will take me. The owners of the *Hindoo* have bought the clipper *Whirlwind*. Both will sail for Melbourne about the middle of March and from there to Calcutta and home. *Hindoo* probably make it in 11 months. *Hindoo* is 25 years old, 586 tons register, 1,200 burden; carries 14 able seamen, cook, steward, two mates and captain—in all 19 men. Sam Miller intends going back to New York on Wednesday. Went skating in afternoon.

"Feb. 5, Mon. Afternoon went to Uncle Dunkin George's office. His boy is sick. Evening Pop met Sam Miller and George Latimer in Chestnut street. . . . Pop asked Sam Miller to tea on Saturday. Very cold.

"Feb. 6, Tues. Very cold; thermometer at Zero.

"Feb. 7, Wed. River blocked up. Commenced snowing. Wind N.E. till night.

"Feb. 8, Thurs. Snowed again all day. In afternoon went sleighing with Uncle Joe Van Dusen.

"Feb. 9, Fri. Clear. Delaware pretty nearly closed. Skated a little on the ice in the afternoon. Saw Augustine on the first ice he had ever been on. Went to Aunt Rebecca Latimer's to tea.

"Feb. 10, Sat. Sam Miller and George and Kate Latimer came about five o'clock and staid to supper. . . . Sam said he had received a letter from his father saying he need not come on to New York until he sent for him.

"Feb. 11, Sun. Clear and cold. Up at Uncle Dunkin's office all the week.

"Feb. 19, Mon.   Came home at night along the wharf.
Saw Augustine on the Brig *Globe* of Bangor, about to
sail for Cuba.   Stopped at Aunt Rebecca's.   Sam Miller had heard nothing from his father.

"Feb. 20, Tues.   Auntie Ann came to our house
to dinner.   Said Sam Miller had heard from his father to go on immediately.   He went on at two
o'clock.   .   .   .

"March 26, Mon.   Uncle Dunkin's in the morning.
Saw in New York papers at Exchange the *Hindoo* ad-
vertised to sail on the 5th of April—a week from next
Thursday.

"March 27, Tues.   Office in morning.   Staid home
in afternoon working on my brig [toy boat].   .   .   .
Before supper went to Aunt Rebecca's.   George received a letter from Captain Miller [Sam Miller, just
made captain].   Said he would sail about Thursday,
April 5, and that he would come on to Philadelphia
on Saturday and stay till Monday and take me with
him.   It surprised them all.

"March 28, Wed.   Went to Uncle Dunkin's in the
morning.   Told him I should not come up any more,
as I had so little time.

"March 31, Sat.   Stayed at home in the morning finishing my brig.   Painted her.   After dinner, my last
dinner at home, went with father and mother to get
our daguerreotypes taken.   Came home and went to
Aunt Rebecca's to supper in company with Cad and
Jennie.   Went home at eight P.M."

Young Samuel W. Miller, then about twenty-five, had
obtained command of the ship *Hindoo*, an old East Indiaman, on which he had formerly sailed as mate under his
father, who was now transferred to a new ship.   At the
suggestion of George Latimer, and after talking with
Henry George's father, he had formally invited young
Henry to sail with him.   For Richard George was a clear-
headed, common-sensed man.   Much as he disliked to
have the boy go to sea, he knew that his son inherited the
longing.   Moreover, knowing the strong, wilful nature of

his son, he feared that if objection was raised the boy might run away, as he had done once before while yet going to school. The lad had made an impertinent reply to his mother, and his father, overhearing it, reproved him with words and a blow. To be struck by his father was so unusual that he was humiliated. He stole away, got his school books and a little cold lunch—all that he could get to eat—and left the house with the resolve never to return again. He remained out until half past nine o'clock that night, when he returned with a tamer spirit and was forgiven. The father had not forgotten this incident, and he was determined that if the boy must go to sea he should go with his parents' consent. So he talked to Captain Miller and suggested to him not to make the boy's berth too comfortable, but to let him see and feel the rigours of a sailor's life, so that by a single voyage the desire for roving should be destroyed. Henry George was then accepted as foremast boy on the *Hïndoo*, bound for Melbourne, Australia, and Calcutta, India.

CHAPTER II.

BEFORE THE MAST.

1855-1856.   AGE, 16-17.

AUSTRALIA and India swam in the boy's fancy as in a shining sea of gold. Australia, the island continent nearly as large as the United States, giving promise of a great rival, English-speaking republic in the southern hemisphere, had riveted attention by its gold discoveries in the early fifties and by the enormous treasure since taken out—equal almost to that of wonderful California. It was the new land of wealth, where poor, obscure men in a day rose to riches. India lay like a counterpoise in the mind's picture. With her jungles and monkeys, tigers and elephants; her painted idols, fantastical philosophies and poppy smokers—this land of mysteries, old when the pyramids of Egypt and Syria were young, shone through partings in her gorgeous tropical foliage with the gleam of gold and precious stones, despite the pillage of the ages. Whatever the boy had read, from Bible to "Arabian Nights," in magazine or in newspaper; and all that he had heard, in lecture or sermon, from traveller or sailor, burned in his imagination and made him eager to be gone.

The *Hindoo* was to sail from New York Harbour early in April. On Sunday, April 1, after Sunday school,

Henry George received a Bible and a copy of "James's Anxious Enquirer"; and the next morning, bidding farewell at the wharf to his father, and uncles Thomas Latimer and Joseph Van Dusen, his cousin George Latimer and his friends Col Walton and Joe Roberts, he and Captain Miller went aboard the steamboat, crossed the Delaware, took train, and four hours afterwards were in New York. Two letters from him, written from the ship before she got away, have been preserved. They are in large, clear, firm hand, with some shading, some flourishes and a number of misspelled words. In the first, under date of April 6, he says:

"I signed the shipping articles at $6 a month and two months' advance, which I got in the morning.

"While we were down town we stopped at the Custom House, and Jim [an ordinary seaman] and I got a protection, for which we paid $1 each to a broker.

"The New York Custom House looks like a cooped up affair along side of the Philadelphia one—there are so many people and so much business and bustle.

"The upper part of New York is a beautiful place— the streets wide, clear and regular; the houses all a brown stone and standing ten or twenty feet from the pavement, with gardens in front."

To the foregoing letter was added this:

April 7, 1855.

"I was stopped [writing] suddenly last night by the entrance of the men to haul her [the vessel] to the end of the wharf and was prevented from going on by their laughing and talking. At about twelve o'clock we commenced and by some pretty hard heaving we got her to the end of the wharf. It was then about two o'clock. So we turned in and slept until about half past five. We got our breakfast, and being taken in tow by a steamboat about 7.30 A.M., proceeded down the stream till off the Battery, where we dropped anchor and now lie.

"The view from this spot is beautiful—the North River and New York Bay covered with sailing vessels and steamers of every class and size, while back, the hills, gently sloping, are covered with country seats. . . .

"I ate my first meals sailor style to-day and did not dislike it at all. Working around in the open air gives one such an appetite that he can eat almost anything. We shall go to sea Monday morning early. I should love to see you all again before I go, but that is impossible. I shall write again to-morrow, and if possible get the pilot to take a letter when he leaves, though it is doubtful that I shall be able to write one."

It was in these days preparatory to starting, when there were a lot of odd things to do, that the boatswain, busy with some splicing, sent the boy for some tar; and when the boy stopped to look around for a stick, the sailor in surprise and disgust cried to him to bring the tar in his hand! Another incident of a similar kind appears in his second letter, which is dated April 9 and is addressed to his Aunt Mary, one of his mother's sisters, a most unselfish and lovable maiden lady who helped raise the large brood of George children, and who, until her death in 1875, had never been separated from her sister, Mrs. George. She was loved as a second mother by the children.

"We are not at sea, as we expected to be by this time, but still lying off the Battery. The ship could not sail this morning for want of seamen. They are very scarce in New York now and all sorts of men are shipping as sailors. Two Dutch boys shipped as able seamen and came on board yesterday afternoon. The smallest one had been to sea before, but the largest did not know the difference between a yard and a block.

The second mate told them to go aloft and slush down the masts. This morning the smallest went up, but the other could not go up at all. So I had to go aloft and do it. The work was a good deal easier than I expected. I don't mind handling grease at all now."[1]

Then the letter proceeds:

"Captain Miller has been ashore all day trying to get men. There is to be one sent on board in place of the largest Dutchman. I pity the poor fellow, though to be sure he had no business to ship as seaman. He says he has four trades—baker, shoemaker, etc. Another man came aboard this morning as able seaman who could not get into the foretop. They sent him ashore. The captain shipped to-day as ordinary seamen two lads, one a Spaniard and the other English, I believe. They are fine sailor looking fellows. The cook, steward and two of the men are from the West Indies. All sailed in whalers. There are no cleaner looking men in Parkinson's.

"We have better living than I expected—fresh and salt beef, potatoes and rice—and all cooked in the finest style; but I cannot like the coffee as yet.

"They have just brought two men aboard and taken the Dutchmen off. This is the last letter that I shall have a chance to send till we get to Melbourne, where I hope there will be letters awaiting me."

April 10.

"We have just been heaving the cable short and shall be ready as soon as the tow boat comes. I hope that by this time Morrie [his baby brother] is well. I could

---

[1] When a boy, his mother would frequently buy a piece of sweet suet and melting it down, would mix with its oil or fat a little bergamot, thereby making a pomade for the hair. Henry George never during his life liked fats with his meat at the table, and at times would say in the family that it was because when a boy he had to put it on his head. Notwithstanding the use of the hair preparation, he and all his brothers followed their father and grew bald early.

spin out four or five pages, but I have not time. I would have written a great many more letters, but could not. When you read this letter you must remember where it was written—on the top of my chest in the after house (where I sleep, along with Jim, the carpenter and the cook). I have to dip my pen into the bottle at almost every word. Good-bye father and mother, aunts and uncles, brothers and sisters, cousins and friends. God bless you all and may we all meet again.

"P. S. I have received letters from Martha Curry and George Latimer and shall reply the first chance."

9.30 A. M.

"We are now going down the bay in tow of a steamboat and shall soon be at sea. I shall get the captain to send this ashore by the pilot. God bless you all. It is cloudy and drizzling—blows a stiff breeze from the south.

"Good-bye,
"HENRY GEORGE."

So it was that the *Hindoo,* a full-rigged ship of 586 tons register—a very large ship at that time[1]—with 500,000 feet of lumber aboard and a crew of twenty men, all told, started on her long voyage; and as she glided down the bay and through the "Narrows" on her way to the ocean, on the left bank, eighty feet above the water, stood an old white house that forty years later, when his fame had spread through the world, was to become Henry George's home and witness the end of his career. But the boy, all unconscious of this, had been set to work, as he says in his sea journal, "in company with the other boys to

---

[1] "In the last generation a full-rigged Indiaman would be considered a very large vessel if she registered 500 tons. Now we are building coasting schooners of 1000 tons"—"Social Problems," Chap. V. (Memorial edition, p. 46.)

picking oakum for the carpenter, who was busy fastening and calking the hatches."

This journal or log, covers most of the voyage, and with the few letters that still exist, and an account of the passage written by Captain Miller for his friend, George Latimer, furnishes pretty full and clear information as to this important formative period. The journal consists of an original in two parts and three incomplete fair copies. The original parts are quite rough and show marks of wear and stains of water. One is of white, the other of blue, unruled, large sized letter paper, folded so as to make neat pages of four by six inches, and stitched together with heavy linen thread, such as might have been used in sewing sails. The entries are mostly in pencil, the spelling not of the best, and the writing not uniform —in some places quite faint—but generally small, condensed, round and clear. The fair copies are in a fine state of preservation. They are written in large, bold hand in commercial blank books and the spelling is correct. Two of them may have been copied while at sea, but the fullest and best looking one was doubtless written in Philadelphia after the voyage.[1]

From Captain Miller's account it appears that when the *Hindoo* cast off the tug that was taking her to sea, the wind was from the south-east and right ahead, and the pilot advised him to anchor at Sandy Hook; "but," says the Captain, "we could not wait. We set all sail and stood E.N.E. until we saw the rocks of Long Island. We then tacked to the south'd and stood down until we were abreast the Capes of Delaware. Then a gale of wind

[1] In the back pages of this little journal are some historical, scientific and other notes probably made while reading. These bear date as late as April 1859, at which time its owner was in California.

From daguerreotype taken March 31, 1855,
just before going to sea.

from the north-west commenced, lasting four days; during which time we made good progress off the coast." The boy's log for these four days runs as follows:

"Tues. 10. . . . About 12 A.M. we passed Sandy Hook, and a slight breeze springing up, set all fore and aft sail. About 3 P.M. discharged the tow boat and pilot. Soon after I began to feel sea-sick, and the breeze dying away, the tossing of the vessel very much increased it. . . . After supper all hands were called aft and the watches chosen. I was taken by the mate for the larboard. . . . It being the larboard watch's first watch below, I turned in at 8 P.M.

"Wed. 11. I was roused out of a sound sleep at 12 o'clock to come on deck and keep my watch. On turning out I found a great change in the weather. The wind had shifted to N.W. and came out cold and fierce. The ship was running dead before it in a S.E. direction, making about 8 or 9 knots an hour. After keeping a cold and dreary watch until 4 A.M. we were relieved and I was enabled to turn in again. All this day sea-sick by spells. . . . It will be a long time before we are in this part of the world again, homeward bound. Twelve months seem as if they would never pass. In the afternoon all hands were engaged in getting the anchors on the forecastle and securing them for a long passage. The colour of the sea is green on sounding, the shade varying according to the depth of water, and a beautiful blue outside, and so very clear that objects can be seen at a great depth.

"Thurs. 12. A brisk breeze all day from N.W. with frequent showers of rain. Numbers of Stormy Petrels or Mother Carey's Chickens hovering about the quarter. Weather rather cool.

"Fri. 13. A fine bright day; wind still the same. Hoisting the lower stun'sail in the forenoon, the halyards parted, and the sail was with difficulty secured. The sea-sickness has now entirely left me."

The old ship after twenty-five years of hard service was pretty nearly worn out, and the log reveals a series of breakages, and some consequent accidents.

"Sat. 14. Commenced with fine clear weather and brisk breeze from N.W. About 5.30 A.M., the larboard watch being on deck, the tiller of the rudder suddenly broke in half. All hands were immediately called and everything let go and clewed up. Tackles were got on the rudder and the ship steered by them, while the carpenter immediately set to work on a new one. While furling the main top-gallant sail a man belonging to the larboard watch, John Frentz by name, fell from the yard to the deck. Luckily the main topsail, which was clewed up, broke his fall, or he would certainly have been killed. On taking him forward, his arm was found to have been broken in three places, but otherwise he had sustained no serious injury. His arm was set and bandaged by the mate. The carpenter finished the tiller about 4 P.M., when, everything being replaced, sail was again made on the ship and she continued on her course with a fair, though light wind. The old tiller which had suddenly broken, and which outwardly appeared so firm and sound, was in the centre completely rotted away. . . . The account which the man who fell from aloft gave of his mishap when he had recovered his senses was that he was pulling on the gasket with both hands when it suddenly parted and he was precipitated backwards. He knew no more until he found himself in the forecastle with his arm bandaged up."

The fifteenth of April is noted in the log as the "first Sunday at sea," and that instead of being seated in St. Paul's Church, they were "ploughing the ocean a thousand miles away." Soon the entries take more of the formal aspect of a ship's log and less of a personal journal, though once in a while they relax into general observation and fancy. On May 3, for instance, the ship, lying in a dead calm, was surrounded by a large school of dolphins, which presented "a most beautiful appearance in the water, changing to brilliant colours as they swam from place to place." On May 24 calms and light airs, with this entry:

"At 8.30 A.M. the mate succeeded in striking one of the porpoises which were playing under the bows. The fish was immediately run up to the bowsprit end by all hands, when a running bowline was put around his tail and he was hauled inboard, where he was soon despatched and dissected. We had a sort of hash of his flesh for supper, which was very palatable, and the rest was hung up to the topsail sheets, where it spoiled in the moonlight." [1]

Thoughts kept reverting to home, and there is more than one entry like: "Would have given anything to have been back to breakfast." Then came the Fourth of July:

---

[1] "In later years I have sometimes 'supped with Lucullus,' without recalling what he gave me to eat, whereas I remember to this day ham and eggs of my first breakfast on a canal-packet drawn by horses that actually trotted; how sweet hard-tack, munched in the middle watch while the sails slept in the trade-wind, has tasted; what a dish for a prince was sea-pie on the rare occasions when a pig had been killed or a porpoise harpooned; and how good was the plum-duff that came to the forecastle only on Sundays and great holidays. I remember as though it were an hour ago, that, talking to myself rather than to him, I said to a Yorkshire sailor on my first voyage: 'I wish I were home, to get a piece of pie.' I recall his expression and tone, for they shamed me, as he quietly said: 'Are you sure you would find a piece of pie there?' Thoughtless as the French princess who asked why the people who were crying for bread did not try cake, 'Home' was associated in my mind with pie of some sort — apple or peach or sweet-potato or cranberry or mince—to be had for the taking, and I did not for the moment realise that in many homes pie was as rare a luxury as plums in our sea-duff."—"The Science of Political Economy," p. 352.

"Wed. July 4.   Commenced with a fresh breeze from
N.   At 5 A.M. wind died away; at 8 A.M. came out from
S.   At 12 M. double reefed topsails and single reefed
mainsail.   During the rest of the day showery.   Lat.
33 S., lon. 6 W.   At 12 o'clock last night the day was
ushered in by three discharges from a small swivel,
which made a great deal of noise, rousing up all who
were asleep.   As soon as the smoke cleared away and
the dead and wounded were mustered, it was found that
it had not been without execution, all the glass on one
side of the house being shattered (a loss not easily repaired) a port blown out; and the waddings (made of
rope yarn, and very hard) had passed, one through the
head of the new water cask, and another through the
new foretopsail, which had not been bent a week.   The
wind, which had been strong from aft the day before,
during the middle watch died away and was succeeded
by a calm until 8 A.M., when a stiff breeze from the
South sprang up, accompanied by showers of rain.   At
12 M. all hands were called to reef.   While reefing the
foretopsail the parrel of the yard gave way, causing a
great deal of trouble and keeping all hands from dinner.   It was 2.30 P.M. before our watch got below to
their plum-duff, which had been allowed in honour of
the day.   The rest of the day was rainy, with wind
constantly varying, keeping us hauling on the braces.
Thus closed the most miserable 4th of July that I have
ever yet spent."

On the ninety-seventh day out the *Hindoo* passed the
Cape of Good Hope, though far to the south of it, and
entered the Indian Ocean.   Thence to Port Philip (Melbourne) came a succession of gales from the westward,
with heavy squalls of hail and rain, but the ship driving
before them made good progress.

"Sun. Aug. 12.   Commenced with cloudy weather and
stiff breeze.   At 6 A.M. shook a reef out of topsails
and set topgallant sails, but at 12 M., wind increasing

and barometer falling, (although the sun shone brightly and gave promise of a fine afternoon) furled topgallant-sails and close-reefed topsails. At 4 P.M., blowing a heavy gale from W. by N., furled mizzen topsails and reefed foresail. At 8 P.M., wind increasing, furled fore topsail. During the night tremendous squalls of wind and hail. Ship constantly heaving water on deck, one sea which she took in at the waist running completely aft and filling the cabin with water.

"Mon. Aug. 13. Strong gales from W. with heavy squalls of hail and rain. Weather very cold, the hail sometimes covering the deck. Looked more like winter than any weather we have yet experienced. It is impossible to describe the wildly grand appearance of the sea and sky."

At last, on the one hundred and thirty-seventh day out from New York, the first land of Australia was sighted, and with that flamed up the desire of the crew to get ashore and strike out straight for the gold districts, where men with little more equipment than pick and pan were, so far as the sailors' knowledge went, still washing fortunes out of the soil.

"Fri. Aug. 24. Commenced with strong wind from N. Furled jib. At 4 A.M. wind hauled to N.W. Course N.E. At 4.30 A.M. hove the lead, without soundings at 60 fathoms. When daylight came at last the anxiously looked for land was nowhere to be seen. Squally and showery, with very hazy weather. At 6 A.M. shook a reef out of main topsail. Two coasting schooners in sight steering about E.N.E. At 10.30 A.M. I had just turned in, having given up all hope of seeing land to-day, when all hands were called to close reef main top-sail and furl mainsail. While reefing the main topsail we were agreeably surprised by the joyful sound of 'Land ho!' from the second mate, who was at the weather earing. 'Where away?' shouted the captain. 'Right ahead,' was the reply; and sure enough there lay the long looked for land directly before us, looming above the horizon like a dark blue cloud, the first solid ground we had looked upon for 137 days. By the time we [the larboard watch] turned out, 12 noon, we were about 2 miles distant, running along the land. Our captain had hit the exact spot, Cape Otway, the light house on which was now plainly to be seen. After dinner all hands turned to get the anchors over the bows. It was a beautiful afternoon. The clouds, which in the morning had obscured the sun, had now vanished. The ship was sailing smoothly along before the wind at the rate of 4 or 5 knots. Numerous birds, a species of Albatross, were flying around us, now and then darting down after a fish. The land was high and apparently thickly wooded, and although winter in this part of the world, presented a beautiful, green appearance. It was looked upon by most of the crew as the Land of Promise, where gold was to be had by all; and most of the men were engaged in laying out what they would do, and where they would go, and how they would spend their money when they got it. While getting the anchors over, one of the small coasters which we had seen in the morning passed our bows under a press of sail, and stood in closer to the land. At 6 P.M. we furled the mizzen topsail, and at 8 P.M. backed the main topsail and laid to all night."

Next day they took a pilot and at 3 P. M. cast anchor in Hobson's Bay, opposite the Light house. Several American ships, some that had sailed before and some after the *Hindoo*, were also at anchor there.[1] Times were

---

1 " Thirty years ago ship-building had reached such a pitch of excellence in this country that we built not only for ourselves, but for other nations. American ships Were the fastest sailers, the largest carriers and everywhere got the quickest dispatch and the highest freights. The registered tonnage of the United States almost equalled that of Great Britain, and a few years promised to give us the unquestionable supremacy of the ocean." —"Protection or Free Trade," chap. XVIII. (Memorial Edition, p. 186). Captain Marryat, a by no means flattering critic of Americans,

reported to be "very hard ashore, thousands with nothing to do and nothing to eat." Notwithstanding this, the crew wished at once to get away.

> "As the captain was getting into a boat to go ashore, the men came aft in a body and requested their discharge, which being refused, they declared their intention of doing no more work. After supper the mate came forward and ordered the men to pick anchor watches, which they agreed to do after some parley. The mate told Jim and me to keep watch in the cabin until 12 and then call him. This I did until 10, when, after having a feast of butter, sugar and bread in the pantry, I turned in, leaving Jim to call the mate."

For several days the men refused to work, demanding to see the American Consul, and on Wednesday, four days after casting anchor, the captain got the Consul aboard. The Consul "took his seat on the booby hatch with the shipping articles before him," and called up the crew one by one. He finally "told the men that, as the passage would not be up until the cargo was discharged, he could do nothing until that time; but that Dutch John (the man who in the early part of the passage fell from the main topgallant yard) was entitled to his discharge if he wished it." The captain then promised that if they would "remain by the ship until she was discharged, he would pay them their wages and let them go in peace." They demanded this in writing, saying that he might change his mind, "but the captain refused to give them any fur-

---

in his "Diary in America" (First Series), Philadelphia, 1839, says, p. 186: "It appears, then, that from various causes, our merchant vessels have lost their sailing properties, whilst the Americans have the fastest sailers in the world; and it is for that reason, and no other, that, although sailing at a much greater expense, the Americans can afford to outbid us, and take all our best seamen."

ther guarantee than his word." As they still desisted from work on the *Hindoo,* they were taken off in a police boat, and sentenced to one month's hard labour in the prison ship, at the end of which time, still refusing to work, they would perhaps have been sentenced to further imprisonment if the captain had not reached court too late to appear against them. Before he sailed, the captain had to ship a new crew.

There is nothing in the journal to indicate that the boy thought Captain Miller unjust, but the incident made an indelible impression, revealing the tremendous powers for tyranny the navigation laws put into the hands of a captain, and this was to inspire a remarkable fight for sailor's rights in years to come.[1]

The ship lay in Hobson's Bay twenty-nine days discharging chargo and taking in ballast. Captain Miller in his account says: "Harry went up to Melbourne once, but did not see much to admire." Perhaps the boy saw more than the captain realised, for thirty-five years later, in a speech in Melbourne, he said, that he had a vivid recollection of it—"its busy streets, its seemingly continuous auctions, its crowds of men with flannel shirts and long high boots, its bay crowded with ships." No letters written from there now exist, but it is clear that the Australia of his dreams did not appear to be such a wonderful place after all; that there was not much gold in sight and that in this respect the "Land of Promise" was something of a disappointment. Land monopolisation and speculation had set in and cut off the poor man's access to nature's storehouse.

Other dreams were to be dissipated on reaching India. The best description of the passage and arrival there is

---

[1] Sunrise Case in San Francisco.

found in a letter to his father and mother, dated Calcutta, December 12, 1855.

"We hove up anchor in Hobson's Bay about 11 o'clock on the 24th of September, made sail, proceeded down the bay under charge of a pilot, and at about 5 P.M. passed the heads and discharged the pilot. After leaving Port Philip and until we had rounded Cape Lewin we had strong winds, mostly head, and cool weather. . . . Then the weather gradually became milder as we got to the northward, with fair, though not very strong winds. Near the line we had light airs, not even sufficient to fill the sails, but under the pressure of which the ship would go two or three miles per hour. We crossed the line November 5, when 42 days out. . . . From this place until we arrived at about 10° north we had the same fair airs as on the other side of the line, with every prospect of a short passage. Then the wind became stronger and more variable, but dead ahead. It would seldom blow from one point of the compass for more than an hour. Indeed, it seemed as if a second Jonah was aboard, for tack as often as we would, the wind was sure to head us off. . . . . Progress under the circumstances was impossible. For over a week we did not gain a single inch to the northward. What she would make one hour she would lose the next. During this time the weather was delightful, warm without being uncomfortably so, and so pleasant that sleeping on deck could be practised with impunity.

"At length on the morning of the 29th of November the colour of the water suddenly changed to green, and by noon we were abreast of the lightship, which marks the outer pilot station. The tide was running so strongly that with the light air we could hardly hold our own against it. About 3 P.M., in obedience to a signal from the pilot brig, we cast anchor with 30 fathoms of chain, furled all sail, and cleared up decks for the night. At 8 P.M. set anchor-watch and turned in for *all night*. . . ."

Then came the first impressions of the country—impressions that always afterward remained vivid and helped before long to direct thought to social questions; that changed the fancied India—the place of dreamy luxury, of soft and sensuous life—into the real India, with its extremes of light and shadow, of poverty and riches, of degradation and splendour; where the few have so much, the many so little; where jewels blaze in the trappings of elephants, but where, as he has since said in talking with his son Richard, "the very carrion birds are more sacred than human life!" These impressions are preserved in a description of the trip to Calcutta up the Hooghly branch of the Ganges River scribbled in pencil on the back pages of one of the journal records.

ARRIVAL AT GARDEN REACH AND FIRST IMPRESSIONS OF THE TOWN.

"Mon. Dec. 3. We turned out about 3 A.M. and after some heavy heaving got up anchor. About 5 A.M. we were taken in tow by the steamer and proceeded up the river. The night air was misty and chilly and a monkey jacket proved very comfortable. The day soon began to break, revealing a beautiful scene. The river, at times very broad and again contracting its stream into a channel hardly large enough for a ship of average size to turn in, was bordered by small native villages, surrounded by large fruit trees, through which the little bamboo huts peeped. As we advanced, the mists which had hitherto hung over the river cleared away, affording a more extensive prospect. The water was covered with boats of all sizes, very queer looking to the eye of an American. They were most of them bound to Calcutta with the produce and rude manufactures of the country—bricks, tiles, earths, pots, etc. They had low bows and very high sterns. They were pulled by from four to ten men, and steered by an old fellow wrapped up in a sort of cloth, seated on a high platform at the stern. Some had sails to help them along, in which there were more holes than threads. On the banks the natives began to go to their daily toil, some driving cattle along, others loading boats with grain, while the women seemed busy with their domestic affairs. As we approached the city, the banks on both sides were lined with handsome country residences of the wealthy English. About 10 A.M. we came to Garden Reach, where, as there was no Harbour Master's Assistant ready to take us up, we were obliged to drop both anchors. After getting fairly moored we had a little time to look around us. The river which here takes a sudden bend, was crowded with ships of all nations, and above nothing could be seen but a forest of masts. On the right hand or Calcutta side, are the East India Company's works, for repairing their steamers, numbers of which, principally iron, were undergoing repairs. On the other side was an immense palace-like structure (the residence, I believe, of some wealthy Englishman) surrounded by beautiful lawns and groves. The river was covered with boats and presented a bustling scene. One feature which is peculiar to Calcutta was the number of dead bodies floating down in all stages of decomposition, covered by crows who were actively engaged in picking them to pieces. The first one I saw filled me with horror and disgust, but like the natives, you soon cease to pay any attention to them.

"Tues. Dec. 4. About 4.30 A.M. the Harbour Master came along side and we were roused up to get up anchors. . . . It astonished me to see with what ease the pilot took the vessel up . . . steering her amidst the maze of vessels as easily as if she was at sea. The port seemed crowded with vessels, a large proportion of them American, some of which I recognised as having seen at Philadelphia. At length about 10 A.M. we cast anchor off our intended moorings. About 2 P.M. we hauled in and made fast along side of an English clipper, the *British Lion*. After getting all fast we had dinner and cleared up decks and squared the yards."

While the ship lay at her moorings, visits were made to Barrapore, eighteen miles away, and other places of interest in the vicinity, and the boy saw those things that are observed generally by travellers. But the event of perhaps most interest to him was the receipt on December 10 of letters from home—the first since he had left. His father sent family news and said: "Your little brig is safely moored on the mantelpiece. First thing when we wake, our eyes rest upon her, and she reminds us of our dear sailor boy."

The mother's letter also touched on family matters, but gave chief place to other things engaging her devout mind.

"And now for the news. The best news just now is the religious news—a great work going on in New York and Philadelphia and all the principal cities of the Union; prayer-meetings all over the land; all denominations uniting together in solemn, earnest prayer; Jayne's Hall (you know its size) is crowded to excess, even those large galleries literally packed with men of the highest respectability—merchants, bankers, brokers, all classes. Those who have never entered a church and have hitherto scoffed at religion meet at this prayer-meeting every day to hear the word of God read and solemn prayer offered for their conversion. . . . I might fill many pages to show you that this is truly the work of God—the out-pouring of the Holy Spirit. . . . That same Holy Influence will be given to all that ask for it in simple faith: 'Lord, teach me to pray.' "

The event to the lad next in interest to the receipt of home letters was the acquisition of a pet monkey, of which he wrote in later years:[1]

----

[1] "The Science of Political Economy," p. 30.

Henry George's mother and sister Jennie.

From daguerreotype taken about 1850.

"I bought in Calcutta, when a boy, a monkey, which all the long way home would pillow her little head on mine as I slept, and keep off my face the cockroaches that infested the old Indiaman by catching them with her hands and cramming them into her maw. When I got her home, she was so jealous of a little brother that I had to part with her to a lady who had no children."

In his account of the voyage, Captain Miller says that the ship left Calcutta with quite a menagerie of monkeys and birds aboard, but that before long "Harry's was the only survivor." The others died or got away, two of the sailors without intentional cruelty throwing theirs overboard to see "which would swim ashore first," but the animals quickly drowned. The boy cherished his little creature most fondly; though for that matter he always showed a warm love for animals, and this was but one of a great number that he had about him during his life.

On the 15th of January, 1856, the *Hindoo* having completed her loading, consisting of nearly twelve hundred tons of rice, seeds, etc., took a new crew aboard and started down the river, homeward bound. Henry George at the time estimated that he would have when he reached New York and settled his accounts "about fifty dollars to take clear of everything—not much for thirteen or fourteen months." The distance down the Hooghly from Calcutta to the sea is eighty miles, but what with head winds, the scarcity of tow boats and a broken windlass, the vessel was twenty days making the passage, during which time the hot weather played havoc with the fresh provisions, so that the crew was the sooner reduced to "salt horse and biscuit." Light winds blew down the bay of Bengal and the ship crossed the equator on the 23rd of February. On the 27th the cook, Stephen Anderson, fell sick and young

George went into the galley temporarily. The journal says:

"Wed. Feb. 27. Cook laid up. Went into the galley.

"(Not having written down the events of the inter-vening space, I do not remember them fully, being obliged to work pretty hard.)

"Sun. Mar. 2. Fine clear day. Breeze from S.W., course, S.S.E. For several days there have been thou-sands of fish playing around, but, although the men tried hard to catch them, they were unsuccessful until this morning, when an albicore was captured. The mate made sea-pie for all hands for supper. 8 P.M. sail in sight.

"Mon. Mar. 3. Calm all day. The cook so weak that he cannot raise a spoon to his mouth. I think it a chance whether he lives.

"Tues. Mar. 4. Calm, fine day. Cook seems a little stronger, but can scarcely speak.

"Wed. Mar. 5. Commenced with breeze from W.N.W.; course S.S.W. Four sail in sight. Last evening the cook appeared a great deal stronger, getting up and moving about, turning in and out; but still could scarce-ly speak. About 7 A.M. he was taken with a fit, when he was brought on deck and laid by the capstan. About 11.30 A.M. he died. He was sewed up and buried at 5 P.M."

The cook having gone, the boy, to his great satisfac-tion, for he had an extreme distaste for the task, was superseded in the galley by one of the crew, who remained there for the rest of the voyage. The ship passed the Cape of Good Hope on April 13 and within sight of St. Helena on the 27th. On May 12 she crossed the equator for the fourth time during the voyage. Long before that date the journal entries had become short, and after May 6 stopped altogether, possibly because there was a great deal of work to do in handling, cleaning,

repairing and painting the ship. April opened with this
entry:

"April 1, 1856.   Lat., 31, S.; long., 40, E.   One year
has passed since the Sunday when I took farewell of
my friends—to me an eventful year; one that will
have a great influence in determining my position in
life; perhaps more so than I can at present see.   O that
I had it to go over again! Homeward bound! In a
few months I hope to be in Philadelphia once more."

And it was not long before he was home, for on June
14, after an absence of one year and sixty-five days, and
from Calcutta one hundred and fifty days, the *Hindoo*
completed her long journey and dropped anchor in New
York Bay.

CHAPTER III.

LEARNS TO SET TYPE.

1856-1857. AGE, 17-18.

ON getting back, home seemed very sweet to the boy on account of the loved ones and comforts, and the association of his boy friends. A year and a half afterwards, when he had gone to California, Jo Jeffreys, at that time the closest of his friends, wrote:

> "Don't you recollect our Byronic quotations? Amusing weren't they? And yet I dare say we had more pleasure in those long moonlight nights spent in conversation—in counsel and reflection—than we had in a like number of hours at any other time. I remember well, too, how night after night we sat together and alone in your little room, smoking slowly and looking —sometimes at the little bed which was to contain us both and which rested in a corner near the door, at the little case of books on the bureau, at the dim gaslight which could so seldom be induced to burn brightly and which shed its dim light upon all around—and then turning from this picture, so familiar to me now (though I have never been in that room since, though often in the rooms beneath it), and gazing upon each other, would talk of the present and the future."

In this little back-attic bed room all the boys at times gathered and talked about books or public affairs or boyish amusements, and it was Henry George's habit, while engaging in conversation, to throw himself down on his bed, and frequently while the discourse was raging he would sink into placid slumbers. It was common enough for the family to see the boys come down stairs alone and hear the explanation: "Oh, Hen's asleep and we think it is time to go."

Thus the home life had much attractiveness for young George, yet he found it full of restrictions, for with all the heavy toil and hard discipline of sea life, there was during the preceding year and a quarter complete freedom of thought, and of actions, too, in the hours off duty. And now to come back to conditions where the most innocent of card-playing was regarded as an evil and riding in a public conveyance on Sunday as a desecration of the Lord's Day, made the energetic, masterful boy, or rather youth, for he was now in his eighteenth year, see new charms in the sea life; and for a time, all efforts failing in the search for employment ashore, his thoughts reverted to the water. Learning of this inclination, Captain Miller, before sailing on a new voyage in the *Hindoo*, wrote to him:

"I hope you will find some agreeable and profitable employment before long. Take my advice and never go to sea. You know of the troubles of a sailor's life before the mast. It never gets any better. A second mate leads proverbially a dog's life. The mate's and captain's are very little better."[1]

[1] This was probably the last letter he received from Captain Miller, and before the *Hindoo* had returned from her voyage and the captain had run on to Philadelphia, Henry George had sailed for California, so that they never again met. The captain died in Brooklyn, in May, 1877, in his forty-eighth year, and his friend, Rev. George A. Latimer, Henry George's cousin, officiating, was buried in Greenwood Cemetery, where Henry George himself, twenty years later, was to rest.

The boy's parents were most anxious not to have him again go to sea, and at last in the fall the father through his former book publishing connections obtained a situation for his son with the printing firm of King & Baird, at that time one of the important printing houses in Philadelphia. The father's idea in putting his son there was threefold: to keep the boy at home, to give him a trade and to teach him to spell. This latter short-coming in the boy was very conspicuous, requiring a second draft or fair copy of letters to insure the correct spelling of many even common words, as drafts of such letters that have survived show.

Learning to set type effected a marked improvement, and the printer's experience later in California perfected it. In after years his letter-writing at times revealed lapses in spelling, but these, as was manifest on the surface, arose from habits of abstraction.

This learning to set type marked another distinct step in the education of Henry George for his life work. Not that it lay so much in type-setting itself, or in correcting his spelling; but rather in bringing him into familiar contact with another field of human activity—among type-setters, who, as a class of men, if they belong to a trade, possess, as a rule, much correct general information and are given to habits of intelligent thought. Edmund Wallazz, who was a type-setter at King and Baird's in 1856, said in after years: "Henry George was a remarkably bright boy, always in discussion with the other boys in the office. He got in the habit of appealing to me (I am seven or eight years older) for support as to his dates and facts, historical and political." Thus through the channel of polemics he was acquiring knowledge of various kinds, and was also learning to observe and to present his thoughts. He had a habit of stowing away things in his memory that would have passed another—things that

Henry George when learning to set type in Philadelphia.

From daguerreotype, 1857.

in his matured years often found expression in his writings. To this period he assigned the first puzzling question in political economy. An old printer observed to him one day that while in old countries wages are low, in new countries they are always high. The boy compared the United States with Europe, and then California and Australia with Pennsylvania and New York, and the old printer's words seemed true enough, though neither the printer nor he could explain why. The thing stuck in his mind and kept rising for answer.

This propensity for investigating and arguing showed itself wherever he happened to be, when with old or with young, abroad or at home. As his Uncle Joseph Van Dusen said: "Henry is not tongue-tied."

For years stories of slave auctions in the South, friction over the return of runaway slaves in the North, the hot agitation of Garrison and Phillips in the East, and conflicts in "Bleeding Kansas" and through the West kept public thought seething. In 1850 appeared Mrs. Stowe's "Uncle Tom's Cabin," and later arose the Republican party with its anti-slavery proclivities and that in 1856 forced the issue and ran John C. Frémont for President. Though James Buchanan, the Democratic pro-slavery candidate, was elected, the new party had waged a fierce fight, and four years later was to elect Abraham Lincoln.

Young George soon after returning from sea showed a lively interest in the slavery question, and, although his father was a Democrat and inclined to support Buchanan, the boy independently took the anti-slavery side, which he discussed with his mother. In the interest of peace and of "property rights,"[1] and doubtless supported in

[1] "I was born in a Northern State, I have never lived in the South, I am not yet gray; but I well remember, as every American of middle age must remember, how over and over again I have heard all questionings of slavery silenced by the declaration that the negroes were the *property* of their

mind by what she regarded as the sanction of the Scriptures, she upheld slavery, not perhaps as a good thing in
itself, but because of the great cost of disestablishment.
The mother in repeating this conversation in after years
to her son's wife said that in arguing she held that the
hardships of slavery "were exaggerated," for, "while some
of the slave owners might be brutal, the majority were
not likely to be so," most of them doubtless being the same
kind of "humanely-disposed people" as she herself. The
boy stoutly held to his position and answered that her
argument rested "on policy, not principle"; that she spoke
of what slave owners *"seemed likely* to do," he of what
they *"could* do"; "for if slaves were property, their masters, having the right to do what they pleased with their
own property, could ill-treat and even kill them if so disposed."

The argument seemed sound enough to the parents,
but the boy was still a boy to them. One night soon after
returning from sea he came home late and his father reproved him. The boy hotly said that he was a child no
longer and then went off to bed. Reflection cooled the
father's anger. He realized that his son was, in mind at
least, maturing to manhood, and that the reproof was not
quite just or wise. He concluded that in the morning
he would talk to his son about it. But when morning
came the son was first to speak, saying that he had thought
upon what had happened, and that while he regarded his
conduct in remaining out as in itself innocent enough,
he now recognised what he had not before observed—his
father's right to object—and that being conscious of having been impudent, he asked his father's pardon. The

---

masters, and that to take away a man's slave without payment was as
much a crime as to take away his horse without payment."—"The Land
Question," Chap. VII. (Memorial Edition, p. 49).

father strained his son to his bosom and thereafter gave him more domestic freedom.

High strung and impetuous, Henry George was at this period prone to sudden resolves. From September, 1856, to June, 1857, he worked steadily at type-setting at King & Baird's, when one afternoon, having a quarrel with Mr. Scott, foreman of the job-room, he left the house's employ. When he told of what had happened, his father found for him an opening with Stavely & McCalla, printers, who offered $2.25 a week for the first year, and afterwards as much as he could earn, providing he remained until twenty-one. The pay was so small that he hesitated. - Just then a boy friend, John Hasson, sent word of a strike in the "Argus" newspaper office. George applied for and obtained employment. To Emma Curry, a girl friend, he wrote (June 29, 1857) explaining some of these matters:

"I left King and Baird's about two weeks and a half ago. I was learning nothing and making little ($2 a week) when I left. The immediate cause of my leaving was that I would not quietly submit to the impositions and domineering insolence of the foreman of the room in which I then worked. Week before last I worked on the 'Daily Evening Argus.' The foreman of that paper and the members of the Printers' Union (who have full control of the various newspaper offices) quarrelled, and they refused to work unless the foreman was discharged. This the proprietor, Mr. Severus, refused to do, and the consequence was that the Union would not allow any of its members to work on the paper. The foreman had, therefore, to get printers who did not belong to the Union. I applied for a situation as a journeyman compositor and got it; but unluckily for me, at the end of the week the Union had a meeting and wisely supported the foreman by a large majority. This compelled the proprietor to discharge us

who were working there at the time and take on the
Union men, who, having control of the other offices,
could have put him to great inconvenience had he refused to do so.

"During the six days I worked there I made $9.50,
the largest sum of money I have ever made in the same
time. I had also the satisfaction of seeing that I was
but very little inferior to any of the journeymen, my
bill for the week being as large as any of theirs, with
the exception of a couple who had worked in the evenings also. I believe that I can set on an average of
5,000 ems of solid matter a day, including distributing
and correcting, which according to the prices you tell
me the printers get in Oregon, would be worth nearly $4."

Emma Curry, her sisters, Martha and Florence, and
their widowed mother, Rebecca D. Curry, had been neighbours of the George family. They had early in the year
gone to Oregon Territory to join the widow's nephew,
George Curry, who had been appointed Governor. Mrs.
Curry was a bright, discerning woman. Her brother, William D. Kelley, from 1846 to 1856 was Judge of the Court
of Common Pleas of Philadelphia and afterwards represented one of the Philadelphia districts in Congress for
almost thirty years and was commonly known as "Pig
Iron" Kelley. Henry George had had many a long, earnest
talk with Mrs. Curry, who took a deep interest in him.
In a letter to her (April 3, 1857) he said:

"I am still at printing and am getting along very
well, considering the time I have been at it. I should
be able to make at least $5 a week were I getting jour-
neyman's prices, but that is impossible here. If you
can find out and will be kind enough to write me the
rates at which printers are paid in Oregon, I shall be
able to tell exactly how much I could make there.

"I commenced last evening to take lessons in penmanship, and if all the old fellow (I mean teacher) says is true, by the time I write my next letter to you my chirography will be so much improved that you will hardly recognise the hand. I have taken your advice and am trying to improve myself all I can. I shall shortly commence to study book-keeping. After I get through that I shall be Jack of three different trades, and, I am afraid, master of none.

"I am still of the same determination in regard to going West. . . . I only wait for your promised account of Oregon, and advice, to determine where and when I shall go."

Before receipt of his letter, Mrs. Curry had already written (April 19):

"We talk and think of you a great deal and I have talked with Mr. Curry [the Governor] about you. He says, 'Do not go to sea, but come here.' He will see what you can make at your business at Salem. He thinks you may do well. He will inquire as soon as possible, and I shall write you. Everything pays well here. He is giving a boy $20 a month for hoeing, chopping wood, washing a little and bringing up the cattle. A man was paid by him in my presence $25 for ploughing from Tuesday noon till Friday noon. Give all attention to your business and you will, I trust, be successful. It is best to have that at your command."

Emma Curry wrote in a similar strain, and to her the boy replied (June 29):

"Give my thanks to the Governor for the trouble he has taken in my behalf and for the information which he has communicated to me through you. Your statement of the prospects that I may anticipate in Oregon has decided me. I *will* go out as soon as possible and in the best manner possible, even if I am obliged to work my way around the Horn—unless by a lucky windfall I shall get into some business."

But the "lucky windfall" in Philadelphia showed no signs of coming. The boy vainly looked for permanent employment. He obtained a position on a weekly paper called "The Merchant," but this proved only temporary, and he became restless and thought the more earnestly of Oregon, and also of California, where he had a cousin, son of his Uncle Dunkin George. But these places seeming remote, again he thought of the sea, if only as a means of livelihood for the time being. He probably was the more restless because of the reaction from the old home rigorous beliefs and restraints. A blank book with some diary entries covering a few days during this period contains this:

"Tues. July 3. Saw Jo Jeffreys in afternoon. In evening Bill Jones and I took Sallie Young and Amelia Reinhart to the Academy of Music. But Sallie Young deserted me there and went with Bill Jones. Curse these girls; they won't fool me so confoundedly again. After taking them home we adjourned to Stead's [cigar store], where Bill Horner was awaiting us. As we came down we stopped at Cook's and Bergner's [taverns]. Coming up again, we serenaded Charlie Walton with the national anthem, after which Bill left us. Horner and I again repaired to Stead's, where after a little while we were joined by Jo and a friend of his, John Owen, by name. They, together with Ebenezer Harrison [a young Sunday School teacher], had been enjoying themselves in Owen's room, drinking punches and making speeches. At the corner of Sixth and Walnut Jo and I commenced to box, when Jo fell down and cut his head awfully. We raised him up, took him to Owen's, washed his wound and then set off to find a doctor. We dragged him around for about two hours before finding any person who could dress the wound. At length we took him to a German physician, who dressed the cut and charged a V for his trouble. We left him at Owen's and returned home about daybreak."

It was at this time that the boys—Jeffreys, Jones, Horner, Walton, Harrison, George and the others—formed "The Lawrence Literary Society" and met in a small building which once had been a church. Two original essays by "Hen" George are still preserved, one on "The Poetry of Life" and the other on "Mormonism," a very hostile view. There also exists a contribution from the pen of Charley Walton treating of the wide-spread industrial depression then prevailing and ascribing its rise to "extravagance and speculation which have since the revolution characterised the American people."[1] But starting with this self-improving literary idea, the "Lawrence" came in the course of things to have other characteristics which Walton later described in a letter to "Hen" (July 29, 1863):

> "I have often thought of the time gone by when the 'Lawrence' in Jerusalem Church was in its palmy days. . . . Can you or I forget the gay, refreshing and kindred spirits that formed that association and gave it a character so unenviable and noticeable as eventually to cause it to be ordered out peremptorily; its sympathy with ghost stories, boxing gloves, fencing foils and deviltry; its exercises tending to promote muscular rather than literary abilities; and its test of merit and standard of membership—to drink Red Eye, sing good songs and smoke lots of cigars?"

---

[1] This essay covers four pages of paper, the first page evidently written with great care, and the last with great carelessness, the whole terminating with the ejaculation, "Thank God, I'm done!"

But however innocent all this may have been, the fact of knowing anything whatever about liquor or of card playing was significant of the break-down of the old home influences; and it partly explains, with the loss of employment and the ambition to be independent, the return of a desire for the sea. At any rate, Henry George embarked on a topsail schooner laden with coal and bound from Philadelphia for Boston. Often afterwards, even towards the end of his life, he spoke with pride of the compliments he received on that voyage. For when he applied as ordinary seaman, the captain measured him with something like contempt and asked what he could do.

"I can handle, reef and steer," was the answer.

"You can't steer this schooner," returned its commander, "but nevertheless I'll try you."

Notwithstanding George's short stature and light weight, the captain found him so useful that at the end of the voyage he paid him off at the full rate of an able seaman, saying that he had been of as much use as any man aboard.

The outlook ashore seemed even worse when he got back from this short schooner trip, as may be seen from a letter to one of his young friends (B. F. Ely, September 30):

"The times here are very hard and are getting worse and worse every day, factory after factory suspending and discharging its hands. There are thousands of hard-working mechanics now out of employment in this city; and it is to the fact that among them is your humble servant, that you owe this letter. If you will send on without delay the V. you owe me you will be doing the State a service by lessening the pressure of the hard times upon one of the hard fisted mechanics who form her bone and muscle, and will at the same time be easing your conscience of a burden, which I have little doubt bears heavily upon it.

" . . . I am pretty hard up at present and haven't as much money as you could shake a stick at. Indeed, I would not have any hesitation in taking a situation on board a good canal boat for a short time, provided that it would pay.

"I have been trying for some time to secure a berth on board the United States Light-house Steamer *Shubrick*, now fitting out at the Navy Yard for California; but she will not sail for two weeks at least, and even then it is very doubtful whether I can succeed and go out in her.

"There is a ship loading here for San Francisco on board of which I have been promised a berth, but in the present stagnation of business it is doubtful whether she will get off before a month or two at least. So that you see I am in a pretty bad fix, having at least two weeks of loafing to look forward to."

Subsequently (October 5) he wrote a letter to Congressman Thomas B. Florence of his district asking his support.

"I have long wished to go to Oregon, where, if I may believe the many assurances I have received, prospects of fortune are open to me which it would be vain to hope for here. But as it is impossible for me to raise means sufficient to defray the expenses of a passage, I must strive to adopt the only plan practicable, and work my way out.

"The Light-House Steamer *Shubrick* will sail in a couple of weeks for California, where she is to be employed. I have been waiting for her for some time, hoping to get a chance to go in her; but I now learn from good authority that in all probability only a few able seamen will be shipped for her, in which case I would be unable to do so, unless I can obtain permission to ship from the Light-House Bureau.

"I have been to sea before, and am competent to ship as ordinary seaman or first class boy.

"If you would be kind enough to write to the proper

authorities at Washington in support of my **application**, it would be of great assistance to me in **obtaining** their permission."

Much to his delight, he not only was accepted for the *Shubrick,* but received the appointment of ship's steward, or storekeeper, at forty dollars a month; though like every one else on board, he was compelled to sign the ship's articles for one year's service, and not for the voyage to California alone, which was all that he wished to do. On December 22, 1857, he said farewell to his loved ones, and the little vessel under Commander John DeCamp of the U. S. Navy steamed down the Delaware River and started on her long journey around the southern extremity of South America.

CHAPTER IV.

WORKS HIS PASSAGE TO CALIFORNIA.

1858.   AGE, 19.

AND now the boy having left home to face the world and seek his fortune in the new country, it may be instructive to get some more definite knowledge of his character. A key to it, or at any rate to his own estimate at that time of it, exists in a phrenological sketch that he wrote of himself while still in Philadelphia. It is in his clear hand-writing and covers two half-sheets of blue, unruled, legal-cap paper, on the back of one of which are the words, "Phrenological examination of head by self." The examination is as follows:

"Circumference [of head], 21⅝; ear to ear, 12½.
1. Amativeness .... Large.
2. Philoprogenitiveness .... Moderate.
3. Adhesiveness .... Large.
4. Inhabitativeness .... Large.
5. Concentrativeness .... Small.
6. Combativeness .... Large.
7. Destructiveness .... Large.
8. Alimentiveness .... Full.
9. Acquisitiveness .... Small.
10. Secretiveness .... Large.
11. Caution .... Large.
12. Approbativeness ....
13. Self-esteem .... Large.

14. Firmness .... Large.
15. Conscientiousness .... Large.
16. Hope .... Large.
17. Marvellousness ....
18. Veneration ....
19. Benevolence ....
20. Constructiveness ....
21. Ideality ....
22. Imitation ....
23. Mirthfulness .... Small.
24. Individuality .... Large.
25. Form ....
26. Size .... Large.
27. Weight ....
28. Colour ....
29. Order ....
30. Calculation .... Small.
31. Locality .... Large.
32. Eventuality .... Full.
33. Time .... Large.
34. Tune ....
35. Language .... Moderate.
36. Causality .... Large.
37. Comparison .... Large.

"An ardent, devoted, fervent and constant lover; will defend the object of his love with boldness, protect his or her rights with spirit. Will feel much stronger attachment than he will express.

"Is not very fond of children. May love them as friends, rather than as children.

"Is strong in his attachments; readily takes the part of friends, resents and retaliates their injuries; yet may occasionally fall out with them.

"Chooses as his friends the talented, intellectual and literary, and avoids the ignorant.

"Is extremely fond of travelling. Has an insatiable desire to roam about and see the world and afterwards to settle down.

"Is patriotic and ready to sacrifice all in defence of his country.

"May get angry quickly, but, unless the injury is deep or intended, cannot retain his anger.

"Will be more likely to make a general than a critical scholar. May have bold and original ideas upon a variety of subjects, yet will not without effort or excitement have a train of connected thoughts upon any.

"Is qualified to meet difficulties, overcome obstacles, endure hardships, contend for privileges, maintain opinions, resent insults and defend his rights to the last; generally takes sides on every contested question; naturally hasty in temper.

"Desires money more as a means than as an end, more for its uses than to lay up; and pays too little attention to small sums.

"Generally keeps his thoughts, feelings, plans, etc., to himself. Will effect his purposes indirectly and without detection. May sometimes communicate his feelings to his nearest friends, yet will seldom do this, and will exercise more attachment than he expresses. May restrain for a long time the anger which is burning in his bosom; yet when he does give vent to it, it will blaze forth in good earnest. Is slow in commencing, yet when once interested in any project pushes it with great spirit. May be timid and fearful until his courage is once excited, but will then be bold and fearless. In cases of danger, will be perfectly self-possessed; and yet will have fore-thought enough to do just what the occasion demands. Cannot soon be worked up to the sticking point; but is determined, if not desperate, when once kindled.

"Is inclined to enter largely into business and to push his projects with so much energy and zeal as to appear rash and nearly destitute of caution; yet will come out about right in the end and will seldom fail entirely in his projects, though he may be obliged to retrace his steps."

This "phrenological examination," tested by what others can remember of him at that period and by the traits shown later in life, must be regarded, so far as it goes, as a fairly accurate presentation of the boy's chief characteristics. But this should not be set down to phrenology, for there is nothing to show that he placed particular confidence, or even had more than passing interest, in that teaching.[1] Nor is it to be set down as a lucky kind of guess about himself. It is in truth, more than anything else, the fruit of a habit of introspection which had begun about the time of the return from the first sea voyage and which was afterwards to be shown more and more strongly.

Meanwhile the little *Shubrick* was boldly pushing her way down the coast. This was her first trip in commission, Henry George having seen her building in the Philadelphia Navy Yard that very year. She was named after Rear Admiral William B. Shubrick, of the U. S. Navy, who had been Chairman of the Light-House Board since 1852. She was to become the first vessel on light-house duty on the Pacific coast, to which service she was now proceeding; and the first tender under steam in the light-house department of the United States. She was of 372 tons burden, 140 feet in length, 22 feet in beam and 19 feet in depth of hold; with black hull, red side-wheels, black funnel and two masts, the foremast square rigged. She looked as sharp and trim as a yacht, but, as in addition to her regular duties of supplying light-houses and maintaining the buoyage along the west coast, she was intended to give protection to government property along

---

[1] Thirty years later, when his son, Richard, manifested interest in phrenology, Henry George discouraged him, saying that though indirectly or collaterally there probably was truth in it, the subject was one that, in his opinion, Nature did not intend to have man know much about, since the discovery of constitutional characteristics would with most men seem to indicate foreordination, and checking free and independent action, would tend to produce fatalism. Moreover, he said, phrenology was not needed for man's progress, for *that* did not depend upon a knowledge of the relative development of the faculties, but rather upon the *use* of the faculties, whatever they might be.

the sea shore of Oregon and Washington from the depredations of Indian tribes, she was armed with six brass guns and a novel contrivance for squirting scalding water on the redskins when at close quarters.

On Christmas day, while the *Shubrick* was steaming along over a sun-kissed sea some distance off the Hatteras coast, the wind, which had been fair, subsided, and then without warning rose into a white squall, blowing from the north-east. The boat's head was swung around and she was brought to under low-steam. At night the wind blew a hurricane, the sea breaking over her fore and aft with great violence. The after part of the wheelhouse, engineer's storeroom and starboard bulwarks were stove in, and everything movable on deck washed overboard, including port shutters, harness-casks, deck engine, and spare spars and lumber. At ten that night, deeming that she was in danger of foundering, thirty tons of sacked coal and some other things were thrown overboard.[1] Many times during his life Henry George spoke of the terrors of this storm, on one occasion[2] saying:

> "A negro deckhand and I worked together throwing over bags of coal to lighten her. The sailing master hung on the bridge shouting to us through the speaking trumpet and barely able to make himself heard, as he told us the work we were doing was for life or death."

This relieved the vessel and at day-light she was enabled to proceed on her course, nine days after leaving

---

[1] Notes from record of *Shubrick*, by courtesy of the U. S. Light-House Board at Washington, D. C., and of Captain Geo. W. Coffin, U. S. N., Inspector 12th Light-House District, San Francisco, Cal.

[2] From shorthand notes by Ralph Meeker of a conversation, New York, October, 1897.

Philadelphia putting into St. Thomas, West Indies, to renew her coal supply and make necessary repairs.

To Jo Jeffreys, his young friend in Philadelphia, Henry George sent from St. Thomas a clear account of the passage and of the danger the ship had been in; but to his parents, under same date (January 6, 1858), he wrote in quite different style to save them from anxiety, omitting all mention of danger. The letter to his parents read:

"Here I am this winter's afternoon (while you are gathering around the parlour stove, perhaps thinking and talking of me) sitting in the open air in my white sleeves almost roasted by the heat. I wish you could view the scene which surrounds me. The noble mountains rising from the water, covered with perpetual vegetation of the tropics and varied in colour by the shadows of the clouds which seem to climb their sides; the little town with its square red-roofed, Dutch houses and white forts, surrounded by the palm and cocoanut trees which line the head of the bay; the ships and steamers which deck the harbour; and the boundless sea stretching away to the edge of the horizon, glittering in the sunlight—form a picture which I know you would enjoy.

"Now that I have tried to give you a faint idea of the scenery that surrounds me, I shall try and give you an account of our passage.

"We had head winds and a rough sea most of the time; and as the steamer was very slow, the spray which incessantly flew over her made the deck very wet and, consequently, unpleasant. However, we made the run in nine days from the time we left the breakwater and arrived here early on Saturday morning.

"I went ashore last Sunday and attended church, and then together with Jim Stanley (the young fellow who I told you was going out as Engineer's Store Keeper) climbed the mountain to the ruins of the castle of Blackbeard, a notorious pirate chieftain, who for a long time made this island his home and stronghold. After coming down, we wandered all over the town and saw all that was to be seen, which I suppose is the same as in the generality of West Indian islands—plenty of darkies—men, women and children—bamboo shanties, soldiers and cocoanut trees. . . .

"I expect our next passage to be much more pleasant than the last, as we shall not be heavily burdened by coal, and important additions have been made in the shape of booby-hatches, etc. . . .

"I know, my dear parents, that you felt deeply the parting with me—far more so than I did. But let the fact that I am satisfied and that my chances are more than fair comfort you. As for me, I, for the first time in my life, left home with scarcely a regret and without a tear. I believed that it was my duty both to myself and to you to go, and this belief assuaged the pain of parting.

"I am now setting out for myself in the world, and though young in years, I have every confidence in my ability to go through whatever may be before me. But of that I shall say nothing. Let the future alone prove."

In reply to the letter he received from St. Thomas, Jo Jeffreys wrote (February 1):

"While such fools and intolerable dolts as James Mc-Mullen[1] live, it is almost impossible to expect your family to be kept ignorant of your great danger. I will elucidate the matter. Some few days since a telegraphic despatch (from Boston, I think) appeared in the 'Pub-

---

[1] "Jim" McMullen, as he was commonly called, was regarded by his boy friends as slow of comprehension. One day wishing to go swimming without McMullen, they tried the expedient of telling him one after another that his head was swollen and that he must be sick. This succeeded so well that the boy went home and to bed in a fever of excite-ment, and they had great difficulty in convincing him that they had been deluding him. The experience so frightened Henry George that he never again indulged in that kind of a practical joke.

lic Ledger' setting forth that the U. S. S. *Shubrick* had put into St. Thomas in great distress, want of coal, etc., etc. This I presumed somewhat alarmed your mother; but she received your letter about the same time, and you saying nothing of any storm, but merely mentioning rough weather encountered in the Gulf, she thought no more of it. But here McMullen steps in on last Saturday night (he called once before since your departure) and after propounding several knotty interrogatories to your father, very kindly informed your mother that he had seen an extract from a private letter written by one of the *Shubrick's* engineers to a friend in this city in the 'Evening Journal' (or as Collis says, the 'Evening Disturber') the purport of which was that the *Shubrick* had encountered a terrific storm, that they almost went down, etc., etc.

"I happened to call in a few minutes after and was subjected to a series of questions which made me wince. I had received a letter from you? Yes. Well, what did you say? You said you were well and in good spirits. Was that all? Yes, about all. I was sorry to say I had left the letter at the office. (It was in the breast-pocket of my coat.) Did you say anything about a storm? (This question was propounded by your mother, who looked me straight in the eye, while Cad, Janie and Kate followed her example, and your father, who was reclining on the sofa, turned round to hear the answer, which, with this awful battery of unflinching eyes in front, and the consciousness that your father might have some information upon the subject which he designed to level at me in the rear, I was endeavouring to manufacture into as ingenious a shape as possible. They looked at me; I returned the gaze as steadily as an honest fellow who knew he was going to dissimulate for the sake of an absent friend—but an awful bad fellow—could do. At last I broke silence.) *No.* You had said, however, that you had encountered rough weather and had got out of coal. (My hair almost stood on end, and the perspiration rolled in mad torrents down the exterior covering of my seething brain.)

To this succeeded a number of questions that ·tortured me almost to martyrdom, for, as you know, my very bowels *yearned* to tell the truth. I, however, satisfied your mother that the 'Evening Disturber' had made false representations, and so ends that difficulty.

" . . . You are right, Hen. 'There never was any affectation of sentiment in speech between us when face to face,' and none shall exist now. How do *you* know that we shall never meet again? I should be obliged to you if you would *not* send such letters to me in the middle of business—letters which are calculated to distract my mind and render me as weak as a child. Your ideas absolutely make me gloomy, truth though they be. You know I love you, Hen, as much *as anyone* in this wide world. . . .

"I have commenced to reform, and Bill Jones and myself have for some time been studying geometry together. I spend but little, 37 cents a week on cigars, and loaf only occasionally. I go to the office sometimes in the evening and study law. Bill and I are to take up natural philosophy and grammar in a few days."

The father's letter soon after the departure of the *Shubrick* shows the man's robust nature.

"My dear boy, we have missed you. I have hardly become reconciled to your absence. It seems that I cannot lock the front door without the thought of your coming in; and when the boys visit us—Jeffreys, Jones and the others—it seems as if it leaves a blank when we find you absent. Don't think I regret the step you have taken. On the contrary, the more I think of it, the more I see the hand of Providence in it. . . .

"Nothing has transpired since you left worthy of note. Things are much as you left them. The times are rather on the mend [industrially]. In political matters things look gloomy. The nigger question, Mormonism and General Walker,[1] etc., will, I think, give us trouble; but notwithstanding all this and as much more, the Union is and will be safe as long as there is bunting to make stars and stripes. They may bluster North, East, South and West as much as they please. Our nation is in the hands and under the guidance of a higher Power, who created this republic for a higher and holier destiny, which is not revealed, and will not be until I am long gathered to my fathers."

From St. Thomas to Barbadoes and thence to Pernambuco and Rio Janeiro the little *Shubrick* proceeded, having fair weather and making fair time. A letter written at Monte Video to one of the young friends in Philadelphia (Charley Walton, February 18) gives some characteristic notes:

"We arrived here yesterday morning after a passage of five days from Rio. We lay five days in the latter port and had very fine weather and a pleasant time generally, marred only by one or two little accidents. . . . The first night we stayed there all hands went ashore, wandered over the island, and as a matter of course, got drunk. A couple of the men in trying to come aboard fell over a precipice about forty feet in height. One escaped uninjured, but the other was nearly killed. He is now recovering fast, but it will be some time before his arm, which was broken, will be entirely healed.

"I enjoyed myself very well while we were coaling, wandering along the rocks, catching crabs and toad-

---

[1] Probably a reference to William Walker of Tennessee, who led a filibustering expedition into Lower California and was driven out. Then he went to Nicaragua, C. A., assumed the title of President of that State, and re-established chattel slavery, which had been abolished. He was driven from power in May, 1857, but escaped to New Orleans. In 1860 he led a filibustering expedition against Honduras, but within four months was captured and shot at Truxillo.

Henry George's father, Richard Samuel Henry George.

From daguerreotype taken in the middle fifties.

fish and paddling from one island to another in a canoe, the exact model of the famous one constructed by Crusoe, and like his, made of a single piece.

"I was ashore in Rio but once—on Sunday afternoon—and saw but little of the town, as it was too infernally hot to walk the narrow streets."

The chief incident of the voyage—an event of singular nature—occurred at the port of Monte Video. Two letters containing a brief mention of it have been preserved, but a full and graphic account appeared under the title of "Dust to Dust" in a sketch written by Henry George eight years subsequently and when he was less than twenty-seven, at the request of his friend Edmund Wallazz, for publication in the "Philadelphia Saturday Night,"[1] a prosperous weekly paper, of which Wallazz was then foreman and part owner.

The story in substance is this. An hour after leaving Rio, yellow fever had broken out on the *Shubrick* and several were taken down. All recovered except the Second Assistant Engineer, S. W. Martin, a popular young man on board.

"The crisis seemed past, and if his strength would only last until he neared the Cape, all would be well. . . . Only one port remained to be passed before we should hail the rain and fog, and strength-giving winds —Monte Video. But when we entered that great stream, more sea than river, the mighty La Plata, on which the city is situated, young Martin was dying. . . .

"For some time in intervals of consciousness, Martin had been aware of his approaching end, and the only thing that seemed to trouble him was the idea of dying so far from those he loved, and of being buried where affection might never mark his resting place. It was his last and earnest request that his grave might be made on shore, where his body could be recognised by his friends, and not committed to the waves; and though it was very doubtful if the privilege could be granted, yet the captain resolved to take the corpse into the harbour, and try to obtain permission to bury it ashore.

"And when night came, sadly we talked in little groups upon the deck, while the sound of hammer and plane from the gangway, told that the 'last house' of one of us was being built. Though no star shed its light, still it was not all blackness. The 'river of silver' beamed with a lustre of its own. Not alone the furrows our prow threw aside, or the broad wake we left behind, but the whole surface of the water glowed with phosphorescent brightness, and we seemed to force our way through a sheet of molten silver.

"All night long we steamed up the river, and when the sun again arose—it showed us the harbour of Monte Video. Out beyond all the other shipping lay a stately frigate, the Stars and Stripes of the great republic streaming from her peak in the morning breeze—the old *St. Lawrence*, flagship of the squadron. . . . We were bringing them news and letters from home, and every port of the great ship thronged with faces eager to see the comer from the land they loved. Running up under her quarter, we were hailed and answered, and after the usual inquiries, our captain mentioned the death of young Martin, and his wish to have him buried on shore; but was told that it was impossible, that we would infringe the quarantine rules by even entering the port with the corpse; and was directed to steam back some miles and commit the body to the waves, before entering the harbour.

"The shrill whistle of the boatswain sounded; a boat dropped from the frigate's davits, reached our side, took letters and papers, and our little steamer turned slowly round to retrace her path. We had felt sad while coming up, but a darker gloom hung over all while going down the river. It seemed so hard that the last and only request of the poor boy could not be complied with.

"But swiftly down the current in the bright, fresh morning dashed our little boat, and when the lofty frigate was hull-down behind us, we turned and stopped for the last sad rites.

"Upon the quarter-deck, in reverential silence, all hands were gathered. The large box-like coffin, in which we had hoped to commit our dead to mother earth, bored full of holes and filled up with heavy materials, was placed by the side, covered with the flag. The beautiful burial service was commenced, its solemn sentences sounding doubly solemn under such mournful circumstances—there was a pause—then came the words, 'We, therefore, commit his body to the deep!' and with a surge the waves closed above the dead.

"Hardly a word was spoken as the wheels again took up their task, and we began to ascend the river, but every eye was fixed on the spot we were leaving, and at the same instant an exclamation sprang from every lip as the coffin was seen to rise! The engine was quickly stopped, a boat lowered, and taking a small anchor and some heavy chain, they tried to secure and sink the box. But it was no easy task in the fresh breeze and short, chopping sea, and the coffin seemed almost instinct with life and striving to elude their efforts. Again and again they were foiled in their attempt to fasten the weights, but were at last successful, and once more the water closed above the corpse.

"After waiting some time, to make sure that it could not float again, we started once more up the river, and this time awe was mingled with our grief. Most men who follow the sea have a touch of superstition. There is something in the vastness with which Nature presents herself upon the great waters which influences in this direction even minds otherwise sceptical. And as we steamed up the river, it was more than hinted among many of us that the strong desire of the dying man had something to do with the difficulty of sinking his body.

"This time we passed the frigate, saluting, but not stopping, and entered the port. It was war time; on the Pampas some phase of the interminable quarrels of this Southern federation was being fought out, and the harbour was crowded with men-of-war. Nearly all the Brazilian navy was there, watching the progress of events; and besides these, and the numerous merchantmen, the ensign of almost every nation was displayed above some armed vessel. By direction of the officer who boarded us, we proceeded past them all, to the farther side of the harbour, where we were ordered to lie in quarantine seven days before being allowed to coal.

"The new scene, the various objects of interest around and the duties of clearing up, conspired to make us forget the events of the morning, but the sun was yet some distance above the western horizon when a startling circumstance occurred to recall them to our minds.

"Nearly all hands were busily engaged below, only two or three loitering around the deck, when the quartermaster, sweeping the harbour with his glass, noticed something floating in, which riveted his attention. Again and again he looked at it; then, with surprise and dismay in his face, called the officer of the deck. The whisper spread through the ship, and in a few minutes all were watching in silence the object that seemed drifting towards us. Onward it came, through all the vessels that lay beyond us—now lost to our view, now coming in sight again—turning and tacking as though piloted by life, and steadily holding its course for our steamer. It passed the last ship, and came straight for us. It came closer, and every doubt was dispelled—it was, indeed, the coffin! A thrill of awe passed through every heart as the fact became assured.

"Right under our bows came the box; it touched our side; halted a moment, as if claiming recognition, and then drifted slowly past us towards the shore.

"There was an excited murmur forward, a whispered consultation in the knot of officers aft; then one advanced—'Man the quarter boat, boys; take pick and spades; tow the coffin ashore, and bury the body!'

"It was the work of a moment—the boat shot like an arrow from our side, the ashen oars bending with the energy of the stroke. Reverently and gently they secured the box, and with slow, solemn strokes, towed it to the foot of the desolate looking hill that skirts the bay. There, breaking it open, they bore the corpse, covered with the flag, a little distance up the hillside, and making in the twilight a grave among the chaparral, laid it to rest, marking the spot with a rude cross, which, concealed from observation by the bushes, would yet serve as a mark of recognition, and secure the grave, should it be noticed, from the intrusion of vandal hands.

"And so, spite of all, that dying wish was gratified, and the body which the waters refused to receive was laid to rest in its mother earth."[1]

From Monte Video the *Shubrick* proceeded to the Strait of Magellan, arriving at Cape Virgin on March 6; for instead of taking the long route followed by sailing vessels around Cape Horn, she was to steam by the short route through the strait. The heavy westerly winds and strong currents peculiar to that region made such boisterous weather that progress was greatly retarded and nearly all the coal consumed, so that the crew had to go ashore and cut fire-wood with which to make the next port.[2] To his family Henry George has described the scenery in the western part of the strait as perhaps the most magnificent and impressive he ever beheld.

"The water was clear and green with depth even up to the banks, which in places were sheer walls of rock running up perhaps three thousand feet and mantled at their summits with dazzling snow. In the valleys between these and the mountains beyond were glacial formations, white and green and iridescent; and at the bases where the land flattened out, were heavy growths of evergreens.

---

[1] If Mr. George had any superstitious feeling at the time regarding the matter — and there is nothing to indicate that he had — he certainly did not continue to entertain it in after years, but believed the movements of the coffin due to the accidental loosening of weights, peculiarities of currents and other natural causes.

[2] '*Shubrick's* log.

"Being short of fuel, we brought the little steamer against a bank, and tieing her there, went ashore and cut wood. This consumed a number of days. We ran into a little harbour in the strait and came upon a schooner which belonged to English missionaries with whom we exchanged letters. The missionaries were praying and working with the native Terra del Fuegians. We saw a number of these natives, and they were not at all attractive. I heard afterwards that the Patagonians killed and ate these missionaries."

On the passage up the Pacific coast the *Shubrick* touched at Valdivia, Valparaiso, Panama, and San Diego, and on the 27th of May, 1858, after a voyage of one hundred and fifty-five days from Philadelphia, arrived at San Francisco.

CHAPTER V.

AT THE FRAZER RIVER GOLD FIELDS.

1858.   AGE, 19

WHEN the *Shubrick* glided through the Golden Gate and cast anchor, it was with mixed emotions that Henry George gazed about him. California, bursting on the world ten years before with her astonishing gold discoveries, had now begun to reveal to the prospectors who found that the mineral regions had meanwhile been ocenpied, a new wealth of soil in her amazing agricultural fecundity. She had now been for eight years a State in the Union, and had a population of about three hundred and fifty thousand, of which her chief city, San Francisco, claimed some fifty thousand.

Like a new Eternal City, San Francisco nestled upon a cluster of hills. These hills rose on a narrow spur or peninsula, washed on the west by the ocean and on the east by the bay; and on the north formed one portal of the Golden Gate. The bell in the little pioneer adobe church of the missionary Franciscan monks still tinkled at the "Mission Dolores," and though many substantial buildings had arisen since the entrance on Statehood, the city for the most part still consisted of "cloth and paper shanties." The whole world was sending the flower of youth and energy into the new city; and to the young and bold and adventurous of spirit, San Francisco, for all her newness and roughness, wore a charm, and even fascination, that only they could understand. Should Oregon fail, this, to Henry George, seemed the place to seek his fortune.

He had expected on reaching San Francisco to find a letter from Mrs. Curry telling him of the Oregon prospects, and perhaps inviting him to come up. When a letter came to hand, several days after his arrival, it contained no information on this subject and gave no counsel, and to it he replied (May 29, 1858):

"About an hour after we dropped anchor my cousin, Jim George, came on board. I went ashore with him and spent the day. He has his family here and is doing well. Although we have been here but a short time, yet I have already seen a good deal of the city and agree with Emma that 'it is a dashing place,' rather faster than Philadelphia.

"My mind is not fully made up as to what I shall do. I should feel grateful for your advice. Please write to me as soon as possible. If you still think I can do well in Oregon I will go up as soon as I can procure my discharge from the ship, which I hope to do in two or three weeks. I do not think I shall remain where I am at present, as I wish to settle down as soon as possible; and the old Oregon fever has not entirely died, as you may judge from the fact that I write from San Francisco. I have worked hard and long to get here and have at last succeeded, and I feel convinced that the same spirit will carry me through."

The "Cousin Jim George" referred to was son of Henry's Uncle Dunkin, his father's only brother. James George was book-keeper for the retail clothing firm of J. M. Strowbridge & Co., doing business at Commercial and Sansome streets, and composed of Jerome and W. C.

Strowbridge and E. F. Childs. Childs had a young brother-in-law there named George B. Wilbur, a Rhode Island Yankee, who had gone to California with the hope shared by almost everyone going there—of finding a fortune. Wilbur and Henry George became acquainted, and Wilbur showed the newcomer around town; thereby beginning a friendship that was to be of mutual use in the near years, and though their aptitude and careers became distinct, was to last to the end of life.

And now since the prizes ashore seemed large and many for him who was free and could move quickly, young George had resolved not only not to remain at sea, but not even to embrace the prospect of a place in the Navy Yard at the head of the bay, which Commander DeCamp, who expected to be stationed there, had talked of helping him to get. Though he had no fixed plans, yet it was the boy's wish to be free, and free at once. The obstacle was the *Shubrick's* shipping articles, which he, like everyone else on board, had been compelled to sign at Philadelphia for one year's service, and which would hold him until November 11, 1858. He talked the thing over with Ellen George, James George's wife, a warm-hearted, sympathetic woman, who showed a lively interest in the youth's affairs. It was agreed that he should go into retirement for awhile, seeking the seclusion of a bed at her house, while she should confer with Commander De Camp, which she did. The Commander, as a consequence, failed to notice the absence of the boy, who, after a short season of this retirement, regarded himself as free of the *Shubrick*[1] and at liberty to go where he would. But as yet

---

[1] Though the *Shubrick's* record shows that later on there were a number of desertions among the officers and crew of the vessel, there is no indication whatever as to when Henry George left, or that he did not remain until the expiration of his term of service — Nov. 11, 1858.

no word of encouragement came from Oregon; nor in
San Francisco, though he looked about him, did any inviting opening appear, so that he was left in idleness, consuming his little store of money consisting of wages earned on
the *Shubrick*. All the while letters were coming from
home which yet had a strong influence over him. From
his mother (April 3, 1858) :

"There is nothing stirring or startling in this great
city. Religion seems to be the all-engrossing subject.
Christians are looking for great results from this out-
pouring of the Spirit. Look to Jesus, my dear child."

From his mother (May 3):

"O my dear boy: how much you occupy my thoughts.
Sleeping and waking your whereabouts, your doings,
your comfort, your conduct, your prospects and a thousand other things fill my mind. Away from all you love
and those who love you and would counsel you, O seek,
my child, that wisdom that cometh from above. Then
you will need no other counsellor."

From his father (May 18) :

"We have accounts to-day that Brigham Young, the
Mormon scamp, has submitted to the United States
authority and that forces are entering Salt Lake City.
I hope it may be true. I should like to see him pun-
ished for his rebellion."

From his Sister Jennie (June 3):

"I dreamed of you, Henry, not long ago for three
nights in succession, and I thought each night that you
had returned home. I thought I came home from
school and saw you sitting in the rocking chair in the

front parlour. I ran to you and just as you kissed me
I woke up. I was glad that I was in time for the kiss
anyhow."

The same intense affection that Henry George kindled
in the friends of his manhood was shown for him by the
friends of his youth. The evidence of this on the part of
Jeffreys we have already seen.[1] A letter from Jennie George
(July 2) tells about Charlie Walton:

"Charlie Walton came around the other evening.
. .. . He said that you had written four or five letters to Jo Jeffreys and but one to him. I never saw
him in such a rage. He really almost cried. I pacified
him as much as I could and he went away a little cooler
than he came. I really believe he thinks more of you
than any of the other boys."

This from Edmund Wallazz who had been a printer in
King and Baird's and who was now a man of about twenty-
seven (July 15):

"Your letters dated the 15 and 19 ult., received
this morning. . . .
"To understand my feeling of a peculiar relation existing between us I will mention the feelings which I
experienced when we first heard of the yellow fever on
board the *Shubrick*. Jeffreys told me of the report
and of your father's fears near midnight of a day, I
think, in the latter part of February or the early part
of March. I was at first stunned; a cold, chilly sensation overpowered me for a few minutes; but after
awhile I said, with an earnestness which made Jeffreys
look surprised: 'Harry is not dead. If he were I should
know it.' He asked if I believed in ghosts. Of course
not, in the vulgar idea of ghosts. And yet I felt certain

---

[1] Page 61.

that if you were dead I should be informed of it. Nay, more. So strong was this feeling that for several days I sat alone in the dark at midnight waiting for you. And in those hours of terrible suspense how often did I think of your probable death, and picture your poor body tossed about by the billows of the Southern Atlantic, far, far from all who loved you! Firmly, I believe, if you had been dead, and if you had come to me, I would not have been frightened at all, only awe-struck, and it may be heart-wrung, by the thought that my advice had much to do with your going. But let this rest forever now. You cannot doubt my love; I cannot doubt yours."

But now Henry George was ready to act. For in June had come the thrilling news of large gold discoveries just over the American line, in the British possessions, on the Frazer River, not far from its mouth. There was much excitement in San Francisco, especially among that multitude of prospectors and adventurers, who, finding all the then known placer lands in California worked out or appropriated, and not willing to turn to the slow pursuits of agriculture, had gathered in the city with nothing to do. A mad scramble for the new fields ensued, and so great was the rush from this and other parts that fifty thousand persons are said to have poured into the Frazer River region within the space of a few weeks. Indeed, all who did not have profitable or promising employment tried to get away, and the *Shubrick's* log shows that most of her officers and crew deserted for the gold fields.[1]

---

[1] "There is no mystery as to the cause which so suddenly and so largely raised wages in California in 1849, and in Australia in 1852. It was the discovery of placer mines in unappropriated land to which labour was free that raised the wages of cooks in San Francisco restaurants to $500 a month, and left ships to rot in the harbour without officers or crew until their owners would consent to pay rates that in any other part of the

James George was doing well with the San Francisco clothing house, but caught in the gold excitement, he thought he saw a chance for a fortune in the sale of miner's supplies; and he formed a co-partnership with O. F. Giffin, of San Francisco, a dealer in nuts, dried fruits, etc., doing business on Front Street, between Sacramento and Clay. The agreement was that James was to go to Victoria, on Vancouver's Island, just off the mouth of the Frazer, and open a miner's supply store.

This project of James George's had much attractiveness for Henry George, but he resolved to be cautious and not venture on reports that might prove to be false. To Martha Curry, who now had become Mrs. Malthrop, he wrote (June 29):

> "I have left the steamer I came out in and am now staying at the same house as my cousin. In all probability I will be able to get employment of some kind in a few days. I think I shall stay here until next spring, and then, if the diggings on Frazer River turn out to be as good as reported, I shall go up there. . . .
>
> "Messrs. Byron and Pipe are both well, though rather the worse for their long journey and long handling."

A few days following this came a letter from Mrs. Curry (July 9) that ended all present thought of Oregon and increased that of the Frazer River. "As for this place," wrote she, "business is dull. The mines seem to be the all-absorbing theme." So with hope of Oregon closed and with no chance of work offering in San Francisco, the

---

globe seemed fabulous. Had these mines been on appropriated land, or had they been immediately monopolised so that rent could have arisen, it would have been land values that would have leaped upward, not wages." — " Progress and Poverty," Book V. chap. ii (Memorial Edition, p. 290).

young man found himself urged along the line of his inclinations—toward the Frazer; and with the promise from his cousin James of employment as clerk in the store, should he fail at the diggings, Henry George's hopes burned high and he wrote home of golden expectations. But the news of his starting for Victoria carried something like dismay to the quiet home in Philadelphia. His mother wrote (August 15):

"I think this money-getting is attended with too many sacrifices. I wished it all in the bottom of the sea when I heard of your going to Victoria, but since it has been explained to me I feel better. . . . I shall never feel comfortable until you are settled down quietly at some permanent business. This making haste to grow rich is attended with snares and temptations and a great weariness of the flesh. It is not the whole of life, this getting of gold. When you write explain about the place and how you are situated. Then we will look on the bright side."

A month later (September 18) she wrote:

"We all feel happy and thankful that you have arrived safely at Victoria and that your prospects appear bright. Don't be too anxious or too sanguine. This making haste to be rich I am afraid of. Remember you are but young. We do not expect great things as yet. You have just passed your nineteenth birthday. Did you think of it, or were you too busy? If you had been home we would have had a jollification. What a kissing time there would have been, playing Copenhagen and so forth. Hen, kissing is quite out of the fashion since you left; no kissing parties at all, I believe."

His father in the same letter wrote:

"Your letter from Victoria came safe to hand and you may be sure we were glad to receive it. I had become quite anxious about you, inasmuch that your last letter gave us the information that you were off on a trading expedition. I did not know how you would be situated, but now I feel more reconciled and think that your chances are fair. But I hope you will not build your castle in the air. Fortunes are not to be made in a hurry; it takes time and application. However, I say again, your prospects are fair. Nurse your means and use all the economy you can and I think in the end a fortune will be sure. Still, my dear son, consider; contentment is better than both hands full with labour and travel."

Henry George, working his way as seaman on a top-sail schooner, reached Victoria when the excitement was at the flood. That place, established in 1843 as a trading-fort of the Hudson Bay Company—those pioneers of commerce through the north-western part of the continent—and beautifully situated on Vancouver's Island in the majestic Puget Sound, had, with the gold discoveries, suddenly swelled in population, until it was estimated that at times ten thousand miners, in sheds and tents, gathered about the more substantial structures.

Henry George arrived at Victoria when the river, still at the season that rains and melting snows on its great mountain water-sheds swelled high its volume, came tearing down its long, twisting course and rushed through its rocky gorges like a roaring flood of destruction, earning the name sometimes given it—"The Terrible Frazer." The gold had been found at Yale and Fort Hope, a hundred miles up stream, in the exposed bars and the bed of the river when the water was low, so that with the water in flood, all gold-seeking operations had to come to a standstill and there was nothing to do but to wait until the water had subsided. The young fortune hunter, therefore, went into James George's store.

The store was in a rough wooden structure of one story and an attic, or rather loft. It stood on Wharf Street, beside the Victoria hotel, facing the harbour. Henry George worked very hard there. Part of the time he slept in the loft, reaching it by a ladder. He fastened a note outside the street door inviting customers who came out of the regular hours to "Please give this door a kick." In a letter to his Sister Jennie subsequently from San Francisco (December 6, 1858) he said:

"You innocently ask whether I made my own bed at Victoria. Why, bless you, my dear little sister! I had none to make. Part of the time I slept rolled up in my blanket on the counter, or on a pile of flour, and afterwards I had a straw mattress on some boards. The only difference between my sleeping and waking costumes was that during the day I wore both boots and cap, and at night dispensed with them."

But the full picture of his condition was not at once revealed to the folks at home. He had on starting for Victoria written of such large expectations that pride now prevented him from saying more than he could help about the poor results. Jo Jeffreys wrote (October 3):

"There is one remarkable thing in your letters, or rather *not* in your letters, which is this, that you fail to say whether you are prospering *at all* in your present business, or even if it supports you, and which I certainly should be glad to hear."

From his Sister Carrie (October 4):

"How I should like to see you in your new situation. Your account of your cooking is quite laughable. I should just like to look in upon you while you were thus engaged and see what kind of a cook you make."

His father wrote him a letter containing worldly wisdom (October 4):

"We have all sorts of things going on here in Philadelphia. On the first of September we had the grand Ocean Telegraph celebration, though the cable has never spoken since, and I have great doubts that it ever will. Yet a great thing has been accomplished; or at any rate, if the practicability of a lightning rod through the ocean be not accomplished in my day, it will be in yours.

"Uncle Joseph Van Dusen took dinner with us yesterday. He seems much pleased with your present prospects and bade me when I wrote to say that if this thing should be successful their house would be glad to send you a load of goods direct which would cost much less than at San Francisco. About that I do not know—I mean as regards cheapness. You know Uncle Joseph and his partners. Show them where they can invest safely and profitably and they have the means and the nerve. This information may in the future, if this thing succeeds, be of great advantage to James and yourself. Recollect old John Sharp's advice: 'When thee makes a friend use him and keep him.'

"We are all well. Tom [one of Henry's brothers] is just promoted in school and is making very good progress. He is sharp, and will, if spared, make a smart and active man. I don't think I told you of his Fourth of July speech at dinner. When we were about half through Tom rose and said: 'Ladies and Gentlemen: This is the first time in my life that I have sat down to a Fourth of July dinner without ice-cream. I will, therefore, put the question. All who are in favour of ice-cream will please say, aye.' Of course it was unanimously carried, to the joy of all present. After he found it so, he very gracefully turned to me, saying: 'It is carried unanimously, Mr. Chairman. Will you please advance the money?' I could not get out of this, and put up fifty cents, which proved to be satisfactory."

Ferdinand Formhals, now a well-known citizen of San Francisco, who had charge of a stove and tinware store beside James George's store on Wharf Street, Victoria, says that he knew Henry George there, and that "George had nothing to say about the single tax or political economy then." Yet that the youth's mind was even then quietly at work is proved by a speech he made in San Francisco thirty-two years later:[1]

"Let me, since I am in San Francisco, speak of the genesis of my own thought. I came out here at an early age, and knew nothing whatever of political economy. I had never intently thought upon any social problem. One of the first times I recollect talking on such a subject was one day, when I was about eighteen, after I had come to this country, while sitting on the deck of a topsail schooner with a lot of miners on the way to the Frazer River. We got talking about the Chinese, and I ventured to ask what harm they were doing here, if, as these miners said, they were only working the cheap diggings? 'No harm now,' said an old miner, 'but wages will not always be as high as they are to-day in California. As the country grows, as people come in, wages will go down, and some day or other white men will be glad to get those diggings that the Chinamen are now working.' And I well remember how it impressed me, the idea that as the country grew in all that we are hoping that it might grow, the condition of those who had to work for their living must become, not better, but worse."

But now something caused a falling out between the cousins. What the trouble was does not appear, though in after years Henry George said that he had "behaved badly towards Jim George." The offence could not have been grave, as they were on the old friendly terms soon again in San Francisco. But however this may be, Henry

---

[1] Metropolitan Hall, Feb. 4, 1890.

left James' employ and went to live in a tent with George
Wilbur, who had come up from San Francisco to dig gold.
Wilbur had since his arrival made an unsuccessful trip
up the river, but was determined to try again. Meanwhile he was driving a water cart for a living. Henry
George proposed to go up the river with Wilbur, but before they could set off they were daunted by the stories
of failure that returning miners were bringing down.
While in this wavering state of mind, Ferdinand Formhals
gave Henry George information that caused him to aban-
don the project. Formhals was something of a chemist
and had from curiosity been analysing some of the sam-
ples of "pure gold from the river" that were being handed
about, and found them to be a mixture of tin, lead and
other metals. He believed that there was some gold at
the diggings, but only a little—not enough to be worth
searching for. Time has confirmed Formhals' judgment,
comparatively little gold having at any time been taken
out of this part of the Frazer River, the really rich deposits being found in the Cariboo region, several hundred
miles farther up; but these places were not discovered for
a number of years afterwards.

Hope of fiuding a fortune at the diggings thus closing
before him, and having no other employment, and for that
matter without prospect of any at Victoria, Henry George
decided to return at once to San Francisco, and when
there, should no opening offer, to take again to the sea,
and keep to it as a calling. With this determination, he
borrowed enough money from George Wilbur and others
to buy steerage passage down to San Francisco. George
Wilbur says of the setting off:

"He had no coat; so I gave him mine. An old fellow named Wolff peddled pies among the tents, and

thinking that Harry would enjoy these more than the food he would get aboard the ship, we bought six of them, and as he had no trunk, we put them in his bunk, and drew the blanket over them so that nobody would see them and steal them. He wrote me from San Francisco when he got down that the first night out he was so tired that he threw himself down on his bunk without undressing, and that he did not think of the pies until the morning, when he found that he **had been** lying on top of them all night."

CHAPTER VI.

TOSSED ABOUT BY FORTUNE.

1858-1859.   AGE, 19-20.

TOWARDS the end of November, 1858, Henry George arrived at San Francisco from Victoria "dead broke." And now commenced a stretch of years notable for a restless pitching about, with shifting scenes of prosperity and adversity—years, though, that showed progress, if irregular and jolting.

This period opened with soft sunshine, for as the impecunious youth walked the streets, meeting only strange faces and getting only rebuffs when he applied for work, and when his mind had again turned to the sea as a means of livelihood, he came face to face with David Bond, a compositor whom he had known at King & Baird's printing house in Philadelphia. Learning of his plight, Bond took him to Frank Eastman's printing office and got him employment to set type. The next letter home breathed of prosperity. To his Sister Jennie (December 6) he said:

> "I am at present working in a printing office and am, therefore, busy all day, and the evenings I spend in reading, unless (as is often the case) I go to see Ellie George.
> "After being deprived of reading for such a time,

it is quite delightful to be able to read as much as I wish. In the house in which I am stopping there is a good library, which to me is one of its prominent attractions. .

"I am glad that you are so nearly through school. How would you like to come out here and teach? Teachers here get very good pay, the lowest—the A, B, C, teachers—getting $50 per month; the principals, $200. Ellie George gets $100 a month. Lady's board costs from $25 to $30 per month.

"Women are sadly wanted here. In Victoria there are hardly any, and you can plainly see the effects of the absence of women on society at large.

"I have few acquaintances either here or in Victoria —I mean boys or men. Don't on any consideration think I have thought of girls, for I haven't seen one to speak to, save those I told you about, since I left Philadelphia. But I suppose in some respects it is much better, as I spend less money.

"I am boarding now, and have been for these past two weeks in the 'What Cheer House,' the largest, if not the finest, hotel in the place. I pay $9 per week and have a beautiful little room and first rate living.

"I get $16 per week the way I am working now, but will soon strike into something that will pay me better. . . .

"I suppose you have all grown somewhat since I left. I have not changed much, except that I am even uglier and rougher looking. You thought I looked hard when I came home from Calcutta, but you should have seen me in Victoria!

"How I should like to be home to-night, if only for an hour or two.

"Give my love and respects to *all*. I would write to them if I wasn't so lazy. (You see I call things by their right names once in a while.)

"So good-bye my *dear* sister. I will write you a longer letter when I feel more like it.

"Your affectionate brother,

"H. GEORGE."

"P. S. Wouldn't that signature look nice at the bottom of a check for $1,000—that is, if I had the money in the bank."

Four years before young George wrote this letter a young man of thirty-two named Ulysses S. Grant had for a short time slept in an attic room in this same hotel, the "What Cheer House." He had come down from Ft. Vancouver, Columbia River, where, utterly disgusted with himself and the life he was leading, he had resigned from a captaincy in the United States Army, and was, when in San Francisco, trying to make his way eastward with a view to going into business or farming. Fame was to claim him in the rapidly approaching events.

The "What Cheer House" still stands and is doing business, though in a humble way. In the fifties it was the best house of its kind in the city. A temperance hotel, and a model of propriety and cleanliness, it was for the accommodation of men entirely. No women were ever received and not one was engaged on the premises. It was established by R. B. Woodward, a New Englander, who from its proceeds founded Woodward's Gardens, famous all over the Pacific Coast for more than two decades as a beautiful pleasure resort, containing a menagerie, a museum, a theatre, an art gallery, an aquarium and a variety of other attractions. One of the distinguishing features of this house was a little library, numbering several hundred volumes, well selected, and among them some economic works. Hon. James V. Coffey, who twelve or fourteen years later became an intimate friend of Henry George's, questioning him as to where he had during his busy life found time and books to read, was told that his solid reading was begun in this little library, while staying at the "What Cheer House" and at intervals following:

"Mr. George told me that he spent much of his time when out of work in that little room and that he had read most of the books. That, he said, was the first place he saw Adam Smith's 'Wealth of Nations,' though I cannot remember that he said he read it then. Indeed, in his last writings, he has said that he did not read a line of Adam Smith until long after this period."

This new state of things gave Richard George, the father, undisguised satisfaction. He wrote (Jannary 19, 1859):

"I rejoice to find that you are doing so well. You now see the propriety of a young man just starting in life having some trade to fall back on in time of need, and you will say, 'Pop was right, not only in this, but in many other things in which I dissented.'
"However, so far God has ordered all things well, and my earnest and sincere prayer is that he may still watch over you until he brings *all* at last to his eternal Kingdom.   .   .   .
"My dear boy, let me say again to you: Be careful and nurse your means; lay up all you can and *owe no man anything* and you will be safe. Do not let others entice you. Act on your own judgment, and I hope and trust before I am called hence, to see you return prosperous and happy, which may God grant."

His mother took up another matter (February 2):

"I am very glad you have left Victoria and have some of the comforts of life, and sorry to hear that Ellen is going there. I should not think that Jim would want her until he could make things more comfortable, and the people were more civilised—better society, a few of her own sex, at least. But this, you say, is what they want—women. Ellen will be a star of the first magnitude. Then I hope she will persuade others to go with her—some that have husbands there. Then there will soon be a better state of things.　A writer of great celebrity has said: 'All men that avoid female society have dull perceptions and are stupid, or have gross tastes and revolt against what is pure.'　One of the great benefits a man may derive from women's society is that he is bound to be respectful to them.　The habit is of great good to your moral man.　There is somebody to whom he is bound to be constantly attentive and respectful.　Moreover, this elevates and refines him.

"What will you do without Ellen and the children? . . . Have you made no other acquaintances?　Is there no other place you visit?"

Jo Jeffreys had a word of advice (February 3):

"After having talked with Ned Wallazz and Billy Jones for some three hours, I turn with great pleasure to the consideration of you, my very respectable and respected friend.

"It was not my purpose to induce you to follow the legal profession, though I think you in every way capable to discharge its responsibilities with honour.　I meant by what I said in a former letter to induce you to adopt *some one particular employment* to the exclusion of *every other*.　*If you mine*, do so *until* you have succeeded in your object.　If you enter a house as clerk, stay at it in God's name.　If you should unfortunately resolve to follow printing, follow it with all your abilities and energy until there shall no longer be any ueeessity for it.　You will allow me to say that your great fault (and I think it is your worst one) is that of half-doing things, *in this sense*, that you vacillate about the execution of that which alone secures permanent success and lasting fame.　Few men are competent in *one* lifetime to win honour by more than *one* employment, and these few you would perhaps find were—unlike you —favoured by circumstances.

"Now you are competent for any labour to which your inclinations may direct you.　You are not competent to succeed at a dozen employments, nor can you hope to amass a fortune by labouring at them alternately. If you live on as you are doing now, why, *you will live on;* you will earn sufficient to maintain you in comfort, *but that is all.* You can hardly hope by mining one month, by printing the next, and by serving in a clerkship a third, ever to arrive at a competence.

"Why you do this is evident. You are dissatisfied, either because you are not advancing or for trivial reasons, and then you undertake something different. Now you cannot expect to avoid unpleasant things, and you cannot expect to jump on a fortune, like a waif thrown away by a thief in his flight. Success is the reward of long exertion, not the triumph of a momentary energy. It is the crown for which, like Cromwell, you must struggle long and well. It is like happiness hereafter, only to be obtained by patient and continued servitude. . . .

"I wish I could make you feel as I do. You wouldn't then complain in after life (as you *will* do without you adopt my opinions) of the caprice and the wanton vacillation of Fortune's Goddess. . . .

"I recognise the difficulties of your position and how you are situated, and am aware that you are not at liberty to strike out into anything, as you were here. But do the best you can. Take my advice wherever it's possible to do it; I mean that which respects your employment and notwithstanding other embarrassing difficulties."

But notwithstanding Jo Jeffreys' counsel, a change quickly came, for business becoming slack at Eastman's and the other printing houses, George was unable to follow his trade. But refusing to remain idle, he obtained a position of weigher in the rice mill of Waite & Battles, on Fremont Street, near Mission. He wrote home (February 16, 1859):

"I am still in the rice mill and like it very well. I

shall stay, of course, until I am sure I can make a change for the better. I have to get up pretty early though, and consequently retire early. Indeed, you would be pleased to see what regular hours I keep. For months past 10 o'clock has invariably seen me in bed, for I have no friends here, and neither the disposition nor the money to go to the theatre or other places of amusement.

"Everything is still very dull, but the late rains, by increasing the gold yield, will tend to make times better."

Soon after this George Wilbur came down from Victoria and Henry George and he went to room together. First they lived in Natoma Street, then one of the quiet residence portions of the city. Afterwards they roomed on Pine Street, Henry George taking his meals at the "What Cheer House." Mr. Wilbur says of his companion at this period:

"Very soon after our acquaintance I discovered that he was studious and eager to acquire knowledge, and when we came to room together I frequently woke up at night to find him reading or writing. If I said: 'Good heavens, Harry, what's the matter? Are you sick?' he'd tell me to go to sleep or invite me to get dressed and go out for a walk with him. A spin around for a few blocks would do and then we'd get to bed again. I never saw such a restless human being."

That Henry George was in other ways restless was clear enough. His active, energetic nature would doubtless have made him restless anywhere, but in California the conditions were peculiarly conducive to it, for it was a country where thousands of active, independent young men like himself were opening up the richest mineral region in the world; a country which, within twenty years from the first gold discovery in 1848, was to yield $800,-000,000 of the precious metal.[1] "California," he wrote to his Sister Caroline in January, "is sadly in want of missionaries and I think it would be a good notion for the Sunday school to send a few out, provided they be gold-fever proof." As shown by his Frazer River adventure, Henry George himself was not "gold-fever proof"; and now he kept thinking of the stories of fortune that were coming in from the California mines, and he talked with a young Philadelphian, Freeman A. Camp, who came to see him at the "What Cheer House," as to the chances they would have there. His mother, doubtless perceiving what was floating through his mind, wrote (March 3):

"Are you getting lazy? You do not write as long letters as you used to, nor tell us much when you do write. You change your business so often I should think you would have a great deal to tell. Remember, everything that concerns you will interest us. . . . I suppose the old proverb does not apply in California: 'A rolling stone,' etc. Be that as it may, we will rejoice when you are settled."

Two weeks later (March 17) his mother again wrote:

"I am sorry Ellie has left you, though it is all right; she certainly should be with her husband. I hope you have found some acquaintances among her friends, where you can go and spend a social evening. I don't believe in living without society, and least of all female society. And here I know you will have to be careful, for if the women are not of the right stamp, instead of elevating and refining you, they may prove your ruin. I like your early hours, but not your lonely ones. You should have a few good friends. Here, as in all other anxieties concerning you, I can only breathe the prayer: 'My Father, be thou the guide of his youth.'"

---

[1] Hittell's "History of California," Vol. III. p. 160.

But even if her son had the disposition to keep steadily
at work, the rice mill gave indications of temporarily closing down.   In April he wrote to his Sister Caroline:

> "We have not been very busy at the mill lately, ex-
> cept for a day or two at a time; but this does not make
> much difference to me, as I have to stay there whether
> busy or not.   I generally get up about 6 A.M., go to the
> hotel and take breakfast, and from there to the mill.   I
> come up again at about half past six in the evening,
> eat supper, go into the library and read until about 9
> P.M., when I come up to the room and write or think
> for an hour or two and then turn in.   A pretty quiet
> way of living; but there is no telling what will turn
> up next."

And what did "turn up next" was anything but quiet,
for the rice mill closing down, he was thrown out of work,
and he started off into the interior of the State for the
mines.

The day had passed when more than the occasional man
could find some overlooked and unappropriated spot on
river bed or bar, where, with no more equipment than
shovel, pick and pan, he could draw forth any considerable amount of the precious metal.   Though the gold-
bearing region of California, including the northern mines
and the southern mines, extended from Mt. Shasta to Mt.
Whitney and embraced an area approximately as great as
England's territory, every river bank, bar or bed giving
the slightest indication of gold had been worked over and
over.   The nature of mining then became different.
From "wet diggings" in the river channels, operations
had turned to "dry diggings" in arid ravines, hill slopes
and elevated flats; which led to "coyote-hole" mining (bur-
rowing into the side of hills or boring wells) ; to "hydrau-
lic mining" (the concentration of a powerful column of

water against a hill or mountain side so as to wash the
gravel or "pay dirt" down through the sluice box or
strainer) ; and lastly to "quartz mining," with its shafts
and tunnels, stamp mills and heavy machinery. Gold mining, therefore, had changed its aspect, so that the average,
common man could no longer expect to find, except occasionally, places unappropriated, where, with no special
knowledge, or special appliances or other capital, he could
find any considerable amount of the precious metal or
where he could "dig" and "wash out" even ordinary
"wages."

What drew most gold seekers, and what drew Henry
George, into the mining regions was not so much the hope
of mining in itself as of "prospecting" or "locating a
claim"—finding on the unworked and unappropriated
lands places that would yield to the newer processes the
precious metal in quantities sufficient to pay for the working. Such a claim might be sold to or worked on shares
by others who had the skill and capital, so that as soon
as the rumour of a rich discovery had spread, multi-
tudes of "prospectors" came rushing to the locality, eager
to "stake off claims." The prospector was, therefore,
essentially one who roamed from place to place at the
beck of the Golden Goddess; and since she was whimsical
and beckoned hither and thither, the prospector was always on the move.

There are no clear evidences as to what locality Henry
George had set his hopes on, though the probabilities are
that hearing in San Francisco confusing reports from a
hundred different points, he concluded to strike off for
some nearer and more advantageous centre, there to determine to which particular mining spot to go; and it seems
likely that his first objective point was Placerville, formerly known as "Hangtown," and before that as "Dry

Diggings." For Placerville had not only developed rich finds in its immediate vicinity, but in some instances large treasure was found by digging into the very ground on which its cabins and houses stood. Moreover, it was on the old emigrant route from the East and the road from the Carson River to the Sacramento valley; and with its stores, hotels and saloons, was a place of recreation and supply for all that region of the Sierras.

To purpose to go to the mines was one thing; to get there was another, but young George was determined. "Having no other way of reaching them," he said subsequently,[1] "I started out to walk. I was, in fact, what would now be called a tramp. I had a little money, but I slept in barns to save it and had a rough time generally." But soon he had to spend his money, and then though slight in build and never what would be called muscular, he was forced to do farm work and other manual labour to keep himself alive. He had got some distance towards the mines, but for sheer want of living necessaries, could go no farther; and with great toil, and some real suffering, he worked his way back to San Francisco.

This covered a period of nearly two months—for physical labour the hardest two months in all his life—during which time he seems not to have written a single letter home. While he was in the mountains, the Currys had written of an opportunity to set type on the "Statesman," in Portland, with pay according to competency; but when he had got back to San Francisco the time to accept had passed. Then it was that he learned of the death at Victoria of his sincere friend, Ellen George, and this news, taken with the experience just closed and a poor out-look for work in San Francisco, depressed his spirits, though

---

[1] Meeker notes, October, 1897.

he tried to write cheerfully home to his Aunt Mary (June 17):

"Jim George has gone up to Victoria again, but will be down as soon as he can settle up his business, which will probably be in two or three weeks. The children are here going to school; they are in the best health and spirits.

"We are enjoying splendid weather, just warm enough, though for the last few days it has been quite hot, reminding one of the summers at home. For some time past we have had plenty of green peas, strawberries and all the early summer vegetables and fruits. In ten or fifteen years this will be one of the greatest fruit countries in the world, for fruit trees are yearly being set out by the thousand and grape vines by the million.

"I am doing nothing just now, but expect to go to work next week. I have given up all idea of going to the mines.

"Frazer River seems to have given out at last, and every steamer that comes down is filled with miners. The rich deposits of a month or two ago appear to have been without foundation.

"I must bring my letter to a sudden close, for the clock has struck eleven, and I will just have time to get down to the post office to mail this. I intended to write a longer letter, but coming up here I stopped to look at the operation of moving a house, which must have consumed more time than I was aware of. The way they raise, lower, and pull big houses around the city here is astonishing."

He had, indeed, given up all hope of going to the mines and also pretty much all hope of remaining ashore, where there seemed to be no work for him and no future. Thoughts of the sea came back in a flood tide. They ranged along the line of ocean heroes, and he asked himself why he should not follow that calling and rise to

fame? He was thinking earnestly of this, and stood at
the parting of the ways, when his career was decided as
if by accident. For the second time David Bond, through
a chance meeting, offered a kindly service and obtained
for his young friend a position as compositor—this time
on the weekly "Home Journal" owned by Joseph C. Duncan. Thought of a career at sea never returned.

Printer's wages in California were at that time still
high, the union rate for piece work being seventy-five cents
a thousand ems and for time work to the average man,
thirty dollars a week. But as George was still a minor,
he got only a boy's pay for work in the regular hours—
twelve dollars a week. He resolved now to keep, if he
possibly could, to type-setting until he should come of age
and be qualified as a journeyman. When somewhat settled he wrote to his Sister Jennie (August 2):

"You ask me about my studies. I am afraid I do
not study much. I have not time and opportunity (or
nearer the truth, perhaps, will enough) to push through
a regular course. But I try to pick up everything I
can, both by reading and observation, and flatter myself
that I learn at least something every day. My principal object now is to learn my trade well, and I am
pitching in with all my strength. So anxious am I
now to get ahead and make up for lost time that I never
feel happier than when at work, and that, so far from
being irksome, is a pleasure. My heart just now is
really in my work. In another year I'll be twenty-one
and I must be up and doing. I have a pretty good
prospect ahead and think that before many months I
shall get into something better where I can make good
wages. . . .

"My time is now pretty well taken up. As soon as I
rise in the morning I go to breakfast and then immediately to work, which I seldom leave until nearly seven
o'clock and once in a while not until one or two in the

morning. There are only three others in the office—
nice social fellows—which makes it pleasant for me.
I do not make much, but I am learning a good deal
and think I have a pretty good prospect, so that I am
quite satisfied."

This contentment of mind was broken by news of the
death of the dearest friend of his boyhood, Jo Jeffreys.
Mrs. George revealed her sympathetic heart (August 18):

"I feel as though I must say something to you, but
my heart is full of the one theme, poor Jeffreys, poor
Jo. O I cannot tell you of the anguish I feel when I
think of him, and I can think of nothing else. . . .
The agonising thought with me is the uncertainty of
his state. O had he time to call upon his Saviour; to
say: 'God, be merciful to me, a sinner.' . . .
"O his youth, his bright mind, his sensitiveness, his
love for you made me feel an interest in him of no common kind. I do mourn for him sincerely. I know
your heart too well to doubt your grief.
"Pop thought you would like to have a lock of his
hair."

By the same mail Will Jones wrote:

"Poor Jeffreys has paid the debt of nature, unan-
ticipated and mourned by all. Brilliant in life, flashing upon our vision as a meteor, and as a meteor so soon
to be lost in the impenetrable gloom of night. . . .
"We buried him at the Odd Fellows' Cemetery, in our
lot there, the last tribute of regard I could offer. None
of his family was there save his two brothers, who came
on from New York to the funeral."

Jo Jeffreys' death was a bitter and heavy loss. It
snapped the tie of boyhood. Henry George's life from
that time forward was the life of the man. In November
(20) he wrote to his mother:

"For the past week we have had beautiful weather, and I have employed every possible opportunity to sun myself. The shortness of the days makes this almost impracticable, except on Sundays, when I generally take a long walk outside of the city.

"There is nothing of any interest going on here now. Even the news of the 'bloody Harper's Ferry rebellion,' couldn't get up the smallest kind of an excitement, except among the political papers. General Scott has returned from San Juan, and therefore, all danger from that quarter has ceased for the present. Even the interior towns have for the time stopped burning down; so that, excepting the non-arrival of the mail steamer, we are left without even a decent topic of conversation.

"Letters from the Currys are getting more and more like angel's visits.

"I am still pursuing the even tenor of my way—working, walking, reading and sleeping.

"Thursday is Thanksgiving day for us Californians, as I suppose it is with you at home. I shall try and observe the day with the usual ceremonies, and will think of home even more than usual. I hope you will have a pleasant time, and oh! how I wish I could share it with you."

He wrote in this slighting manner of public matters in California doubtless to calm his mother's mind should she hear rumours from the West; for as a matter of fact most sensational events growing out of the slavery struggle there were crowding into this period. Only the year before the Supreme Court of the State had delivered a decision in the case of a negro named Archy which was described as "giving the law to the North and the nigger to the South." And now, on the just past 7th of September (1859), after the most bitter and tumultuous political campaign ever held in California, the Lecompton, or proslavery, party swept the State. Bad blood raised during the canvass left many scores to be settled after election,

the most conspicuous resulting in a duel between David
S. Terry, Chief Justice of the California Supreme Court,
a pronounced pro-slavery supporter, and U. S. Senator
David C. Broderick, the foremost anti-slavery man west of
the Rocky mountains. Eighty persons were present to
witness Broderick get a death-wound and Terry go un-
scathed. Broderick was carried to San Francisco and
half-hourly bulletins were posted before a surging and
excited multitude. He was accorded a public funeral and
his name became a rally-word in the anti-slavery cause on
the Pacific Coast.[1]

Henry George was not unconscious of such events; on
the contrary he took a burning and apprehensive interest
in them. His father's mind, also, was filled with apprehension arising from similar events in the East, for he
wrote (December 3):

"We have had a high old time with the Harper Ferry
'rebellion,' (as it is called) and John Brown. The abo-
litionists are making all the capital they can out of this
poor fanatic. He is magnified and glorified beyond
anything human, and dies a martyr, according to their
belief. It is having a great effect upon business, and
has thrown trade into something of a panic. Our iron
men suffer, I am told, on account of the Southern merchants everywhere refusing to have anything to do with
Northern men. What the result will be none can tell.
I have always been of the opinion that this Union could
never be dissolved, but if the present feeling is kept
up and we do not get another Andrew Jackson for our
next President, I fear I shall be mistaken in my opinion.

"Brown was hanged yesterday at 15 minutes past 11
without any disturbance. But the end is not yet."

---

[1] "Broderick and Gwin," by James O'Meara, pp. 225-254. Terry was
shot and killed by a Deputy U. S. Marshal in 1889, when committing
an assault upon U. S. Supreme Court Justice Field, growing out of a
case in which Terry had been committed to jail by Judge Field for contempt of court.

CHAPTER VII.

SIX PRINTERS AND A NEWSPAPER.

1860-61.   AGE, 21-22.

THE year 1860 opened auspiciously for the young printer. He was earning steady if small wages at his trade, and purposed not to be diverted, but to keep at it until he came of age in the following September, when he would qualify as a journeyman, and could then demand a man's full pay. To his father he wrote (Jannary 4):

"Christmas and New Year's days were passed by me as pleasantly as could have been expected. The weather, however, on both days was bad, although fine both before and after. On New Year's day I took supper with two of the *Shubrick's* boys, and a friend of mine who likewise hails from Philadelphia. We had a very social, pleasant time, talking over our old adventures; and in the evening we went to the theatre to see Richard III. I have been to a play but three or four times since I have been in the country. I haven't much taste that way, and unless the performance is very good, I would rather be reading or talking. . . .

"I intend to stay where I am until my next birthday —if the paper lasts that long—when I will be admitted to the Union, and to all the rights and privileges of a journeyman printer; and then to work as hard and save as much money as I can, and in a year or two to come

99

home, for a visit, at any rate. A couple of hundred (at the present rates of fare) would enable me to come home, stay a little while, and then come back, if it were best; and it does not take long to raise that if a person can get work."

It may have been to this performance of Richard III. that Henry George referred more than thirty years later in life (February 4, 1890) in a speech in San Francisco, when, tracing the genesis of his thought on social questions, he said:

"I remember, after coming down from the Frazer River country, sitting one New Year's night in the gallery of the old American theatre—among the gods— when a new drop curtain fell, and we all sprang to our feet, for on that curtain was painted what was then a dream of the far future—the overland train coming into San Francisco; and after we had shouted ourselves hoarse, I began to think what good is it going to be to men like me—to those who have nothing but their labour? I saw that thought grow and grow. We were all—all of us, rich and poor—hoping for the development of California, proud of her future greatness, looking forward to the time when San Francisco would be one of the great capitals of the world; looking forward to the time when this great empire of the west would count her population by millions. And underneath it all came to me what that miner on the topsail schooner going up to Frazer River had said: 'As the country grows, as people come in, wages will go down.' "

Many times such thought was to recur and, as he said, "to grow and grow"; but just now a matter of very different nature was to attract his attention. In a letter to his Sister Jennie (February 4) he referred to the newly discovered gold and silver mines in the Washoe mountains in Nevada Territory, just over the California line, perhaps a hundred miles beyond Placerville and not far from Carson. The stories coming in seemed incredible, yet this region was in the next ten years to yield $80,000,-000 worth of bullion, mostly silver; to make celebrated the "Comstock Lode"; and to raise to world renown the names of the "Bonanza Kings," Mackay, Flood, O'Brien and Fair. The letter ran:

"Our library is closed for the present, as they are removing to a new building, put up expressly for the purpose, where there will be ample room. However, I have out a bulky folio—'Constitutional History of the United States'—so that I am well supplied with reading matter. Do you read much? What books do you read, tell me? How I would like to read with you. We can hardly enjoy alone, and my list of acquaintances contains hardly one who reads more than the newspapers. . . .

"We have reports of several rich discoveries of the precious metals, but I hardly think much faith can be placed in them. From present indications there will be a great rush to Washoe in the spring. There is silver there in plenty—of that there can be little doubt—but still there will be many disappointments. One thing is certain—you don't catch me running off anywhere until pretty certain that there is something to be made. I have given up the notion of mining—at least for the present."

Other letters to and from home throw light upon events. From his mother (February 3):

"I really think you are not doing anything more there than you would do at home, at least it amounts to the same thing after expenses are deducted. I hope when you are of age you will see it so, and conclude that *fortunes* can be made at home as well as abroad. We all say, as with one voice, when we get you home we will keep you. No more roving."

From his father (April 16):

"Mr. Brown has a letter of introduction to you. He spent last evening with us. I found him to be a great egotist, but he is an Englishman, and that accounts for it. Treat him politely."

From Henry George to his Sister Jennie (April 18):

"Washoe is walled up by snow at present, preventing both shipping of the ore and prospecting. In another month when it begins to thaw up in the mountains we will have some definite news from that locality. . . .

"I am still on the 'Home Journal.' On the 2d of September next I will be twenty-one years old, and then, if nothing happens, I will have a pretty good thing (comparatively) and be able to make better pay. It is only four months off, and they will fly pretty quickly. . . . I don't expect to work at printing very long after I am of age. I will then have a chance to look around and get into something that will pay better. If Washoe only equals the expectations entertained of it by sober, sensible men, times will be brisk here this summer, and everyone will have a chance for 'a gold ring or a broken leg.'

"Duncan the proprietor of the 'Home Journal,' bought an interest in a silver lead a short time since for a paltry sum which he could sell to-day for $15,000, and which, if it holds out as rich as the assay shows, will be an independent fortune.

"I don't read much now except the newspapers and you are getting far ahead of me in that line. It takes pretty much all my spare time to keep posted on the current topics of the day. What a time we live in, when great events follow one another so quickly that we have not space for wonder. We are driving at a killing pace somewhere—Emerson says to heaven, and Carlyle says to the other place; but however much they differ, go we surely do.

"I am invited out to-morrow evening to join a reading circle, and if it don't rain will make my *début* in polite society on the Coast. Would you like to see me make my bow, or hear me break down when I come to some hard word? But I will do no such thing. I am not as bashful as I used to be. . . .

"You 'do' some pretty heavy reading for a young girl. I wouldn't be so afraid of novels. A good one is always instructive, and your taste is sufficiently cultivated to allow you to like no other. I never read them, but then it is solely because I have not time and am obliged to take my mental food in as condensed a form as possible.

"I have changed my quarters again, and am now rooming in the northern part of the town. I have a long walk to breakfast, but it gives me a good appetite.

"I am sorry anything was wrong about X——'s marriage. However, the more I see of men and things, and the more I examine the workings of my own heart, the less inclined am I to judge anybody else."

It was at this period, that, urged on by his mother's strong counsel, Henry George pushed out to make social acquaintances. He won the friendship of two young men named Coddington and Hoppel, and through them became acquainted with some young ladies. Both of these young men were ardent Methodists—Hoppel an enthusiast, almost a fanatic, and he urged George to attend his church. The young printer had for several years inwardly shrunk from a literal acceptance of the scriptures, such as he had been taught at old St. Paul's and in the family circle. Roving had bred, or at any rate quickened a revolt, so that, though he said little to hurt the feelings of others, and especially of the dear ones at home, he had come to reject almost completely the forms of religion, and with the forms had cast out belief in a life hereafter. He inclined towards materialism. But the burning enthusi-

asm of Hoppel, even if it expressed in the main only
personal magnetism, was contagious to a sensitive, sympathetic nature; and George began to have new thoughts
about religion.   Drawn by this, and the desire to make
acquaintances, he accepted Hoppel's offer, and went with
him to the Methodist place of worship, where an upright,
earnest, broad-minded man, Rev. S. D. Simonds, preached.
Then the young printer wrote home that he had joined a
church.   Understanding this to mean more than he intended to convey, the quiet circle at Philadelphia received
the news with a delight that was only little lessened when
they afterwards learned that it was the Methodist and
not the Episcopal Church to which he had attached himself.   His mother wrote to him (July 2):

"With what thrilling joy did we read your last letter.
Good news!   Good news!   Indeed, so unexpected, so
intensely joyful that copious tears streamed from my
eyes; but they were tears of joy and gratitude.

"Oh, how much better the Lord has been to us than
we have deserved.   How weak our faith, that God's rich
blessings and overflowing goodness and sure promise
should take us by surprise.   I now desire to say, 'Bless
the Lord, O my soul and all that is within me, bless
His holy name.   For Thou hast delivered the soul of
my child from death, and his feet from falling.   I will
offer to Thee the sacrifice of thanksgiving and call upon
the name of the Lord.'

"Your father will tell you, too, the heartfelt joy with
which he received the news.   Not all the wealth of California would have caused a tithe of it.   We feel now
that our boy is safe; his feet are upon the rock.   Let
the waters lash and surge, the trials and troubles of
life come, he is safe as long as he clings to the Cross
of Christ in humble, trusting faith.   You know our
beautiful hymn, 'Rock of Ages.'   Turn to it if you have
forgotten it.   How soothing and comforting its language!   With God for your guide, my dear child, you
will be safe and happy everywhere.

" 'He that dwelleth in the secret places of the Most High shall abide under the shadow of the Almighty. I will say to the Lord, He is my refuge, and my fortress; my God, in Him will I trust.' "

On September 2, 1860, Henry George came of age. He immediately joined the Eureka Typographical Union, and leaving his old boy's position, obtained work as substitute type-setter on the daily papers at journeyman's wages. This irregular work lasted but a short time. He soon returned to the "Home Journal" as foreman at thirty dollars a week, and allowed the use of his name as publisher. But shortly afterwards he wrote home that, the paper being weak, he did not know how long the position might last.

Up to this time frequent reference was made to a desire to visit home, but on the 12th of October, while he was yet foreman on the "Home Journal," Henry George for the first time met, through the offices of his friend, George Wilbur, a girl who was to affect the whole course of his career—Miss Annie Corsina Fox—the occasion being the quiet celebration of her seventeenth birthday.

Miss Fox was an orphan who had just returned from a convent school at Los Angeles, California, which was then a pretty Spanish town. She was of Catholic faith, and of mingled English and Irish blood. Her father, John Fox, an officer in the British army, was of English parentage and Protestant faith. He was thirty-six years old when he married, in Australia, Elizabeth A. McCloskey, a strict Catholic and scarcely out of her sixteenth year. Miss McCloskey was one of the four children, two sons and two daughters, of Henry McCloskey, who was born in Limerick, Ireland. His wife, Mary Ann Wall, born in Ennis, County Clare, came of an educated family, having three brothers graduated from Trinity College, Dublin, two of whom had become clergymen in the English Established

Church. She herself was a woman of refined and intellectual mind, and strong, commanding nature. Henry McCloskey inherited an established business and was himself a successful man. He had the roving spirit and took his family to Australia and thence to California, stopping for a period in the Hawaiian, or as they were then more commonly called, Sandwich Islands. In Sydney and in Honolulu the family lived in ample means, Henry McCloskey carrying on an important iron-mongering business, and deriving large profits from government contracts which were invested in real estate. He settled his family in California in 1851, and two years later returned to build a railroad in South Australia, where he contracted a fever and died. He was then fifty-four years old and on his way to a big fortune.

But before the family left Australia Major Fox had come to a disagreement with his wife's mother. She had urged the marriage, and when asked subsequently how it was that though staunch Catholic and intense Irish patriot, she had consented to her daughter's marrying a man who was a Protestant and wore a red coat, the reply was that she had been "a mother first and a Catholic afterwards," and had given her sweet, gentle daughter to a soldier and gentleman who could protect her in the new, rough country that Australia then was. Discord between the gentleman and his wife's mother at length ran so high that he requested his wife to choose between them. Elizabeth Fox, feeling a stronger sense of duty towards her mother than towards her husband, chose to stay with the former. The Major then took his last farewell and they never met again. The young wife realising her attachment for him after he had irrevocably gone, fell to grieving, which brought on consumption, of which she died in San Francisco at the age of twenty-nine.

Annie C. Fox (Mrs. George) at seventeen.

From daguerreotype taken in San Francisco, 1860.

Teresa and Annie were the two daughters of this marriage. Teresa had early shown a serious bent of mind, and at the age of eleven, while reading at her dying mother's bedside, had formed the desire to become a religious. Hope of some day meeting and comforting her father confirmed her in this desire, so that at seventeen she became a member of the Order of the Daughters of St. Vincent de Paul, better known as Sisters of Charity, retaining her name and being subsequently known as Sister Teresa Fox. Many times in after years the sisters tried to get some word of their father, but in vain. He had left the army in Australia, and all trace of him was lost. Sister Teresa died of influenza in St. Louis, Missouri, on January 6, 1899, after a service in the order of forty years to the day.

On leaving school, Annie Fox made her home with her grandmother, who was now broken in health, and her aunt, Mrs. Flintoff, of San Francisco. The keen eyes of the grandmother apparently saw the trend of affairs between Annie and Mr. George, and though she was the kind of woman who could recognise and admire the quality of mind the young man exhibited, she regarded him as physically weak and endeavoured to divert the girl's attention, saying: "Annie, that Mr. George is a nice young man, but I fear he is delicate and will die of consumption." But the girl kept her own counsel. She was at that time engaged to a gifted and handsome young man, who had promise of a competency; but, under the ardent wooing of Henry George, a change of feeling came over her.

Meanwhile the calendar of outside events was being rapidly filled. The remarkable campaign of 1860 ended in the victory of the new Republican party. Henry George, now of age, cast his first vote for Abraham Lincoln. A few weeks later, December 20, the State of South Carolina formally seceded from the Union. R. S. H. George about the same time (December 19) wrote to his son:

"Things look dark and gloomy; men seem dismayed at the prospect before them; they confess that they cannot see through the gloom. . . . Can it be that these United States, formed for the refuge of the downtrodden and oppressed of the earth, shall be destroyed, and that that glorious flag which is their protection throughout the world shall be trodden under foot? I can't think so; no, never!"

The minds of most men were charged with apprehension as the year 1861 was ushered in. The States of Mississippi, Alabama, Georgia, Florida and Louisiana followed South Carolina's example and passed ordinances of secession. On March 4 the passive Buchanan went out of office and Abraham Lincoln was inaugurated President of the United States.

At this time Henry George was adrift again. Duncan had sold the "Home Journal" and George turned to "subbing" on the daily papers. For a time he considered a mining project of which he speaks in a letter to his Sister Caroline a year later (July 5, 1862):

"A large amount of silver is coming out of Nevada near Virginia City and the amount of goods going up there is astonishing. One of the companies lately declared a dividend of $1,400 per share. Their claim, however, is situated on the famous Ophir lead, probably the richest in the world. A company in which Charlie Coddington held some stock struck the same lead a couple of weeks ago, raising the value of shares to a price which will give him quite a nice little start, and which will make his partner rich, if he has not sold out. Hoppel and I and Charlie were going to buy twenty feet together, when I went into the 'Evening Journal,' which knocked it in the head—I choosing, as I thought, a certainty for an uncertainty. At present prices that is worth $10,000 ($500 a foot) and if it proves as rich as Ophir, will be worth much more."

The "Evening Journal" with which Henry George now became connected, grew out of a campaign newspaper called the "Constitution," which had been run in support of the Union party presidential condidates in the 1860 campaign—Bell and Everett. Five printers—James J. Knowlton, Abel Gee, son of the Major Gee who was to keep the Andersonville prison during the war; John G. Smith, afterwards an Episcopal clergyman in Missouri; Anson C. Benham, and Freeman A. Camp—entered upon a partnership to revive the paper under the name of the "Evening Journal." They all were poor, but they agreed in addition to gathering most of the news themselves to put in what at that time in California constituted the chief item of expense in newspaper making—their printer's services—each man to give his entire time and labour.

For telegraphic news, up to the time the "Journal" was started, did not occupy much space in West Coast papers. There was no wire connection with the East, and telegrams had to travel a long part of the distance on the "Overland Stage." But now a quicker means of transmission was established in what was known as the "Pony Express." Two relays a week of fast pony riders ran over the fifteen hundred miles of prairie and desert separating St. Joseph, Missouri, and Carson City, Nevada, to connect the Eastern and Western telegraph systems. But this was very expensive, and besides its infrequency or intermittent nature, almost nine days were required for so-called telegraphic transmission from New York or Washington to San Francisco.[1] Under such circumstances

Pacific Coast newspapers did not carry much telegraphic matter, the columns being almost entirely filled with local news and comment[2] and when intelligence of secession and hostilities began to come in from the East the general feeling was that these were only temporary things—mere ebullitions, or "flashes in the pan!" And its promoters believed that if the "Journal" could live the short time until peace and quiet should be restored it could then fall back on the local news and be on equal terms with its contemporaries.

Regarding the new daily as a good venture, Henry George bought an equal share with the others for something over a hundred dollars—money he had saved while foreman

---

[1] The chief business of the Pony Express was to carry mail between St. Joseph, Missouri, and Sacramento, California; St. Joseph being the western limit of the Eastern railroads, and Sacramento being connected with San Francisco by river steamers. The distance to be ridden was 1900 miles, going by way of South Pass, Salt Lake, Humboldt River and Carson Valley. There were 190 stations at intervals of about 25 miles ; and 200 station keepers, 80 riders and nearly 500 western native ponies. Postage was $5 for each half ounce. Carson City was on the way, and there telegrams were picked up or dropped. Hittell's "History of California," Vol. IV, pp. 266-268.

[2] For a time the editorial writer on the "Evening Journal" was John R. Ridge, a strikingly handsome man, whose mother was a cultured Connecticut woman, and whose father, educated in Connecticut, was a full-blooded Cherokee Indian, a member of one of what were known as the Civilised Tribes. In later years Henry George wrote of him in "Progress and Poverty," Bk. X, Chap. ii ("Memorial Edition," pages 490-491). " I once knew a man in whose veins ran the blood of Indian chiefs. He used to tell me traditions learned from his grandfather which illustrated what is difficult for a white man to comprehend — the Indian habit of thought, the intense but patient blood thirst of the trail, and the fortitude of the stake. From the way in which he dwelt on these, I have no doubt that under certain circumstances, highly educated, civilised man that he was, he would have shown traits that would have been looked on as due to his Indian blood ; but which in reality would have been sufficiently explained by the broodings of his imagination upon the deeds of his ancestors."

on Duncan's paper—and agreed with the others to give his whole time to the enterprise. He wrote to his Sister Jennie (April 10, 1861):

"For the past week I have been working very hard. I have bought an interest in a little paper, copies of which I send you by this mail. We are pushing in—bound to make it a paying concern or perish in the attempt (that is, the paper, not your respected brother). I think we have a good prospect and in a little while will have a good property, which will be an independence for a life-time. Then, and not till then you may begin to fret about a sister-in-law!

"Since I came in the paper has been enlarged and considerably improved, and probably the next copies I send you will present a much better appearance, as we are yet hardly in the working trim. . . .

"I am very tired to-night. This working on a daily paper the hours that we do is harder than digging sand or wielding a sledge."

On April 12 the astounding news spread over the North that the South had fired upon the United States flag at Fort Sumter. Owing to the slow means of communication, this information did not reach California until some days later; but when it did come it produced an extraordinary sensation.

Henry George had invited Miss Fox out to walk that evening, and he was so absorbed that she asked the cause; and when he said, "The terrible news," and told what had happened, she exclaimed: "Is that all? Why, I thought your dear old father was dead." He turned in astonishment: "All!" he said in some excitement; "why, what could be a greater calamity to this country?"

It was not to be wondered at that a young girl born in another country, and just fresh from a convent school, should, in San Francisco, far removed from the seat of the struggle, not at once grasp the significance of events; but the family in Philadelphia thoroughly understood, Mrs. George writing to her son (May 20) a few days after the President had called out seventy-five thousand volunteers for a three months' service:

"We are now, as it were, holding our breath; waiting for the news of the first battle. It is thought by all that it will take place in a few days at Harper's Ferry. O this horrible, calamitous and most sorrowful of all wars; when and what will be the end? I firmly believe the Lord of hosts is with us, and the God of Jacob will be our defence. Though we have sinned against Him, He will not give us to anarchy and confusion, but will right our wrongs and make us again a happy, united people. O pray for this, my dear boy."

His Sister Jennie (by same mail) wrote:

"Mrs. Browning moves two nations with one song. Have you seen her last poem, written at Turin, I think, termed 'Mother and Poet'? It is magnificent. It commences:

" 'Dead! One of them shot by the sea in the east,
     And one of them shot in the west by the sea.
   Dead! both my boys! When you sit at the feast,
     And are wanting a great song for Italy free,
     Let none look at *me*.'

"It is all we women can do—give up our husbands and brothers cheerfully. A great many we know are going, some your old friends."

Later (June 10) his father wrote:

"You cannot feel it as we do. All around is warlike, and young men are crowding into the ranks of the forces being raised. Nothing now but the sound of the drum and the march of troops South. . . .
"But, my dear boy, this is what I think I predicted

to you long ago. We are now approaching times and scenes such as never have been seen in these United States; and we old men have come to the conclusion that it is best that it should now be declared whether we are a National Government or not, that our children may know the truth, and what they are to depend upon.

"The new Collector has taken his seat and is cutting right and left. I feel that my time at the Custom House is short, and what to do I know not. Commerce is suspended, and I do not know to-night but that I shall be a pauper to-morrow. . . . If I am discharged I know not what will become of us. And yet all I know are in the same boat—all on a par, like a ship at sea without rudder or compass. But blessed be God. We can and do look up to Him for guidance and deliverance. I feel satisfied that He will not leave or forsake us in this our time of need."

The dismissal from the Custom House which R. S. H. George feared came soon after this. At sixty-four years of age, and when business was demoralised, he was forced to seek means of livelihood. His son Henry, in his prosperous periods had been accustomed to send money home, and even during the hard struggling months on the "Evening Journal" had sent a few remittances. When he heard of his father's threatened plight he at once offered to sell out his interest in the paper for whatever it would bring and send the money on. But the old gentleman would not listen to this. He replied (August 3):

"Your kind letter was to me worth more than silver and gold. It showed me that my dear son far away from us was willing to make any sacrifice to help his parents in distress. And so with all my dear children. Surely my grey hairs will not go down in sorrow to the grave on account of the want of love and affection on the part of my dear children."

He told his son that he had hopes of success in a ship-brokerage business which he and a Custom House associate, who also had been displaced, intended to enter upon.

A never failing complaint in the communications from home at this period was that there were so few and such meagre letters from California. There was ground enough for these complaints, for all connected with the "Evening Journal" had to work long and hard. In a letter to his Sister Caroline (August 19) Henry George shows this:

> "I am still on the paper—working hard to make it go, and as yet without any decided success. We are making now about $6 apiece per week—rather small wages you will justly think for California. But then they are slowly but surely getting larger, and I think the prospect ahead is worth some industry and self-denial."

The little band of poverty-stricken printers pressed resolutely on, with the earnest hopes of Henry George's folks at home. Indeed, the latter took so much interest in the enterprise that when her brother had written that he would sell out at any price to send his father some money, his Sister Jennie had replied (August 29): "I hope you won't sell your share in the paper. It seems hard to think of your commencing all over again. We all cried when we got your letter; it seemed so hard on you."

The bond between this brother and sister, always close by reason of congenial tastes, seemed now to grow more tender. By his encouragement, she wrote several long news letters from Philadelphia for his paper, and in her personal letters she constantly referred, with something like wistfulness, to the days that seemed long gone when they were happy children together:

> "Uncle Thomas took us all on an excursion Tuesday.
> . . . He told us that a number of years ago he went

on a similar excursion to Pennsgrove and took you with him. He was very much amused with you. While you were eating your breakfast they gave you some very strong coffee. (I suppose you were not used to it.) All of a sudden you laid down your knife and fork with a very grave face, and they asked you what was the matter. You said quite soberly: 'Why, I do believe the coffee has flew to my head.' "

A long letter to his Sister Jennie at this time (September 15) shows with some clearness the state of the young printer's mind:

"I have been very dilatory about writing and more especially about answering the long letters received from you about two weeks ago, but now I will try to make amends for it, if I can. In the first place, I have been working quite hard, from morning to night, without any intermission, and it is quite a strain. In fact, to sit down and write after the day is over, is but a continuation of the use of the same faculties, which in my trade have been so heavily drawn upon during the day, and though I might at one time send you a few lines, yet I wanted to write you a good long letter, such a one as I used to write, and such as you sent me. Again, I have felt unsettled and worried about business, hoping that each day would make some change that I might tell you of; in fact, until a few days past, hardly knowing whether our paper would get through the next day, as I feared something would occur to bring it to a close, and in truth, feeling something like the sailor in a calm wishing for even— .

" 'Storm or hurricane,
Anything, to put a close
To this most dread, monotonous repose !'

"But the days have followed each other, and pretty much like each other, too, and nothing has happened— no prospect of war with European powers, no uprising of Secessionists, no appearance of the Sheriff's officers, nor even of that individual with more money than brains, and an exceedingly strong desire to go into the newspaper business in a small way, whom I have been hoping would come along and buy me out. So we go. What a constant reaching this life is, a constant stretching forth and longing after something. But you know what Emerson in the 'Sphinx' makes his 'Œdipus' say:

> " 'The fiend that man harries
> Is love of the Best;
> Yawns the pit of the Dragon
> Lit by the rays from the Blest.'

And so it is—and so it will be until we reach the perfect, and that you and I and every son of Adam and every daughter of Eve, each for himself, knows we are very far from.

> " 'For the longing I feel is a part
> Of the hunger and thirst of the heart—
> The frenzy and fire of the brain—
> That yearns for the fruitage forbidden,
> The golden pomegranates of Eden,
> To ease off its hunger and pain.'

"Truly it seems that we have fallen upon evil days. A little while ago all was fair and bright, and now the storm howls around us with a strength and fury that almost unnerves one. Our country is being torn to pieces, and ourselves, our homes, filled with distress. As to the ultimate end, I have no doubt. If civil war should pass over the whole country, leaving nothing but devastation behind it, I think my faith in the ultimate good would remain unchanged; but it is hard to feel so of our individual cases. On great events and movements we can philosophise, but when it comes down to ourselves, to our homes, to those *we love*, then we can only feel; our philosophy goes to the dogs. . . .

"In the meantime we eagerly wait the arrival of each pony. Twice a week it arrives, and from the outer telegraph station in Nevada Territory the news is flashed to us in San Francisco. The last two or three times the news has seemed to me rather more encouraging, not so much by reason of anything that has been done, as by the evident determination of the loyal North to see the thing through.

"I do not get much time to read now. In fact, I have read very little for eighteen months—hardly more than the newspapers; certainly not enough to keep me posted on the current literature of the day. How I long for the Golden Age—for the promised Millenium, when each one will be free to follow his best and noblest impulses, unfettered by the restrictions and necessities which our present state of society imposes upon him— when the poorest and the meanest will have a chance to use all his God-given faculties, and not be forced to drudge away the best part of his time in order to supply wants but little above those of the animal.

". . . . I had a dream last night—such a pleasant, vivid dream, that I must tell you of it. I thought I was scooping treasure out of the earth by handfuls, almost delirious with the thoughts of what I would now be able to do, and how happy we would all be— and so clear and distinct that I involuntarily examined my pockets when I got up in the morning, but alas! with the usual result. Is it an indication of future luck? or do dreams always go by contraries, and instead of finding, am I to lose? But the latter supposition will not worry me, for 'he who lies on the ground cannot fall far.' No, I suppose I dreamed as starving men are said to of splendid feasts, or thirsty desert wanderers of shady brooks and spray-flinging fountains. 'Lust for Gold!' Is it any wonder that men lust for gold, and are willing to give almost anything for it, when it covers everything—the purest and holiest desires of their hearts, the exercise of their noblest powers! What a pity we can't be contented! Is it? Who knows? Sometimes I feel sick of the fierce struggle of our high civilised life, and think I would like to get away from cities and business, with their jostlings and strainings and cares altogether, and find some place on one of the hillsides, which look so dim and blue in

the distance where I could gather those I love, and live
content with what Nature and our own resources would
furnish; but, alas, money, money, is wanted even for
that. It is our fate—we must struggle, and so here's
for the strife! . . .

"The days and weeks and months never flew so fast
with me as they do now. Time we measure by sensa-
tions, and working so steadily, there is not room for
many. I do not like my trade when forced to work
at it so steadily—there is not action enough in it, hardly
a chance for the movements of the mind. But it will
not always be so. 'It is a long lane that knows no turning,' they say, and I hope the turn will come soon, for
I really feel tired.

"It is harder for me to write to you than to anyone
else. When I have business to write about I can sit
down and spin it right off, but when it comes to writing home, I scrawl a few words and find myself lost in
reverie, when I sit and think, and bite my pen, while
Memory is busy till the hours fly away unnoticed.

"I am glad Bill Horner and Jim Stanley have gone
to the wars. I should like to see them. If I were home,
and situated as they are, I would go, too. Not that I
like the idea of fighting my countrymen—not that I
think it is the best or pleasantest avocation, or that the
fun of soldiering is anything to speak of; but in this
life or death struggle I should like to have a hand. If
they die, they will die in a good cause; and if they
live, they will always feel prouder and better when this
time is mentioned than if they had remained safely at
home while others faced the danger and did the work.
I have felt a great deal like enlisting, even here, and
probably would have done so, had I not felt that my
duty to you all required me to remain, though I did
not, and do not, think our volunteers are really needed
or will do any fighting that will amount to anything;
but I should like to place my willingness on record, and
show that one of our family was willing to serve his
country. We cannot tell. It may be my duty yet,
though I sincerely hope not.

"I never hear from the Currys now, except through

the medium of your letters, and at present there is no probability of my going up there. . . .

"We have been having our usual fine summer, but the rainy season will soon set in and then we will make up for it. Rain is a very nice thing once in a while, but when it gets into the habit of coming down for a month at a time, you almost cease to appreciate it, and would be willing to have it change to snow. It is very little colder, however, in winter than in summer, and I wear precisely the same clothing the year round. . . .

"I have been some time writing this much, but I think we will be able to make arrangements that will place us in a better position. As soon as they are completed I will write, probably in a day or two."

The "arrangements" that the young printer spoke of which should place those on the "Evening Journal" in a better position could not have been completed, or being completed, could not have been of more than temporary duration, for in a short time all connected with the paper were hard-driven again. "I worked," said he afterwards,[1] "until my clothes were in rags and the toes of my shoes were out. I slept in the office and did the best I could to economise, but finally I ran in debt thirty dollars for my board bill."

Miss Fox called at the "Journal" office with some friends one day at this period, after the paper had gone to press. Mr. George was the only person there. He was standing at a case in his shirt sleeves distributing type. On seeing the visitors, he hurried to wash his hands, brush and put on his coat and make himself presentable. He showed Miss Fox about the little office and presently pointed to a kind of folding cot, with mattress, grey blankets and a pillow, that were under one of the imposing-tables. When he told her that that was his bed, the young girl exclaimed,

---

[1] Meeker notes, October, 1897.

"Oh, I hope your mother does not know of this." "Why," he replied, "this is nothing after a life at sea."

What brought the crisis on the "Journal" was the completion of the trans-continental telegraph in October. With the wire joining them to New York, Washington and all the East, the papers that were in the press association monopoly had so much advantage that Henry George concluded that for him to stay longer and fight at such odds would be worse than foolish. He expressed his desire to withdraw. Some friction had grown up between the other owners of the paper and so it was concluded towards the middle of November, 1861, to dissolve partnership. Of this Mr. Knowlton, one of the partners, has since said:

> "It was agreed on Mr. Gee's proposal that each of the six partners should make a bid for the 'Evening Journal,' and to write his bid, without showing it to the others, on a slip of paper, which was to be folded and dropped into a hat. Then all the slips were to be taken out and opened. The makers of the three highest bids were to stay in, and of the three lowest bids to go out. George, Camp and Smith were lowest, their bids together making, I believe, $800, or averaging something over $266 apiece."

Even this sum—small, indeed, for the months of strain and privation—would have enabled Henry George to square his debts and have a little remaining with which to make a fresh start, but the instaying partners could not at once pay. In June he had written home that he had been "given a one-third interest in a gold lead in Butte County," but this too, had failed; so that when he went out of the "Journal" to look elsewhere for work his prospects were desperate. At this critical point in his affairs he was called upon to face one of the most important crises of his life.

CHAPTER VIII.

COURTSHIP AND RUNAWAY MARRIAGE.

1861.   Age, 22.

MISS FOX'S family must have marked a change in the appearance of young Mr. George, who at first had dressed well, but whose clothes now, though neat, showed wear. The grandmother had died after displaying every sign of tender care and affection for her daughter Elizabeth's children, orphaned as she felt by her unwise, though most loving interference. Matthew McCloskey, Miss Fox's uncle, had now become virtually the young girl's guardian, and careful man that he was, he wrote privately to Philadelphia to learn something of the young suitor's antecedents, which he found to be satisfactory.

Matthew McCloskey shared his mother's force of character. He was one of those strong, commanding men seen at greatest advantage in pioneer conditions. In "Happy Valley," the section of the city in which he lived and owned considerable real estate, his word was his bond, and his conclusions in ticklish land-title disputes, which his neighbours brought to him to settle rather than go to law, had the respect accorded to decisions of court. And while a just man, he had the generosity of a courageous man, one night during the campaign of '60 going home in a passion because he had been unable to prevent a mob of Douglass Democrats stopping a Breckinridge Democrat from making a public speech; for though a strong Douglass Democrat himself, he wanted all men to have a fair chance to be heard. Thus no man in his neighbourhood was better known or more highly respected. His house, a frame building, like many others at that time, made in Australia and brought to California in sections, was when erected one of the best in that part of the city.

Matthew McCloskey took no exception to the character or possible abilities of young George, but his own nature was too masterful long to brook the same trait in the young man who came courting his niece. For the time he said nothing; while all unconscious, or careless, of smiles or frowns from such a quarter, the young printer was showing in his wooing the strength of his nature and bent of his mind. He brought Miss Fox books, mostly of verse, and they had reading tasks together. One work used in this way was Charles A. Dana's "Household Book of Poetry," a large volume just published containing an admirable collection from the writings of the great poets of the language. The lovers read, memorised and discussed.

One day Henry George said he had just heard his rival's love story, and that he thought the other man ought to have the right to press his suit, and that he himself ought to withdraw. The lady intimated that the other gentleman had few friends at court, whereas Mr. George was well represented. The young printer needed no further word of encouragement, and at all hours, early in the morning, at midday or late at night—for one hour was as pleasant to him as another—he came dropping in at the Flintoff's on Twelfth Street, near Folsom, until unexpectedly the storm broke and Matthew McCloskey, who came out that night to his brother-in-law's, told Mr. George that until he could show more evidence of prosperity—for he was now out of the "Evening Journal," and indeed, of all regular employment—he should make his visits less frequent. The young fellow replied with spirit, and the two quick, hot tempered men would have come to blows had not Miss Fox, who had been the terrified spectator of the quarrel, rushed between them. Her uncle, forgetting that his brother-in-law and not he was master there, ordered the young man from the house and forbade him ever again to enter it.

Much of that night Miss Fox spent praying and next morning, December 3, 1861—a stormy, rainy morning—when Henry George came out, she said that she would no longer remain under the roof of either of her uncles, and had resolved to go to Los Angeles and accept a position as teacher in the school of the Sisters of Charity.

The young man said: "If you go I'll not see you," to which the girl replied that since she could not stay with her relatives in San Francisco, she saw nothing else to do. The young man drew from his pocket a single coin. "Annie," said he solemnly, "that is all the money I have in the world. Will you marry me?"

She gravely answered: "If you are willing to undertake the responsibilities of marriage, I will marry you."

He told her when he came again later in the day that at nightfall he would send a carriage for her to the door inquiring for "Mrs. Brown" and that she should be ready at once to leave. All day long she sat in the parlour of Joseph Flintoff's house waiting for night and the carriage, while Henry George was off telling some of his friends of the matter, getting credit for two weeks' board for two persons, borrowing a little money and some better-appearing clothes than his own, and hiring a carriage. There was some difficulty about the carriage, for when the driver grasped the fact that he was about to take part in a runaway marriage, and that he was to get into the very thick of it by inquiring at the door for "Mrs. Brown," he declined, saying that he already had "a bullet in one leg" for participating in another just such affair. But he agreed to hold his conveyance in readiness at a discreet distance from the residence. Isaac Trump, one of George's *Shubrick* friends, with coat collar turned up and soft felt hat drawn down, went to Mr. Flintoff's residence and asked for "Mrs. Brown." Miss Fox was ready, and followed him out, handing him a heavy cloth-covered package, which from its form and feeling he afterwards said he thought must be boxes of jewels, but which to his astonishment turned out to be the "Household Book of Poetry," and all the other volumes that Henry George had given the young lady, she preferring to take these to any other of her personal possessions. Presently Mr. George joined them and they proceeded to the carriage where the lady that Isaac Trump was engaged to marry was awaiting them. Rev. S. D. Simonds, the Methodist clergyman whom Henry George had been going to hear the year before, was to perform the ceremony. But he was out of town at that hour and would not be back until nine that night. The party, therefore, went to a restaurant to supper. After the repast they walked to Mr. Simond's little Methodist church called the Bethel. The night was bright with moonlight, but wet under foot from the day's storm and when they came to a pool, Henry George lifted his bride-elect over it—a habit which the young man continued, at night at least, for many years.

Charles Coddington and Mrs. Simonds, the wife of the clergyman, were waiting at the church. James George could not get there, but his newly wedded wife, Sophia George, came and brought his hearty good wishes.

Miss Fox, a Catholic in good standing, would have preferred her own church for the place of the marriage, but fearing the delay that that seemed to present, was willing to have Mr. George's Methodist friend, Rev. Mr. Simonds, perform the ceremony, though soon afterwards in Sacramento she had Rev. Nathaniel Gallagher of St. Rose's Church give the Catholic sanction. Broad-minded man that the Rev. Mr. Simonds was, he voluntarily read the service of the Episcopal Church in which the bridegroom had been bred, and which, as he said, "more nearly approached the Catholic" than his own short Methodist service. And in this way Henry George and Annie Fox —the one twenty-two, the other eighteen—became husband and wife, the ring being the one used at the wedding of Miss Fox's grandmother.

When the ceremony was over Mr. George wrote out and sent advertisements to all the newspapers; and the clergyman took down Charles Coddington's name as one of the witnesses. He then turned to Mr. Trump, who was to be second witness, but whom he did not know. "I. Trump," the witness responded. "I perceive that you do," said the clergyman, "but what is your name?" and it was several minutes before the reverend gentleman could be made to believe that the witness was not joking, and that "I" stood for "Isaac."[1]

There was no honeymoon trip for this bridal pair; in-

---

[1] Six months later, (July 5, 1862) writing from Sacramento to his Sister Caroline, Henry George said : "Both friends who were at our marriage are now in the same fix — Ike Trump and Charlie Coddington (of whom I have spoken in connection with Hoppel). Charlie ran away with his girl, or rather Hoppel did it for him, and they had a queer old time. When I was in San Francisco I met Hoppel with a big revolver buckled around him and he told me the whole story. Ike's girl went up to Marysville last week to be married to him, he writing to me to hurry her along ; for if she lost a day the new licence law would go into effect and he would have to pay $3 for the privilege."

deed, the young groom arose at five o'clock next morning to go out and look for work. This he found as a "sub" type-setter, and worked all day; and in the evening getting another chance, he worked that night until the small hours next morning. By irregular "subbing" of this kind he was able to earn enough to pay their board bills. After a few days, learning of an opening in Sacramento, the Capital of the State, he went up and got "subbing" work on the "Union," a morning daily, and earned good wages. He at once sent for his wife and for a time at least felt some sense of security, though adversity was soon again upon him.

All this while the George family was without knowledge of what had happened, nor did any but his Sister Jennie even so much as know of the existence of Miss Fox. Before the crisis came in the love affair, and before he had drawn out of the "Evening Journal," he had written in confidence to his sister to tell her of his affection, withholding the intelligence from the others because he would not have his father and mother think that he would so much as contemplate the taking on of new responsibilities at a time when they were down in their fortunes, and when he could do so little to help them—a time, indeed, when, under the circumstances, he could only with difficulty support himself. His sister's reply, without date, bears evidence of great haste, and runs:

"I felt a sudden choking, a sudden loneliness and jealousy, when I first read your letter. I have got over that now; and first of all, no matter what else I say, my advice to you is: If you *really love Annie, you marry her as soon as you are able to support her.* I have no doubt you are sure of loving her . . . though you cannot be too sure.

"I am sorry she is a Catholic, very sorry. Be careful about that. You say you often talk on religious subjects; let them not be doctrinal points. The ground is dangerous to you, no matter how well balanced your mind may be. I know that our family will object to that, Ma especially; but still I do not think she will withhold her consent on that account. The great objection is that you should be married away from home. Do not, I beg of you. Come home and bring her with you. I will love her; so will they all, I know.

"I love her already—at least I feel as if I had found a new friend somewhere by the name of Annie. I call her Annie to myself; her name is familiar to me now. . . . Marry her if you love her, for love is too precious a thing to be thrown away. 'For beauty is easy enough to win, but one isn't loved every day.' . . .

"In the meantime do not forget me; do not cease to love me as much as ever, will you? There can be two places in your heart—one for Annie and one for me."

When he wrote in November that he was out of the "Evening Journal" his mother answered (December 11):

"I see, my son, that you get the blues sometimes as well as other folks, and I don't wonder. I think you have had a hard time of it, but don't, I beseech you, ever allow that to prevent you from writing home. Remember, a whole household is made blue in that case, though they say they are not, to keep up the mother's spirits. Keep up your spirits, my dear boy. All will yet be well. I feel persuaded you will yet come out right. You know the darkest hour is just before day. I have always boasted of your happy, cheerful, encouraging tone. Never till late have I detected a shadow of gloom. Put your trust in God, my dear child."

Then, owing to the disturbed condition of the country, mails accumulated, and there was a three months' silence from California. When the mails resumed, a bunch of letters arrived together, among them one from the son telling of his marriage and one from his wife, for both of them wrote just after the wedding. Perhaps the folks were too happy on hearing from their son once more in those troublous times and too much astonished at the news that the letters brought, to think of deprecating his marriage. At any rate, the whole family united in a warm and earnest welcome to the new daughter and sister, and nearly all of them wrote messages of love by the next mail. His Sister Kate wrote (March 4):

"My new relationship never struck me so forcibly as it did last night at family prayers, when father prayed for his beloved son and daughter. Before we used only to pray for our dear absent one; now it is for our dear absent ones."

The young couple had on their side waited with something like trepidation through the long months for word of recognition from home, and though neither spoke of it, both had almost settled down into despair when the bundle of letters came to hand, telling of the warm taking into the heart, and then the time slipped merrily along. But his mother and his Sister Jennie pleaded with them in every letter to come home. To her brother, Jennie wrote with a tender love (April 20):

"There are a great many more things here to remind us of you than there are out there to remind you of us. . . . Here everything is associated with you. We live the same as we did when you went away; in the same house, doing the same things over and over again, only each time we do them less light-heartedly, feeling that we are gradually growing older, that things will not always be so.

"We had pretty nice times when we were children, didn't we? Yesterday I was forcibly reminded that every one of us is growing older. You know it was Easter Saturday. Don't you remember Ma always dyed us two or three eggs apiece? Well, yesterday she did not dye one. She never thought of it and none of the children asked for it.

"What nice times we used to have Christmas, too. How sleepless we used to be all night. You used to be up about 4 o'clock in the morning.

"Hen, in the Spring we used to have such a time planting seed in our garden. What a handsome garden! Time has not improved it. It is the same little 'snub' it used to be. We thought it was nice though, didn't we? Don't you remember Tom and Val used to plant things and pull them up about a week after to see if they were growing?

"Tell Annie about Tom sitting in the air. I tell him that that one act is enough to immortalise and hand his name down to posterity."[1]

The bond between brother and sister was never closer than now, as shown by his letter a couple of months later:

Sacramento, June 5, '62·

"MY DEAR JENNIE: We are having Summer at last; and hot enough it certainly is. I feel it more, perhaps, than I would otherwise from the fact that since leaving Panama I have experienced no really warm weather, the winds which draw in through the Golden Gate, making San Francisco almost as cool in summer as in winter. But we are now living in one of the pleasantest parts of the town—a square from the State Capitol —and surrounded by trees of all kinds and the largest growth, and roses in greater profusion than I ever saw

---

[1] Tom George, the brother next in age to Henry, had been told that sitting in the air was possible. So following directions, he procured one of the household wash tubs, filled it with water, placed a board across it, stood on the board and then told a younger brother and sister to draw the board away when he leaped up into the air. He leaped and they pulled — and then, of course, down he came and took an unpremeditated bath.

before.   Aunt Mary would be delighted with this country, barring the floods.

"A short distance from the house is the slough—
formed by the back water of the American River, which
unites with the Sacramento at this point—a beautiful
sheet of water on which we have a boat, and over which
we frequently sail.   In a word, we are as pleasantly
situated as we could desire, but Annie will tell you all
about how we are fixed.   She will write to-night, being
at the present moment 'amusing' herself by nursing
a baby, the property of one of the ladies in the house,
and of which I must in justice say that I have not yet
heard it cry.   She is a regular woman, and has all the
notions and fancies that seem so strange to a man.

"But while we are so pleasantly situated, 'Old Adversity' walks as close behind as ever.   The Legislature
has adjourned, as I told you before, and though the
weather and roads have much improved, the Overland
Mail stage has not yet commenced running.   We were
under the impression that it had started from the other
side and the first budget of news would be here in a
few days, but on Sunday a telegraphic despatch was
received from New York dated May 26 stating that
operations would probably be resumed in about fifteen
days.   This is disheartening, for to its regular arrivals
we are looking for the revival of our business, which just
now is unprecedentedly dull.   The proprietors of the
'Union' state their determination to commence to run
two double sheets a week as soon as the Overland Mail
resumes, which will give me all the work I care to do.
But we have been expecting and looking for it so long
that it seems that it never would come.   I am not one
of those who love work for its own sake, but feeling
what it brings, I love it and am happiest when hard at
it.   It is no wonder that wealth is sought by all means,
good or bad, for it expresses almost everything.   With
it, it seems to me, I should be supremely happy (perhaps that is the reason I have it not).   It is but the
want of a few dollars that keeps us separate, that forces
us to struggle on so painfully, that crushes down all
the noblest yearnings of the heart and mind.   I do not

complain that no special miracle is worked in my behalf, that by none of those lucky windfalls which sometimes come to fools, I am enriched; but it really seems that strive as hard in whatever direction I may, the current still turns against me. But I will not believe that it will be so always. At any rate I will do the best I can, make the most of my opportunities, and for the rest trust to God.

"Though I have a great deal of time on my hands, I do not think it is wholly lost. I employ it in the development of either body or mind, in rowing or swimming or in reading. Marriage has certainly benefitted me by giving a more contented and earnest frame of mind and will help me to do my best in 'whatever station it pleases God to call me.' This is the only difference I can perceive. Annie and I are so well matched in years and temperament that there was no violent change in either. I feel no older, and my dear sister, I love you as much as ever, and I believe, long to see you more. But I am afraid it will be some time before we can get home, and in the meantime we want to try and get one of you out here. The fare will be reduced in some way or other before long, and when I once get *on the train,* it will not take long to find the means. I wish you were all here, I think you would like the country, or that we were all home, which would be better still. However, we must hope on.

"Every day the telegraph is in working order it brings us the news of the success of the armies of the Republic. I cannot help feeling regret that the contest will be over and the victories won without my having taken the slightest part in it. If I am East after the war is ended I will feel abashed among its heroes. If I had been home I would have gone if I possibly could, but here there was no chance unless one could pay his passage to New York, for those who were raised here were merely to garrison posts and fight Indians, though now a column is being pushed across the deserts to Arizona, though it is very doubtful if they will see any fighting.

"What has become of Will Jones and Charley Walton? You have not told me of them, but I suppose they are in the army.

"Times must be improving now at home. The worst of the war will soon be over and then I think there will be a great revival. Considering the effects of the floods and the northern gold fevers, everything is becoming quite brisk here.

"In future direct to the 'Union' office at Sacramento, and if I am not here my letters will be forwarded immediately. I think, however, that I will stay here for some time, and if I get a situation within a short time, I will be sure to do so.

"For the present I must say good-bye. Give my love to all.

"Your affectionate brother,
"HENRY GEORGE."

"P. S. I have just received a call to go to work, so excuse my abruptness."

And so the current of affectionate communion passed between brother and sister, when one afternoon, returning from an outing for his early evening dinner, the young wife noticed that her husband was depressed and preoccupied, that he ate little, and that when he spoke it was as with an effort to be cheerful. He went off to his printer's work as usual, but when he came home in the early morning she asked his trouble. He said that letters from home bore heavy news which he had withheld as she was to be alone during the long night hours. Now he was ready to tell her—his Sister Jennie was dead! He handed her a letter from his mother, and unable longer to control himself, broke into a flood of passionate tears. The letter, which was unsigned, ran:

Philadelphia, August 7, 1862.

"MY DEAR SON: Uncle Thomas has imparted to you by this mail the dreadful, heart-crushing news. God, I hope, has given you strength to bear it. After my

first gush of agony, and I could think at all, my cry
went up for my boy, Lord, sustain him in this great
trouble.　Oh, if he were here to witness the dying scene
and weep with us it would not seem so hard.　And then,
dear Annie, your image came up with inexpressible comfort—a dear wife to sympathise with him, on whose
breast he can pour out his agonising cry, tears to mingle with his tears.　O I blessed God that he had a wife.

"It is nearly two weeks since we laid our darling
Jennie in the grave, and we miss her more and feel more
desolate than we did at first.　O every article, and every
spot, and everything in the house reminds us of her.
O· how we mourn our precious child. . . . My
heart would burst without tears.

"I suppose Uncle Thomas gave you particulars of her
death and the impression with her from the first that
she would die.　In her first conversation with me (she
had been in bed several days and seemed to be easier
and more quiet, her sickness at first being characterised
by great restlessness and excessive debility by turns)
she said: 'Ma, I want to see Uncle Thomas, and Dr.
Goddard and Dr. Reed.'[1]　She had just been telling Pop
before I came in the room the same thing, mourning
over her coldness and hardness of heart, and saying that
she had not lived as she ought and that she was afraid
to die, that her Saviour would not receive her and that
she would not go to heaven.　All day when I thought
her easy and quiet she had been struggling and praying.　'O Ma,' said she, 'how everything earthly sinks
into utter nothingness at the prospect of death!'　I
tried to comfort her (Pop could not command his voice),
told her neither we nor the doctor had a thought of
her dying, she would get well; but I said, 'Dear, Uncle
Thomas cannot help your peace of mind; no earthly arm
can give you peace.'　'I know it,' she answered quickly,
'but I would love to have him talk and pray with me.'
'Jesus alone,' I again said, 'is all you want.　Simply
look to Him; cast yourself upon Him, in all your sin-
fulness and weakness, as you did, my child, when you

---

[1] Drs. Goddard and Reed were clergymen.

first came to Him years ago.   He is the same precious
Saviour.'   I repeated the hymn 'Rock of Ages,' slowly
and with emphasis—

> " 'In my hand no price I bring,
>   Simply to thy cross I cling.'

'Yes, yes,' she whispered.   .   .   .
  "O then the cruel, crushing blow came.   I would not
listen to any of them, not until dinner time would I
believe my child was going to die.   No, no, no; not my
Jennie.   Others might lose their children, but O no, this
could not be.   This rebellious spirit lasted some time
after she breathed her last, though after the first out-
burst I was enabled to choke down the agony and appear calm until it all was over.   She died peacefully
and gently, as an infant just sleeping away.   .   .   .
  "Henry, how her mind developed!   It was too much
for her frail body.   She read too much—nearly every
day at the library, besides bringing home books.
  "A piece of hair for Annie."

After his wife had read the letter the young man, springing to his feet and pacing the floor, as was his habit when
mentally roused, protested that he could not bring himself to believe that his dear sister was dead; and with the
manner of sudden conviction, said that there *must* be,
there *is*, another life—that the soul *is* immortal.   But his
words expressed his longing, rather than his conviction.
Immortality he now earnestly wished to believe in.   But
the theology of his youth did not persuade him, and it
was not until many years afterwards when pursuing the
great inquiry that produced "Progress and Poverty" that
he perceived the "grand simplicity and unspeakable harmony of universal law," that beneficence and intelligence
govern social laws, instead of blind, clashing forces; and
then faith from reason came and immortality became a
fixed belief.

CHAPTER IX.

SUFFERS EXTREME PRIVATION.

1861-1865.   Age, 22-26.

THE city of Sacramento, built on the sloping east bank of the Sacramento River, at the junction with the American River, is protected from overflows by a levee. For several weeks at the close of 1861 heavy rains had fallen throughout the State, so that the great Sacramento and San Joaquin river systems had over-flowed their natural banks, and in January, when Mrs. George was sent for by her husband to come to Sacramento, the rainfall amounted to twenty-four and one half inches, the heaviest monthly fall recorded in California. Under the stress of water, the levee broke and the low part of the city was submerged, most of the one-story buildings being entirely covered. Outside the city the entire country as far as the eye could reach, north and south, and as far west as the Coast Range of mountains was a sheet of water, the river course being told only by the tops of trees that grew along the banks.[1]

The Georges at first lived in the old City Hotel on K Street, just around the corner from the "Union" office where the husband worked. One morning Mr. George sent a hurried message to his wife to get her lunch, that

---

[1] Hittell's "History of California," Vol. IV., pp. 294–295.

he would join her at once, for the water was coming.
The hotel dining-room was on the ground floor, and out
in the street had accumulated a small pool, and so rapidly
did the water rise that before the hasty repast was over
all in the dining-room were standing on their chairs and
left the room on a bridge or pathway of them.

But everybody was showing what is said to be an American characteristic—good humour in face of the inevitable.
People abandoned first stories and lived and did business
above.   Printers in the "Union" office came to the City
Hotel over roof tops.   The members of the legislature
moved about in boats, as did everyone else who could get
them; and failing boats, used wash tubs, bath tubs and
rafts.   All things seemed to pass the hotel, and among
them came a section of sidewalk bearing a man and his
dog, the man on a stool, calmly contemplating the watery
aspect of city and country.   Bakers' ovens were early submerged, so that for a time fruit cake in stock became a
substitute for bread.   Spirituous liquors were, also, for a
time exceedingly scarce—a serious deprivation in a community, where, as in every new country, custom had made
drinking of some sort one of the common marks of cor-
diality in daily social life.   This afforded Henry George
special opportunity for amusement.   While on the "Evening Journal" he had obtained from a druggist, who had
no other way of settling an advertising bill, some toilet
articles, and among them twelve bottles of "New England
Rum," all of which he had given to Miss Fox, and which
were sent to her with her personal effects by her relatives
after her marriage.   Mr. George now took the "New England Rum" to his thirsty printer friends, and to his intense amusement, they emptied the bottles in a twinkle.
When Mrs. George heard of this she was in consternation.
"It was not for the stomach, but for the head—a hair

tonic," she said.   One of the printers ventured to explain that what was good for the hair must be good for the stomach, and that at any rate the liquid had tasted well and had produced no ill effects.

After perhaps four months' residence at the City Hotel, the Georges went to boarding and then to housekeeping, taking one house after another.   They were so restless that in answer to an acquaintance's question afterwards as to what time of year they cleaned house, Mr. George jokingly said: "We didn't clean house; we moved, instead!"   In October of 1862 he wrote home to his sisters:

"I have not written for some time—much longer than I should have neglected it; but I have been very busy all this time—busier than I have ever been before. I have been working steadily and literally working all the time.   Up to a couple of months ago I could not get enough to do, but since then the Overland Mail has been arriving with great regularity, and I have not missed a day, except when I took a run down to San Francisco for a couple of days on business, trying to get the balance of the pittance for which I sold my share in the 'Evening Journal.'   Had not my ueeessities been so great I would not have worked as I have during that time, for no one can do so for any time and retain good health.   But I wanted so much that I could not idle away a day on which I had a chance to work.   But we are getting along very well and I will not do so in future.   I have been making from $36 to $40 every week, and to do that I have had to be at work constantly, for the work on the 'Union' is what the printers call 'lean,' and every cent made is fully earned.   I have not even read the papers; barely glanced over the outlined news each day, and on the one day of the week when I had any time to spare it has been so filled up with things that should have been attended to during the week and I have been so tired out that I have hardly had time to write."

On November 3 (1862) the first child was born, a boy, who was named after his father. Added responsibilities made the young printer ready to turn his hand to whatever would bring him a living. And it happened that a young newspaper man named Samuel L. Clemens, who, under the *nom de plume* of "Mark Twain," had won a reputation on the Coast as a humourist of a dry and original quality, came to Sacramento to lecture. Another newspaper man, Denis E. McCarthy, acting as manager, hired Henry George to take tickets at the door.

Close, hard work had enabled Mr. George to pay up pretty much all that he owed in San Francisco at the time of his marriage. Then getting some money ahead, he had, following the old infatuation, invested it in mining stocks. But these stocks, instead of yielding dividends or even advancing in value, brought constant assessments, which meant privation or more indebtedness, and frequently both. He had in these mining ventures gone in with Isaac Trump, who was deeply interested in what was known as the Gettysburg and Swansea Mining Company, working a copper claim. The situation is explained in letters to and from Trump.

Sacramento, October 12, 1863.

"DEAR IKE: As you cannot come down and I cannot go up, I will write you as much as possible of my views and wishes about our investments. I don't want to bother you and will be as brief as possible.

"It is now eight months since we determined to make our fortunes, and I am afraid, in spite of our sanguine hopes, we have failed. 'Hope deferred maketh the heart sick,' and that is my case, if not yours. From the hopes of making a big raise, I have come down to think if I can get my money back I will be in luck. I need it badly and want to get it as soon as possible. . .

"I asked you the actual, cash value of my stock, and as you say nothing in answer, I suppose you consider the question already answered in your previous letter. In that you set down Swansea at $3 per foot and everything else, exclusive of Banner and Gray Eagle, at $1. That would make the account about this:

100 feet	Swansea	$300.00
100 "	Pine Bark...............	100.00
37½ "	Red Rock...............	37.50
25 "	Yorkville	25.00
		$462.50

The others, I don't suppose you count at anything. If this money could be got, however, I would be very well satisfied, you may be sure. I would be willing to take almost half that amount for everything.

"You tell me to sell down here, but that is a sheer impossibility. The claims are not known here. If they were Sacramento companies it might be different. As it is, I could only sell to one who would take my word for their value, which no one but a very intimate friend would do, and to such I would not sell in that way. I suppose it would be a like impossibility with you to get in cash anything like the figures you have named, but I suppose something could be got.

"Outside of the Swansea I should like to sell everything for whatever it would bring. I can't pay any more assessments without getting something back—with my liabilities it is impossible. Twenty-five or fifty feet of the Swansea I would like to hold. The remainder I want to sell.

"The year is fast closing and prices are not likely to improve before another season. I am deeply in debt and I want to make another effort by Spring at farthest and think the sooner we realize what we can the better it will be for us.

"I write you as well as I can what I think and want,

and leave you to act. If you don't want to sell, but can sell for me, without injuring yourself, do so.

"Yours sincerely,

"HENRY GEORGE."

Marysville, Nov. 8, 1863.

"DEAR HARRY: I received your note a few days ago. I do not think I will be able to come down for a month yet. I cannot raise the money. Unless something turns up before Christmas I am gone in. I have gone everything on copper and now I see no way of extricating myself, unless I give up near all my 'feet.' Plenty have Swansea who will not sell at any price, and others again can hardly give it away. We are about giving a contract to sink a shaft 35 feet deeper. The majority of the company think it will pay its own way after we get down 10 feet farther. An assessment on the Swansea is levied—ten cents a foot, payable before the 20th of this month.

"It is very uncertain about my stopping here any length of time, for I am very much discouraged and feel like starting out on the hills to prospect. I want excitement and think I could get plenty of it on a prospecting tour. I have a good locality in view where they have struck the richest kind of copper (so it is said). If I could only hold onto my stock a few months longer I feel confident I *must* come out all right.

"Harry, the Swansea is actually worth $6.00 per foot, but people here have paid out considerable this summer, and likewise the market is over-stocked with 'feet,' and folks have been 'stuck' so often that it is almost impossible to get men to purchase in any claim no matter how cheap it is offered. If one offers to sell low they come to the conclusion it is a *sell*, no matter how good your prospect is. And so it is, and so it will be, so long as men will be found who are ever willing to swindle their fellow men for the sake of a few paltry dollars. If I had been mean enough to take advantage of parties who had placed confidence in me since I have been on the 'copper lay,' I could have come out considerably ahead by this time. I do not regret acting honourably to them, but I do think there is a mighty slim chance for 'the poor whites' ever making anything by acting on the square.

"I feel quite depressed in spirits, but nevertheless, I am determined to persevere and try it again. As Mc-Fadden said: 'It is a gold ring or a wooden leg.'

"I have had sad news from home—a death in, the family and my mother in poor circumstances. And to think I cannot send her one dollar at present! 'It is hard, but I suppose fair.' If I live, by the help of God, *I will* come out all right yet.

                              "My love to all,
                                   "ISAAC TRUMP."

In the end—and the end was soon after the interchange of these letters—the mining ventures involved the two speculators in the loss of nearly all that they had invested. In his efforts to "get his nose out of the space box," George had been trying about this time to promote a project for a newspaper in the mining region of Reese River, but this, too, had failed, and the year was closing with him in what to a man in his circumstances were embarrassing debts.

It had been a year of hard work and considerable worry with the young printer, affording little time for attention to occurrences beyond his own small sphere; yet two events of first magnitude engaged his earnest thought. On January 1, 1863, President Lincoln issued his Emancipation Proclamation, which forever killed chattel bondage in the United States, and in the eyes of the world changing the issue from secession to slavery, gave the North new vigour for the conflict and cut off the South's hope of foreign aid.

The other event that intensely interested George was close at hand. Leland Stanford, a grocery and provision dealer in Sacramento, had been elected to the office of

Governor of California on the new Republican party tidal wave. He was also president of the Central Pacific Railroad Company and on the 8th of January, 1863, amid a crowd of people at the corner of Front and K Streets, Sacramento, he turned the first shovelful of earth in the construction of a railroad system which at that time looked puny enough, but which, under the extraordinarily energetic, able and unscrupulous management of Stanford, Charles Crocker, a Sacramento dry goods merchant, and Collis P. Huntington and Mark Hopkins, Sacramento hardware dealers, was within the next half dozen years to cross the State, climb over the mountains, span the Nevada desert, and meeting the line coming from the Missouri River, join with unbroken track, the West with the East. The young hard-working printer took an intense interest in what nearly everyone in the State at the time seemed to hail with applause. He may, indeed, have been one of the unnoticed men in the crowd at the initial ceremonies; but his mind beginning to open, questions were beginning to creep in, and he was before long to see that the enterprise—and likewise every such enterprise—in private hands, must involve gigantic public evils. And taking a clear mental stand against this, thought was to expand to other and deeper problems, and at length bring the obscure type-setter into the world's gaze as a new champion of equal rights. But no outward sign of such thought was to appear for years yet.

The first break in Mr. George's affairs at Sacramento was on the 26th of January, 1864, after he had been working on the "Union" for more than a year. That evening, after the midnight lunch, he got into an altercation with the foreman, John Timmins, about some matter that does not now appear clear, and was discharged. He was too proud to linger around or try to get back, and two days later left by steamer for San Francisco to look for work there.[1] The day after his arrival in San Francisco he wrote to his wife:

"Times seem pretty dull here, but I think I can get along. Anyhow we will try. I staid at the 'What Cheer House' last night. My darling, I don't know how much I love you until I am separated from you. I don't believe I could live without you. And the dear little fellow—how I love him!"

The young wife, with the baby, at once followed her husband to San Francisco where they went for a few days to the old Oriental Hotel, then very much run down, and afterwards took private rooms. The husband was on the alert for work from the moment he had arrived. Nothing whatever presented itself until Knowlton of the "Evening Journal" suggested that he canvass for subscribers for that paper on a commission basis. Isaac Trump, pursued by hard luck, had meanwhile come down from the mountains and was trying to see what he could do at selling clothes wringers, and he suggested that George should sell some wringers at the same time that he canvassed for the newspaper. George started out vigorously on the plan, but after five days of hard walking and talking through the suburban parts of Alameda County, just across San Francisco Bay, he returned without having sold a single wringer and with scarcely more than half a dozen subscribers. Then he went to setting type on the "Evening Journal," though the paper was in an obviously shaky

---

[1] A few years later, when Charles De Young was about to start the "Daily Chronicle," with Henry George as managing editor, the latter recommended Timmins for the position of foreman, saying that though he and Timmins had parted in ill-feeling, Timmins was an excellent workman and worthy of the post. Timmins obtained the place.

condition, and he had difficulty in getting his wages. Indeed, the money due for his share in the paper sold more than two years before had not yet been fully paid him. But for a time no other position opened to him. He was now nearly two hundred dollars in debt, with no prospect of steady employment. However, one of the regular typesetters on the "Evening Bulletin" being taken down with a serious illness, George received a call to the place as substitute and made good wages while the position lasted.

In April he left the "Bulletin" and went on the "American Flag." A little later, having got somewhat out of debt, he and his wife took a little house on Russ Street, or rather the upper flat of a two-story wooden house, and paid eighteen dollars rent. A change came in the "Flag" office on October 18, when the foreman, Mr. Bradford, discharged Mr. George for "claiming an advertisement." Next day the young man asked for a meeting of the "chapel" (the body of journeyman printers in the office), and after a hearing, was justified and under the typographical union rules was entitled to go back to work, but feeling that the foreman had taken a dislike to him, he concluded to resign. This threw him back upon "subbing" and he worked around odd days and nights wherever a friend laid off and gave him a call. All during the year he had at various times been talking with first one and then another about newspaper schemes that would give him better wages, in the future if not at once, and a chance to do something more than set type. He talked of the Sonora "Eagle," and of starting papers at Silver Mountain, Susanville, and La Paz, but none of these schemes took form, and when Isaac Trump suggested going into a partnership with him and a skilled job type setter named Peter Daley in a job-printing office, he decided that that was the thing to do.

Isaac Trump was a square, generous-minded man, of restless nature, sanguine temperament and great energy. With small schooling, he had a shrewdness and quickness of mind that adapted him to circumstances, and a love of mechanical contrivances that made him ready to turn his hand to anything. The ways that Trump had tried during the past few years to make a living were legion. He had learned the trade of gas fitter in his native city of Philadelphia, had shipped on the *Shubrick* for California as coal passer, had attempted farming on landing,[1] had lived for a while by mending pumps and when that failed took to mending watches, though he knew little about either; had "gone broke" at mining, and when he had done a job of wall papering and the complaint was made that the figure in the paper was up-side-down, he admitted that that was so, but that he had supposed the job was to be done in "first-class Eastern style" where it had become the fashion to invert the paper! He had got a delivery route on the "Flag," but sold it and now panted for a job-printing office, suggesting that he should solicit business while Daley and George should set type and do the mechancial work. The "Evening Journal" had at last died in June and its plant of type was lying idle. In December, 1864, George purchased some of this plant for the new business, agreeing to pay $400 and give $100

---

[1] In "The Science of Political Economy," Henry George makes reference to Trump's farming (p. 500). "On going ashore in San Francisco, a shipmate of mine, who could not tell a scythe from a marlinspike, hired out to a farmer in haying-time for $5 a day. At his first stroke with the scythe he ran it so deep in the ground that he nearly broke it in getting it out. Though he indignantly denounced such antiquated tools as out of fashion, declaring that he was used to "the patent scythes that turn up at the end," he did not really feel wronged that the farmer would not pay him a cent, as he knew that the agreement for day's labour was really an agreement for so much mowing."

worth of work, making money payment in what cash he could borrow and giving notes for the remainder.

Thus heavily weighted at the outset, the three men opened their office. But hard times had come. A drought had shortened the grain crop, killed great numbers of cattle and lessened the gold supply, and the losses that the farming, ranching and mineral regions suffered affected all the commercial and industrial activities of the State, so that there was a general depression. Business not coming into their office, the three partners went out to hunt for it; and yet it was elusive, so that they had very little to do and soon were in extremities for living necessities, even for wood for the kitchen fire. Henry George had fitfully kept a pocket diary during 1864, and a few entries at this job-printing period tell of the pass of affairs.

"December 25. Determined to keep a regular journal, and to cultivate habits of determination, energy and industry. Feel that I am in a bad situation, and must use my utmost effort to keep afloat and go ahead. Will try to follow the following general rules for one week:

"1st. In every case to determine rationally what is best to be done.

"2nd. To do everything determined upon immediately, or as soon as an opportunity presents.

"3rd. To write down what I shall determine upon doing for the succeeding day.

"Saw landlady and told her I was not able to pay rent.

"December 26. 7 A.M.:

"1st. Propose to-day in addition to work in office, to write to Boyne.

"2nd. To get wood in trade.

"3rd. To talk with Dr. Eaton, and perhaps, Dr. Morse.

"Rose at quarter to seven. Stopped at six wood yards trying to get wood in exchange for printing, but failed. Did very little in office. Walked and talked with Ike. Felt very blue and thought of drawing out. Saw Dr. Eaton, but failed to make a trade. In evening saw Dr. Morse. Have not done all, nor as well as I could wish. Also wrote to Boyne, but did not mail letter.

"Jannary 1. (Sunday) Annie not very well. Got down town about 11 o'clock. Went with Ike to China-man's to see about paper bags. Returned to office and worked off a lot.

"Jannary 2. Got down town about 8 o'clock. Worked some labels. Not much doing.

"January 3. Working in office all day. DeLong called to talk about getting out a journal. Did our best day's work."

From time to time they got a little business, enough at any rate to encourage Trump and George to continue with the office, though Daley dropped out; and each day that the money was there the two partners took out of the business twenty-five cents apiece, which they together spent for food, Trump's wife being with her relatives and he taking his dinner with the Georges. They lived chiefly on corn meal and milk, potatoes, bread and sturgeon, for meat they could not afford and sturgeon was the cheapest fish they could find.[1] Mr. George generally went to the office early without breakfast, saying that he would get it down town; but knowing that he had no money, his wife more than suspected that many a morning passed without his getting a mouthful. Nor could he borrow money

---

[1] Unlike that fish on the Atlantic Coast, sturgeon on the Pacific Coast, or at any rate in California waters, is of fine quality and could easily be substituted on the table for halibut.

except occasionally, for the drought that had made general business so bad had hurt all his friends, and indeed, many of them had already borrowed from him while he had anything to lend; and he was too proud to complain now to them.   Nor did his wife complain, though what deepened their anxieties was that they looked for the coming of a second child.   Mrs. George would not run up bills that she did not have money to meet.   She parted with her little pieces of jewellery and smaller trinkets one by one, until only her wedding ring had not been pawned.   And then she told the milkman that she could no longer afford to take milk, but he offered to continue to supply it for printed cards, which she accepted.   Mr. George's diary is blank just here, but at another time he said:[1]

> "I came near starving to death, and at one time I was so close to it that I think I should have done so but for the job of printing a few cards which enabled us to buy a little corn meal.   In this darkest time in my life my second child was born."

The baby came at seven o'clock in the morning of January 27, 1865.   When it was born the wife heard the doctor say: "Don't stop to wash the child; he is starving. Feed him!"   After the doctor had gone and mother and baby had fallen asleep, the husband left them alone in the house, and taking the elder child to a neighbour's, himself went to his business in a desperate state of mind, for his wife's condition made money—some money—an absolute and immediate necessity.   But nothing came into the office and he did not know where to borrow.   What then happened he told sixteen years subsequently.

---

[1] Meeker notes, October, 1897.

"I walked along the street and made up my mind to get money from the first man whose appearance might indicate that he had it to give. I stopped a man—a stranger—and told him I wanted $5. He asked what I wanted it for. I told him that my wife was confined and that I had nothing to give her to eat. He gave me the money. If he had not, I think I was desperate enough to have killed him." [1]

The diary notes commence again twenty days after the new baby's birth and show that the struggle for subsistence was still continuing, that Henry George abandoned the job-printing offiee and that he and his wife and babies had moved into a smaller house where he had to pay a rent of only nine dollars a month—just half of his former rent. This diary consists simply of two half sheets of white note paper, folded twice and pinned in the middle, forming two small neat books of eight pages each of about the size of a visiting card. The writing is very small, but clear.

"Feb. 17, 1865. (Friday) 10:40 P.M. Gave I. Trump this day bill of sale for my interest in office, with the understanding that if he got any money by selling, I am to get some. I am now afloat again, with the world before me. I have commenced this little book as an experiment—to aid me in acquiring habits of regu-

---

[1] Henry George related this incident to Dr. James E. Kelly in a conversation in Dublin during the winter of 1881–82, in proof that environment has more to do with human actions, and especially with so-called criminal actions, than we generally concede ; and to show how acute poverty may drive sound-minded moral men to the commission of deeds that are supposed to belong entirely to hardened evil natures. Out of long philosophical and physiological talks together at that time the two men formed a warm friendship, and subsequently, when he came to the United States and established himself in New York, Dr. Kelly became Henry George's family physician and attended him at his death-bed.

larity, punctuality and purpose. I will enter in it each evening the principal events of the day, with notes, if they occur, errors committed or the reverse, and plans for the morrow and future. I will make a practice of looking at it on rising in the morning.

"I am starting out afresh, very much crippled and embarrassed, owing over $200. I have been unsuccessful in everything. I wish to profit by my experience and to cultivate those qualities necessary to success in which I have been lacking. I have not saved as much as I ought and am resolved to practice a rigid economy until I have something ahead.

"1st. To make every cent I can.
"2nd. To spend nothing unnecessarily.
"3rd. To put something by each week, if it is only a five cent piece borrowed for the purpose.
"4th. Not to run in debt if it can be avoided.

"1st. To endeavour to make an acquaintance and friend of every one with whom I am brought in contact.
"2nd. To stay at home less, and be more social.
"3rd. To strive to think consecutively and decide quickly.

"Feb. 18. Rose at 6 o'clock. Took cards to woodman. Went to post office and got two letters, one from Wallazz and another from mother. Heard that Smith was up and would probably not go down. Tried to hunt him up. Ran around after him a great deal. Saw him; made an appointment, but he did not come. Finally met him about 4. He said that he had written up for a man, who had first choice; but he would do all he could. I was much disappointed. Went back to office; then after Knowlton, but got no money. Then went to 'Alta' office. Smith there. Stood talking till they went to work. Then to job office. Ike had got four bits [50 cents] from Dr. Josselyn. Went home, and he came out to supper.'

From daguerreotype taken in 1865, showing Mr. George at 26, just after job printing office experience.

"Got up in good season.

"Tried to be energetic about seeing Smith. Have not done with that matter yet, but will try every means.

"To-morrow will write to Cousin Sophia,[1] and perhaps to Wallazz and mother, and will try to make acquaintances. Am in very desperate plight. Courage!"

"Feb. 19. (Sunday) Rose about 9. Ran a small hill with Wessling for flour, coffee and butter. After breakfast took Harry around to Wilbur's. Talked awhile. Went down town. Could not get in offiee. Went into 'Alta' office several times. Then walked around, hoping to strike Smith. Ike to dinner. Afterwards walked with him, looking for house. Was at 'Alta' otfiee at 6, but no work. Went with Ike to Stickney's and together went to 'Californian' office. Came home and summed up assets and liabilities. At 10 went to bed, with determination of getting up at 6 and going to 'Bulletin' office.

"Have wasted a great deal of time in looking for Smith. Think it would have been better to have hunted him at once or else trusted to luck. There seems to be very little show for me down there. Don't know what to do.

"Feb. 20. Got up too late to go to the 'Bulletin' office. Got $1 from woodman. Got my pants from the tailor. Saw Smith and had a long talk with him. He seemed sorry that he had not thought of me, but said another man had been spoken to and was anxious to go. Went to 'Alta' office several times. Came home early and went to 'Alta' office at 6 and to 'Call' at 7, but got no work. Went to Ike Trump's room, and then came home.

---

[1] She was now a widow, James George having died in the preceding August.

"Was not prompt enough in rising. Have been walking around a good part of the day without definite purpose, thereby losing time.

"Feb. 21. Worked for Ike. Did two cards for $1. Saw about books, and thought some of travelling with them. Went to 'Alta' before coming home. In evening had row with Chinaman. Foolish.

"Feb. 22. Hand very sore. Did not go down till late. Went to work in 'Bulletin' at 12. Got $3. Saw Boyne. Went to library in evening. Thinking of economy.

"Feb. 26. Went to 'Bulletin'; no work. Went with Ike Trump to look at house on hill; came home to breakfast. Decided to take house on Perry Street with Mrs. Stone; took it. Came home and moved. Paid $5 of rent. About 6 o'clock went down town. Saw Ike; got 50 cents. Walked around and went to Typographical Union meeting. Then saw Ike again. Found Knowlton had paid him for printing plant, and demanded some of the money. He gave me $5 with very bad humour.

"Feb. 27. Saw Ike in afternoon and had further talk. In evening went to work for Col. Strong on 'Alta.' Smith lent me $3.

"Feb. 28. Worked again for Strong. Got $5 from John McComb.

"Feb. 29. Got $5 from Barstow, and paid Charlie Coddington the $10 I had borrowed from him on Friday last. On Monday left at Mrs. Lauders [the Russ Street landlady] $1.25 for extra rent and $1.50 for milkman.

"March 1. Rose early, went to 'Bulletin'; but got no work. Looked in at Valentine's and saw George

Foster, who told me to go to Frank Eastman's [printing office]. Did so and was told to call again. Came home; had breakfast. Went to 'Alta' in evening, but no work. Went to Germania Lodge and then to Stickney's.

"March 2. Went to Eastman's about 11 o'clock and was put to work.

"March 3. At work.

"March 4. At work. Got $5 in evening."

The strength of the storm had now passed. The young printer began to get some work at "subbing," though it was scant and irregular. His wife, who paid the second month's rent of the Perry Street house by sewing for her landlady, remarked to her husband how contentedly they should be able to live if he could be sure of making regularly twenty dollars a week.

CHAPTER X.

BEGINS WRITING AND TALKING.

1865-1866.   AGE, 26-27.

HENRY GEORGE'S career as a writer should be dated from the commencement of 1865, when he was an irregular, substitute printer at Eastman's and on the daily newspapers, just after his severe job-office experience. He now deliberately set himself to self-improvement. These few diary notes for the end of March and beginning of April are found in a small blank book that in 1878, while working on "Progress and Poverty," he also used as a diary.

"Saturday, March 25, 1865. As I knew we would have no letter this morning, I did not hurry down to the office. After getting breakfast, took the wringing machine which I had been using as a sample back to Faulkner's; then went to Eastman's and saw to bill; loafed around until about 2 P.M. Concluded that the best thing I could do would be to go home and write a little. Came home and wrote for the sake of practice an essay on the 'Use of Time,' which occupied me until Annie prepared dinner. Went to Eastman's by six, got money. Went to Union meeting.

"Sunday, March 26. Did not get out until 11 o'clock. Took Harry down town and then to Wilbur's. Proposed to have Dick [the new baby] baptised in afternoon; got Mrs. Casey to come to the house for that purpose, but concluded to wait.   Went to see Dull, who took me to his shop and showed me the model of his wagon brake.

"Monday, March 27.   Got down to office about one o'clock; but no proofs yet.   Strolled around a little. Went home and wrote communication for Aleck Kenneday's new paper, 'Journal of the Trades and Workingmen.'   Took it down to him.   In the evening called on Rev. Mr. Simonds.

"Tuesday, 28.   Got down late.   No work.   In afternoon wrote article about laws relating to sailors.   In evening went down to Dull's shop while he was engaged on model.

"Wednesday, 29.   Went to work about 10.30.   In evening corrected proof for 'Journal of the Trades and Workingmen.'

"Thursday, 30.   At work.

"Tuesday, April 4.   Despatch received stating that Richmond and Petersburgh are both in our possession.

"Wednesday, 5.   Took model of wagon brake to several carriage shops; also to 'Alta' office.   In evening signed agreement with Dull.

"Saturday, 8.   Not working; bill for week, $23. Paid Frank Mahon the $5 I have been owing for some time.   Met Harrison who has just come down from up the country.   He has a good thing up there.   Talked with Dull and drew up advertisement.   In evening, nothing."

Thus while he was doing hap-hazard type-setting, and trying to interest carriage builders in a new wagon brake, he was also beginning to write.   The first and most important of these pieces of writing mentioned in the diary notes—on "the use of time"—was sent by Mr. George to his mother, as an indication of his intention to improve himself.   Commencing with boyhood, Henry George, as has been seen, had the power of simple and clear statement, and if this essay served no other purpose than to show the development of that natural power, it would be of value. But as a matter of fact, it has a far greater value; for while repeating his purpose to practise writing—"to acquire facility and elegance in the expression" of his thought—it gives an introspective glimpse into the naturally secretive mind, revealing an intense desire, if not for the "flesh pots of Egypt," at least for such creature and intellectual comforts as would enable him and those close to him "to bask themselves in the warm sunshine of the brief day." This paper is presented in full:

Essay, Saturday Afternoon, March 25, 1865.

"On the Profitable Employment of Time."

"Most of us have some principal object of desire at any given time of our lives; something which we wish more than anything else, either because its want is more felt, or that it includes other desirable things, and we are conscious that in gaining it we obtain the means of gratifying other of our wishes.

"With most of us, this power, in one shape or the other—is money, or that which is its equivalent or will bring it.

"For this end we subject ourselves to many sacrifices; for its gain we are willing to confine ourselves and employ our minds .and bodies in duties which, for their own sakes are irksome; and if we do not throw the whole force of our natures into the effort to gain this, it is that we do not possess the requisite patience, self-command, and penetration where we may direct our efforts.

"I am constantly longing for wealth; the wide difference between my wishes and the means of gratifying them at my command keeps me in perpetual disquiet. It would bring me comfort and luxury which I cannot now obtain; it would give me more congenial employment and associates; it would enable me to cultivate my mind and exert to a fuller extent my powers; it would give me the ability to minister to the comfort and enjoyment of those whom I love most, and therefore, it is my principal object in life to obtain wealth, or at least, more of it than I have at present.

"Whether this is right or wrong, I do not now consider; but that it is so I am conscious. When I look behind at my past life I see that I have made little or no progress, and am disquieted; when I consider my present, it is difficult to see that I am moving towards it at all; and all my comfort in this respect is in the hope of what the future may bring forth.

"And yet my hopes are very vague and indistinct, and my efforts in any direction, save the beaten track in which I have been used to earn my bread, are, when perceptible, jerky, irregular and without intelligent, continuous direction.

"When I succeed in obtaining employment, I am industrious and work faithfully, though it does not satisfy my wishes. When I have nothing to do, I am anxious to be in some way labouring towards the end I wish, and yet from hour to hour I cannot tell at what to employ myself.

"To secure any given result it is only necessary to rightly supply sufficient force. Some men possess a greater amount of natural power than others and produce quicker and more striking results; yet it is apparent that the abilities of the majority, if properly and continuously applied, are sufficient to accomplish much more than they generally do.

"The hours which I have idled away, though made miserable by the consciousness of accomplishing nothing, had been sufficient to make me master of almost any common branch of study. If, for instance, I had applied myself to the practice of bookkeeping and arithmetic I might now have been an expert in those things; or I might have had the dictionary at my fingers' ends; been a practised, and perhaps an able writer; a much better printer; or been able to read and write French, Spanish or any other modern or ancient language to which I might have directed my attention; and the

mastery of any of these things now would give me an
additional, appreciable power, and means by which to
work to my end, not to speak of that which would have
been gained by exercise and good mental habits.

"These truths are not sudden discoveries; but have
been as apparent for years as at this present time; but
always wishing for some chance to make a sudden leap
forward, I have never been able to direct my mind and
concentrate my attention upon those slow processes by
which everything mental (and in most cases, material)
is acquired.

"Constantly the mind works, and if but a tithe of
its attention was directed to some end, how many matters might it have taken up in succession, increasing its
own stores and power while mastering them?

"To sum up for the present, though this essay has
hardly taken the direction and shape which at the outset
I intended, it is evident to me that I have not employed
the time and means at my command faithfully and ad-
vantageously as I might have done, and consequently,
that I have myself to blame for at least a part of my
non-success. And this being true of the past, in the
future like results will flow from like causes. I will,
therefore, try (though, as I know from experience, it is
much easier to form good resolutions than to faithfully
carry them out) to employ my mind in acquiring useful information or practice, when I have nothing leading more directly to my end claiming my attention.
When practicable, or when I cannot decide upon anything else, I will endeavour to acquire facility and elegance in the expression of my thought by writing essays
or other matters which I will preserve for future comparison. And in this practice it will be well to aim at
mechanical neatness and grace, as well as at proper and
polished language."

Of the two other pieces of writing spoken of in the
diary notes, the "article about laws relating to sailors,"
has left no trace, but a copy of the one for the "Journal
of the Trades and Workingmen," has been preserved. It

was a long letter to the editor, signed "H. G." urging working men to think about political and social questions, and find if it be possible to "check the tendency of society to resolve itself into classes who have too much or too little." In closing, its author said:

"And so, Mr. Editor, I hail with joy your establishment of a paper which shall speak for the working classes, and through which their most enlightened views may be diffused, which may lead them to think upon problems for which it is to their best interests to find a solution. At a time when most of our public prints pander to wealth and power and would crush the poor man beneath the wheel of the capitalist's carriage; when one begins to talk of the 'work people' and 'farm servants' of this coast, and another to deplore the high rate of wages, and each and all to have quick reprobation for any effort of mechanics or labourers to obtain their dues, but nothing to say against combinations to deprive them of their rights, I, for one, feel that your enterprise is one which we all should feel the necessity of, and to which we should lend our cordial support. In the columns of your paper I hope to see fearless opinions of men and measures ably maintained, and the intelligence of our class brought to the solution of questions of political and social economy which deeply affect us; that we may bring our united efforts to the advancement of those great principles upon which our republican institutions rest, and upon which we must depend to secure for us and our children our proper place and rights, and for our country her proud and foremost rank among the nations."

It was about this time that in addition to the writings mentioned in the diary, Henry George wrote a fanciful sketch entitled "A Plea for the Supernatural," which was published in the "Californian" and soon afterwards republished by the Boston Saturday "Evening Gazette."

The "Californian" was a San Francisco weekly literary
paper founded in 1864, and which, under the editorship
of Charles Henry Webb and the contributing pens of
Mark Twain, Bret Harte and a lot of other bright writers,
had a brilliant, if short, career—being spoken of as having
"lived to be three years old and never died." A. A. Stickney, a printer friend, who, while they were in Sacramento
working on the "Union" together, induced George to join
the Odd Fellows' Order, had bought into the "Californian," and it may have been through his influence that the
young printer's sketch was published. But however published is not important, nor is the sketch itself, further
than to furnish cumulative evidence of the feverish energy
the young man was evincing in pursuit of his purpose to
practise writing—a spirit forming one of his most marked
characteristics when acting upon an important resolve.
He had proved to himself that he could write, and the use
to which he put his power came suddenly, unexpectedly
and in a way to affect his whole after life.

The Civil War was now about over. On April 9, 1865,
Lee's army surrendered. The South, worn out by the
terrific struggle and by starvation, lay prostrate, and the
whole North and West indulged in demonstrative rejoic-
ings over the prospect of peace and harmony throughout
a reunited country—when, on the night of April 14,
flashed the appalling news that President Lincoln had been
shot. Never before was seen such excitement in excitable
San Francisco. This deed seemed like the last desperate
act of the slave-power, and all manner of rumours of a vast
Southern conspiracy of assassination were afloat. The
next day general business was suspended. It was now
known definitely that the President, while sitting in a
proscenium box at Ford's Theatre, Washington, witnessing
the comedy, "Our American Cousin," was shot in the back

of the head by John Wilkes Booth, an actor, who had stealthily approached from behind, and brandishing a knife, had leaped from the box to the stage, crying out in the hearing of the dumb-stricken audience, *"Sic semper tyrannis:* the South is avenged!"

When news came that Lincoln had died of his wound excitement in San Francisco ran mad. To many the first impulse was to destroy the newspapers which had fostered secession; and the "Democratic Press" edited by Beriah Brown, the "Occidental" edited by Zachariah Montgomery, the "Monitor," a Catholic weekly, edited by Thomas A. Brady, and the "News Letter" edited by Frederick Marriot had their plants demolished and cast into the street. Mr. George had been terribly wrought up over the news of the assassination, and talking about the "copperhead" newspapers with Ike Trump and others, had determined to lead an assault upon the "News Letter"; but when he reached the spot he found Trump gallantly leading a party that were hurling type, furniture and machinery into the street with such a spirited and liberal hand that little remained to be done to complete the job.

After this physical venting of feeling, higher sentiments took possession of the young printer, for next day he sat down in his little Perry Street home and wrote out new thoughts that were surging through him. He put them in the form of a newspaper communication, which he addressed to the editor of the "Alta California," the paper on which he had been setting type when opportunity afforded. When the communication was finished he took it to the office and slipped it into the editor's box. Next day it appeared with an editorial note preceding it, for the editor had learned who the writer was. Communication and note appeared as follows:

[The following stirring article on the great patricide of the age was written by a printer in the office of the "Alta California"]:

SIC SEMPER TYRANNIS!

"A man rushed to the front of the President's box, waving a long dagger in his right hand, exclaiming, '*Sic semper tyrannis!*'"

"*Alta*" despatches, April 15.

"What a scene these few words bring—vivid as the lightning flash that bore them! The glitter and glare, curving circle and crowded pit, flash of jewels and glinting of silks—and the blanched sea of up-turned faces, the fixed and staring eyes, the awful hush—silence of death!

"And there, before all—before all mankind forevermore—stands, for an instant, the assassin, poised for the leap, the gleaming steel in his right hand, and his cry of triumph, of defiance, ringing throughout the house, '*Sic semper tyrannis!*'

"Is it a wonder they are spellbound! They came to laugh at a comedy—and a tragedy is before them which will make a nation weep—and whose mighty import centuries may not guess! Their frightened eyes look on a scene in the grand drama whose first act was the creation and whose last will be the procession of the white-robed and the shouts of the redeemed. Well may they gaze, awe-stricken, speechless, for the spirits of the mighty dead, and generation after generation that shall be, look with them, and the past that has gone, and the future that is to come, join their voices in the shout, '*Sic semper tyrannis!*'

"Poised there for an instant, that black, daring heart—that spirit incarnate of tyranny and wrong—feels the import of the act, and with voice of inspiration, shouts its own doom—'*Sic semper tyrannis!*'

"Amen! and thus it will be. They have struck down the just because of his justice, and the fate they have fixed upon him shall be theirs!

"What fitting time! Good Friday! At this very moment, before bare and black-draped altars, sounds the solemn wail of the Tenebræ, and mournful music bears the sorrow which shall burst into the joy of the resurrection—for, on a day of which this is the anniversary, One died that there might be life, and Death and Hell heard their doom. And now (as close as human type may approach the divine) again has Evil triumphed, and the blood of its victim sealed its fate.

"While the world lasts will this scene be remembered. As a martyr of Freedom—as the representative of the justice of a great nation, the name of the victim will live forever; and the Proclamation of Emancipation, signed with the name and sealed with the blood of *Abraham Lincoln* will remain a landmark in the progress of the race.

"In the hearts of a people whose number shall be as the sands of the sea, his memory will be cherished with that of Washington. And to the ends of the earth— from the frozen sea of the North to the ice fields of the South, in every land on which the sun in his circuit shall look down, whenever the standard shall be raised against a hoary wrong, his name shall be a watch-word and an inspiration.

"And when, on plains and uplands where now the elephant and spring-bok roam, farms shall be tilled and homes arise; and on great lakes and rivers, now the haunts of the hippopotamus—a thousand paddles shall beat, the mothers of nations yet unborn shall teach their children to call him blessed!

"*Sic semper tyrannis!* Blazoned on the shield of a noble State by the giants of the young republic, their degenerate sons shall learn its meaning! The murderer's shout as Lincoln fell, it will be taken up by a million voices. *Thus shall* perish all who wickedly raise their hands to shed the blood of the defenders of the oppressed, and who strive, by wickedness and cruelty, to preserve and perpetuate wrong. Their names shall become a hissing and a reproach among men as long as the past shall be remembered; and the great sin in whose support they spared no crime is numbered henceforth with the things that were. *Sic semper tyrannis!* Amen.

"H. G."

"San Francisco, April 16, 1865."[1]

A few days later the editor of the "Alta" engaged the printer as a special reporter to write in conjunction with others a description of the Lincoln mourning decorations throughout the city, and this was the first newspaper writing for which Henry George received pay. But he had more than a reporter's thoughts in him; and again he sat down in the parlour of his little Perry Street home and wrote a communication to the editor and signed it with his initials. It was on the character of Lincoln. This, like the former one, he put in the editor's box. Next morning he looked to see if it had been printed, and lo! like Ben Adhem's name, "it led all the rest." It did not bear his signature, nor was it printed as a letter to the editor, for it had been made the chief editorial of the paper. A few short extracts will suffice:

"No common man, yet the qualities which made him great and loved were eminently common. . . .

"He was not of those whom God lifts to the mountain tops, and who tell of His truth to ears that will not hear, and show His light to eyes that cannot see— whom their own generation stone, and future ones worship; but he was of the leaders who march close before the advancing ranks of the people, who direct their steps and speak with their voice.

" . . . No other system would have produced

---

[1] This article is copied from a printed proof pasted in a scrapbook kept by Mr. George and containing his early published writings. But since the file of the regular issue of the "Alta California" fails to reveal it, the conclusion is drawn that the communication must have appeared in a special edition of that newspaper.

him; through no crowd of courtiers could such a man
have forced his way; his feet would have slipped on the
carpets of palace stairs, and Grand Chamberlains ordered him back! And, as in our time of need, the man
that was needed came forth, let us know that it will
always be so, and that under our institutions, when the
rights of the people are endangered, from their ranks
will spring the men for the times."[1]

This experience led to the "Alta's" agreement to take
from Mr. George some news letters relative to a Mexican liberating expedition in which he was about to embark. While
the United States were engaged in their civil war Napoleon
III. had sent an army into Mexico to establish an imperial
government and place Austrian Arch-duke Maximilian on
the throne. The resistance of the Mexican patriots under
Juarez excited strong sympathy through all that part of
the United States adjacent to Mexico; and ardently desirous of striking a blow for that republic, especially as
circumstances had prevented him from engaging in the
war in the United States against slavery, Henry George
joined an expedition that was being organised to help the
Juarez party. He talked it over with his wife, with whom
now, after three and a half years of wedded life and extreme trials of poverty, he was sealed in the closest possible relations of confidence and affection. Though the
prospect of parting and the danger he would run were sore
to bear, and though the peril of being left destitute with
two babies was imminent, she would not withhold him, but
on the contrary did what she always afterwards did—encouraged him to follow the promptings of what he con-
ceived to be his duty.

He, therefore, arranged with the "Alta California" peo-

[1] "Alta California," April 23, 1865.

ple to send his wife whatever money should come from the news letters that he should write, which he thought would be sufficient to maintain her; and then with his wife, took the new baby to St. Patrick's Catholic church, in deference to her, and had him baptised Richard Fox, the first name after his father and the second in honour of his wife's family. Then the couple went back to their home, and kneeling down beside their babies prayed together; after which, kissing his darling ones good-bye, the young man set off for the meeting place. He has described this:[1]

"I was to be first lieutenant in a company commanded by an Indian fighter named Burn; with an acquaintance of mine, Barry, as major; and Hungerford, afterwards father-in-law of Mackay, the millionaire, as colonel. We swore in a good many men, and went down to Platt's Hall to prepare to make a start in a vessel which should be secretly provided. We gathered there in the early evening, but hour after hour passed without receiving the order to start. Finally, at daylight next day we were told where the vessel was, but it was well on in the morning before we made for her.

"When we got down we found an old bark, the *Brontes*, to be the one selected for us. She was short of provisions and equipment for such a company. She had aboard 10,000 American condemned rifles, half a dozen saddles and a few casks of water. We had hardly got aboard before a revenue cutter dropped anchor in front of her and blocked the way. This ended our expedition. The Federal authorities had shut their eyes as long as they could to what was going on, but now could do so no longer.

"Among those who were going with us, and who would have been little less than a crowd of pirates if we had got down, were some who got up a scheme to seize a French transport, and I believe, to capture one of the

---

[1] Meeker notes, October, 1897.

mail steamers which then left for Panama twice a month with shipments of gold from California to New York. This got wind and some half dozen or so were arrested and put on trial for intended piracy.

"This was the *Brontes* expedition, which led to the charge in some San Francisco papers when I ran for Mayor in New York years afterwards, that I had been engaged in a piratical expedition. This is the nearest I ever came to engaging in war, and I will never forget the willingness with which my wife, with her two little children, agreed to my leaving her to go on an expedition that I now know could have had no possible good end."

A little later Henry George helped in the establishment of the Monroe League, which was to send an expedition to the Mexican patriots, a newspaper man named Linthicum to head it. They swore men in on a bare sword and the republican flag of Mexico, and Mrs. George was sworn as the only woman member. Nothing came of the League, though its failure is not explained.[1] By this time Mr. George saw a good opening in Sacramento to set type on a

---

[1] Nearly two years subsequently (July 3, 1867) when managing editor on the San Francisco "Times," Mr. George wrote in an editorial relative to the downfall of the Mexican tyranny and the execution of Maximilian: "We should not allow either his position or his private character to blind our eyes to his public crimes. The men who have inflicted the greatest evils upon their kind, have not been always the worst men in their personal relations. Charles I. was a good husband and kind father, but he was not less the enemy of liberty, and his death was not less a salutary example. . . . . That the execution of Maximilian will excite a deep sensation in Europe cannot be doubted, but its effects will not be entirely without benefit. It is a protest against the right of kings to cause suffering and shed blood for their own selfish ends. It is a vindication of justice upon an offender of a class whose rank has hitherto sheltered them from the punishment due to their crimes. It will teach princes and princelings to be more cautious how they endeavour to subvert the liberties of a free people."

contract for State official work, and so he went there, taking his family with him and settling down at housekeeping. Touching his personal matters he wrote to his Sister Caroline (December 3):

"I am, for the present, only ambitious of working, and will look neither to the right nor left, until I have 'put money in my purse'—something it has never yet contained. I have abandoned, I hope, the hand to mouth style of living, and will endeavour, if not absolutely forced to do so, to draw no drafts on the future. By next year we hope to have enough money saved to return home, and will do so, unless it should seem very inadvisable. I will come, anyhow, as soon as I can, for I have made up my mind it is my duty to do so. I am going to work on the State work as soon as it commences (this week I think) and expect to have steady work for the best part of a year and perhaps more. Since we came up here I have done pretty well—have made a living, paid expenses of coming up, got what was necessary, and owe nothing at all here, and feel more comfortable and hopeful than ever since we have been married."

For nearly a year Henry George, following his trade of type-setting, continued at State work. He lived quietly, and since his wife and he had modest habits, very comfortably. He had joined the Odd Fellows' Order during his former residence in Sacramento, through the advice of his printer friend, A. A. Stickney; and now in 1866 he joined the National Guard, though he soon dropped out of it; and a literary organisation, in which for a while he engaged in discussions on public questions. One of these discussions was of great importance in his life, since it marks another stepping-stone in his thought—his conversion from a belief in the protective principle to the opposite principle of the entire freedom of trade. In "Protection

or Free Trade?" Mr. George has spoken of his strong protection views at this time.[1]

"I was for a number of years after I had come of age
a protectionist, or rather, I supposed I was, for, without
real examination, I had accepted the belief, as in the
first place we all accept our beliefs, on the authority of
others. So far, however, as I thought at all on the subject, I was logical, and I well remember how when the
Florida and *Alabama* were sinking American ships at
sea, I thought their depredations, after all, a good thing
for the State in which I lived—California—since the
increased risk and cost of ocean carriage in American
ships (then the only way of bringing goods from the
Eastern States to California) would give to her infant
industries something of that needed protection against
the lower wages and better established industries of the
Eastern States which the Federal Constitution prevented
her from securing by a State tariff."

The way in which this belief was changed is more fully
explained in another place:[1]

"One night in Sacramento I went with a friend to a
debating society and there heard a young fellow of great
ability, William H. Mills, the present Land Agent of the
Central Pacific Railroad, deliver a speech in favour of
protection. I was a protectionist when he began, but
when he got through I was a free trader. When they
asked me what I thought of it I told them that if what
he said was true, it seemed to me that the country that
was hardest to get at must be the best country to live in;
and that, instead of merely putting duties on things
brought from abroad, we ought to put them on things
brought from anywhere, and that fires and wars and
impediments to trade and navigation were the very best
things to levy on commerce."

---

[1] Chapter IV (Memorial edition, p. 29).
[2] Meeker notes, October, 1897.

Mr. Mills says that he remembers "with reasonable distinctness the incident referred to by Henry George":

"The debating society was known as the 'Sacramento Lyceum.' The subject for the evening was a general consideration of a national tariff, whether for revenue or for protection. I was the leading speaker for the evening and took a position in favour of a protective policy as that best calculated to produce the broadest industrial skill of our people, develop the natural resources of the country, give the largest diversity of employment, confer the highest intelligence, employ a greater proportion of our people in skilled labour which always receives the highest reward and generally confer industrial and commercial independence upon the nation.

"As one of the speakers of the evening, Henry George controverted the doctrine that nationalism was the goal of civilisation, pleading for a broad cosmopolitanism. He contended that national policies should interpose no barrier to harmonious relations between nations of the earth; that if the doctrine enunciated to sustain a policy of high protection were true, absolute national isolation would be the condition best calculated to promote national development; that as relative evolutionary forces, the policy of protection created antagonism between the nations, isolated them, augmented their selfishness, intensified the military spirit, and made standing armies and vast navies necessary to the peace of the world; while free trade, as an evolutionary force, made nations dependent, promoted peace among them and urged humanity on toward a higher plane of universal fraternity.

"In conversation with Mr. George since then, he said to me that while he went to the Lyceum meeting a protectionist, he left a free trader, because protection was defensible only upon the theory that the separation of mankind into nations implied their industrial and commercial antagonism."

But while this period marked what he considered a great step in right thinking, Henry George did not neglect writing. It was now that he wrote for Edmund Wallazz's paper, the "Philadelphia Saturday Night," the account of the *Shubrick* burial[1] under the title of "Dust to Dust." The sketch was republished by the "Californian." For the latter publication he also wrote a fanciful sketch entitled "The Prayer of Kohonah—a tradition of the northwest coast." Both of these, like the Lincoln article, gave proofs of a vivid imagination and a high order of descriptive power, and it is certain from casual notes in his pocket diaries during the next two or three years that he was thinking of writing a novel; so that perhaps it wanted but the accident to have turned his abilities and energy into the realm of fiction instead of to a search for the eternal verities underlying social order.

But public affairs attracted and absorbed more and more of his attention, and he gave vent to his sentiments in the "Daily Union" through the medium of letters to the editor, which he signed with the *nom de plume* of "Proletarian"; and in September, 1866, when printing became slack, he wrote for San Francisco newspapers a number of letters relative to the State fair then being held in Sacramento. Then his newspaper ambition took a leap forward. A daily paper to be named the "Times" was to be started in San Francisco, and he made application for a writing position upon it. A letter to his father (August 8) told about it:

"When you next write direct to San Francisco, for I expect to go down there in about two weeks. The paper that I wrote you of is to start there in about that time. I do not know whether I will get the situation I asked for as reporter or assistant editor, but I can have a position in the composing room, at any rate, with a chance to go in the editorial department in a little while. I can have steady work here if I stay, but have concluded to go down, as I will have a better chance down there. The foreman has given me a case, which is in itself desirable, as it will be a good paper to work on, and will be a steady thing. But even if I do not get a better position than that at the start, I am promised one shortly afterward. And if things go as I wish them to, I may by the first of the year make $50 or $60 a week. I don't say that I will, or even that I expect to, but I see where there is a chance. However, I won't say anything about it until I see more clearly.

"This I hope, is our last move until we step on board the steamer. Our desire to return home increases daily, and all my plans tend to that object. I do not think, though, that we can come till spring, but I hope that this delay will be of benefit, in better enabling me to come home and to do better when I do come. I want, if possible, to secure some little practice and reputation as a writer here before going, which will not only give me introduction and employment there, but help me in going and enable me to make something by corresponding with papers here. If I do not overrate my abilities I may yet make position and money."

He was not destined to go to Philadelphia in the following spring, for fortune threw upon him larger responsibilities than he had dreamed of.

CHAPTER XI.

MANAGING EDITOR AND CORRESPONDENT.

THE San Francisco "Times" was started on November 5, 1866, with Henry George in the composing room setting type. James McClatchy, who, as editor of the "Sacramento Bee," had won a reputation as a forcible writer, became editor of the new paper, and it was mainly through him that George's hope of advancement lay, having won McClatchy's friendship while in Sacramento. McClatchy, having a clear, sound mind himself, was liberal enough to recognise and encourage merit in others. He may be said to have seen signs of promise in the young printer. At any rate, three editorial articles from George were accepted and published in quick succession. The first, for which he received $5, was entitled "To Constantinople," and was published eleven days after the paper was started. It treated of the destiny of Russia to carry the cross to the Bosphorus, and there, overruling the Turk, to make its seat of empire in the city founded by the great Constantine to be the new capital of the Roman world. But after only three weeks' career as editor of the "Times," James McClatchy disagreed with the paper's owners, and stepping out, returned to the "Sacramento Bee."

Noah Brooks, who in later years has become best known

in the East as the author of "Washington in Lincoln's Time," tales of the early California days, and juvenile stories, had been chief editorial writer. He now became editor, with William Bausman and N. S. Treadwell as editorial writers. O. B. Turrell was foreman of the composing room and was very friendly to George. Indeed, he next to McClatchy had encouraged the young printer to think of advancement, and now suggested that he submit an article to the new editor. Noah Brooks tells of his side of this transaction:

"Mr. Turrell, the foreman, had come repeatedly to me to recommend a young printer as a writer, and I said that I would look at some of his work. Turrell brought an article that was in editorial form and written in neat, regular and rather small hand, with the lines far apart, on buff sheets of paper such as was used for wrapping and sending the newspaper through the mails. I glanced at the article and then read it somewhat carefully, for it showed a style and largeness of thought that made me suspect that the young man had been borrowing. So I laid the matter aside for a day or two and meanwhile took a glance over the current magazines and other periodicals, but could find no signs of appropriation. I spoke to the foreman and he said that I need have no thought of irregularity—that the young man was bright and original, and that he was entirely honest and would not think of offering another's thoughts. So I put the article in the paper.

"Turrell told me where I should find the printer who had written the editorial. That day I passed through the composing room and saw a slight young man at work at the case Turrell had named. He was rather under size, and stood on a board to raise him to the proper height to work at his case. I was not prepossessed with him and little dreamed that there was a man who would one day win great fame—as little dreamed of it, as no doubt, he did.

"I invited him to write at our regular editorial col-umn rates, which he did for a while, continuing at the same time at his printer's case. Afterwards I called him into the reportorial department, and then, on the death of Mr. Treadwell, invited him to become a regular editorial writer. Soon after this I fell out with the president of the board of trustees of the paper, Mr. Annis Merrill, and resigned, taking Mr. Bausman with me. My quarrel was not Mr. George's quarrel, and he remained, and took charge of the paper."

As reporter of the "Times," Henry George earned $30 a week; later, as editorial writer, $35 a week; and as man-aging editor, from the beginning of June, 1867, $50 a week. An incident about this time showed his great ten-derness for his wife. One evening word was brought that his wife, who was expecting her third child, had fallen down-stairs. The husband ran most of the way home. The doctor feared consequences. But the medicine he gave was effective, for the patient by midnight grew quiet and fell asleep. Her husband, half leaning on one elbow, half bending over her, reclined beside her intently watch-ing, all his clothes on and with hat in hand, ready at the first unfavourable symptom to spring up and run for the physician. When the grey streaks of dawn came, four hours afterwards, the wife awoke, greatly refreshed, to find her husband with unchanged position and tense eyes re-garding her. When she spoke of this he simply said that all had depended on her sleeping. The wife fully re-covered from the shock, and the child, born three months later, came into the world strong and sound of body and mind, and named Jennie Teresa, after its father's dead sister and its mother's living sister, grew up into beautiful womanhood.

Henry George became managing editor of the "Times"

in the beginning of June, 1867, under the chief-editorship of Dr. Gunn, well known in San Francisco political affairs in that day, and who had bought into the paper. George retained the position of managing editor until he left the paper on August 12, 1868. During the interval, besides the regular office work, he was conducting occasional correspondence with the Hawaiian "Gazette" and other newspapers, so that his income was much larger than ever before in his life. Moreover, his work was telling, making him friends and extending his influence.

But more important than anything else during the "Times" period was the preparation he was going through for his life work. This related to style in writing and development in thinking. While his style always had been free and natural, he had from the beginning aimed at compactness, and it was to the necessity of re-writing news articles and compressing them into condensed items while he was sub-editor on the "Times," that, when reviewing his life, he said he had obtained valuable practice in terse statement. The development in thought was manifested in editorials on the larger questions of the day, such as free trade, government paper money and interconvertible bonds in place of national bank notes; personal or proportional representation; public obligations attached to public franchises; and the abolition of privilege in the army.

But perhaps the most important advance in thought appeared in an article entitled "What the Railroad Will Bring Us" in the "Overland Monthly" in October, 1868, just after Mr. George left the "Times." That San Francisco periodical was then in its fourth number, having started in July of that year, and was edited by Bret Harte, who, with two of its contributors, Mark Twain and Joaquin Miller, constituted "The Incomparable Three" of lighter literature in California. Noah Brooks was one of the assistant editors and numbered in the long list of bright, original writers who made the pages of the magazine, like those of the "Californian" which had preceded it, of exceptional brilliance—the more undoubted since most of the writers were new, and all wrote anonymously. The "Overland" as originally cast did not last very long, but long enough to call the world's attention to Bret Harte's "Heathen Chinee," and other productions.

"What the Railroad Will Bring Us" was a forecast of the era of California which the operation of the then almost completed trans-continental railroad would usher in —adding enormous artificial advantages to the already great natural advantages that San Francisco possessed, and laying foundations for her rapid rise to a commercial and intellectual greatness that should not only make her mistress of all the coasts washed by the vast Pacific, but, indeed, as to population, wealth and power, cause her eventually to overtake and surpass New York and London, and make her the greatest city in the world.   But, as if reverting to the question that had arisen in his mind years before when, sitting in the theatre gallery, he saw the advent of the railroad pictured on the new drop curtain[1]—the author asked, would California, with her great population and wealth, and culture, and power, have so even a distribution of wealth as in her earlier, pioneer days?   Would she show so much general comfort and so little squalor and misery?   Would there then be so large a proportion of full, true men?

"Amid all our rejoicing and all our gratulation let us see clearly whither we are tending.   Increase in population and wealth past a certain point means simply an approximation to the condition of older countries—

[1] Page 100.

the Eastern States and Europe. Would the average Californian prefer to 'take his chances' in New York or Massachusetts, or in California as it is and has been? Is England, with her population of twenty millions to an area of not more than one-third that of our State, and a wealth which per inhabitant is six or seven times that of California, a better country than California to live in? Probably, if one were born a duke or factory lord, or to any place among the upper ten thousand; but if one were born among the lower millions—how then?

"For years the high rate of interest and the high rate of wages prevailing in California have been special subjects for the lamentations of a certain school of local political economists, who could not see that high wages and high interest were indications that the natural wealth of the country was not yet monopolised, that great opportunities were open to all—who did not know that these were evidences of social health, and that it were as wise to lament them as for the maiden to wish to exchange the natural bloom on her cheek for the interesting pallor of the invalid.

"But however this be, it is certain that the tendency of the new era—of the more dense population and more thorough development of the wealth of the State—will be to a reduction both of the rate of interest and the rate of wages, particularly the latter. This tendency may not, probably will not, be shown immediately; but it will be before long, and that powerfully, unless balanced and counteracted by other influences which we are not now considering, which do not yet appear, and which it is probable will not appear for some time yet.

"The truth is, that the completion of the railroad and the consequent great increase of business and population, will not be a benefit to all of us, but only to a portion. As a general rule (liable of course to exceptions) those who have, it will make wealthier; for those who *have not,* it will make it more difficult to get. Those who have lands, mines, established businesses, special abilities of certain kinds, will become richer for it and find increased opportunities; those who have only their own labour will become poorer, and find it harder to get ahead—first because it will take more capital to buy land or to get into business; and second, because as competition reduces the wages of labour, this capital will be harder for them to obtain. . . .

"And as California becomes populous and rich, let us not forget that the character of a people counts for more than their numbers; that the distribution of wealth is even a more important matter than its production. Let us not imagine ourselves in a fool's paradise, where the golden apples will drop into our mouths; let us not think that after the stormy seas and head gales of all the ages, *our* ship has at last struck the trade winds of time. The future of our State, of our nation, of our race, looks fair and bright; perhaps the future looked so to the philosoophers who once sat in the porches of Athens—to the unremembered men who raised the cities whose ruins lie south of us. Our modern civilisation strikes broad and deep and looks high. So did the tower which men once built almost unto heaven."

For this "Overland" article, seven thousand words in length, Henry George received $40. To many who have knowledge of California's progress during the past three decades a remarkable feature about the article is the prophecy of hard social conditions which have since enveloped the masses and checked—and almost stopped—the State's growth. But to others its political economy is a still more remarkable feature. For though there is in the article what he subsequently may have called a confusion of what is rent with what is interest, there is in the tracing of high wages and high interest in California to the fact that the "natural wealth of the country was not yet monopolised—that great opportunities were open to all"—a distinct foreshadowing of that formulation of the laws of wages and interest which ten years later, in "Progress and Poverty," he put in these terms—that "wages depend upon the margin of production, or upon the produce which labour can obtain at the highest point of natural productiveness open to it without the payment of rent"; and that "the relation between wages and interest is determined by the average power of increase which attaches to capital from its use in reproductive modes—as rent rises, interest will fall as wages fall, or will be determined by the margin of cultivation."

In August, 1868, Henry George left the "Times." He had asked for an increase in salary. This not being granted, he withdrew, though on good terms with and at the convenience of the management. While continuing to send remittances home, he had been able by economy during the stretch of prosperity to save a little money and to open a bank account. He now resolved to carry out the long-cherished plan of going to Philadelphia, and he sent his family East under escort of his brother, John Vallance George, who had come to California three months before— Henry George intending himself to follow as soon as opportunity permitted.

Just then Mr. George was invited by Charles DeYoung to help him develop a morning newspaper from the "Dramatic Chronicle." He was engaged to be managing editor, and at his suggestion, DeYoung made John Timmins foreman—the same John Timmins who was foreman in the Sacramento "Union" office in 1864 and had discharged George. But Mr. George's connection with the "Chronicle" lasted only a few weeks, as he disliked DeYoung's policy.

The success of the San Francisco "Times" in breaking into the press telegraph monopoly had encouraged the starting of other papers, of which the "Chronicle" was one and the San Francisco "Herald" another. There were not many important Democratic papers in the State and

John Nugent's idea was to establish a good one by reviving the San Francisco "Herald," and he engaged Henry George to go to New York and try to get the paper admitted to the Associated Press, or if that should be refused, to establish there a special news service for the paper. Charged with this commission, the young man about the beginning of December started East on the overland and stage route.

"It was just before the completion of the transcontinental railroad, and I crossed the plains in a four-horse 'mud wagon.' I spent many nights sitting at the driver's side, and I was all the more impressed, therefore, when we reached the railroad and got a sleeping-car. We had to sleep two in a berth, however."[1]

He went first to his old home in Philadelphia where he found father and mother, sisters and brothers, as well as wife and children eager to welcome him. After a short season there, he engaged John Hasson, one of his boyhood friends, to go in with him, and then went to New York and made formal application for access of the San Francisco "Herald" to the Associated Press news service. Writing early in January (1869) to Charles A. Sumner, managing editor of the paper, he said:

"Nobody received me with open arms, unless I except the Peter Funks. I have made no acquaintances beyond those necessary for my purpose and not yet delivered any letters except business ones. The newspaper offices here are like big manufactories and they don't seem to be in the habit of asking strangers to take seats and look over the exchanges. The bosses come down for a few hours occasionally; the managing editors get down about twelve and leave about four or five in the after-

---

[1] Meeker notes, October, 1897.

noon; and I don't think the smaller guns begin to work as hard as those on the Pacific Coast."

Before the "Herald" business had advanced far, the active and courageous spirit of the young man manifested itself by a signed letter in the "New York Tribune" (March 5) attacking two of the great corporations in California—the Central Pacific Railroad and the Wells, Fargo Express, the former for its excessive charges; the latter for reckless treatment of the newspaper mails in the stage-coach intervals on the plains between the yet incompleted Union Pacific and Central Pacifio lines. As to the Central Pacific Railroad he said:

"So far as cheapening the cost of transportation is concerned, the Pacific Railroad has, as yet, been of no advantage to the people of the Pacific Coast, who have to pay just as much as, and in some cases more than, when they relied on horse or ox flesh. There would be some excuse for this, if the road had been constructed by private means; but it has been, and is being, built literally and absolutely by the money of the people, receiving liberal aid from cities, counties and State of California, as well as the immense gratuity of the general government. . . .

"But minor grievances sink into insignificance when the enormous political power which these great Pacific Railroad corporations can wield is considered. The Central Pacific can dictate to California, Nevada and Utah, and the Union Pacific to the States and Territories through which it passes more completely than the Camden and Amboy dictated to New Jersey, and each or both will be able to exert an almost irresistible pressure upon Congress in any manner in which their interests are involved. I don't know about the Union Pacific, but the Central already influences conventions, manages Legislatures, and has its representatives in both Houses at Washington. And it is already buying up other corpor-

ations, and bids fair to own the whole railroad system of
the Pacific. . . ."

But returning to the San Francisco "Herald," the Board
of Directors of the Associated Press, after many vexatious
delays, refused its service to that paper, and an independent service had to be made up. Concluding that Philadelphia would suit their purpose better than New York,
Henry George and John Hasson opened their press bureau
in a little coal office occupied at the time by Henry George's
father, on Third Street, almost opposite St. Paul's church
Here they collected by wire from various sources their
news, and dressing it to fit their California requirements,
putting as much as possible in a prearranged cipher, to
save expense, telegraphed it by the Western Union Company, which controlled the only route to San Francisco, at
a rate fixed by a clear agreement and based upon a schedule
adopted before any news war was in sight. In exchange
for the full credit, access was given to the "New York Herald's" special despatches, and in this and other ways a good
news service was supplied; so much better, indeed, than
that which the Associated Press papers in California received that they made a great commotion inside the association, and that body urged the Western Union Telegraph
Company to interfere. The latter hesitated to do so directly, but on the ground of interference with the rules,
refused to allow the use of the cipher code or to receive the
service from Philadelphia; and then finding that the agent
of the California paper at once moved to New York and
continued the service, the company took summary action
by giving short notice of a new schedule of rates, which
in effect increased the San Francisco "Herald's" charges,
while it reduced those of the Association. The "Herald's"
agent vigorously protested and was invited to call upon

Vice-President McAlpine of the Western Union. In a letter of April 21, to John Nugent, the San Francisco "Herald's" owner, Henry George recounts what occurred:

"I saw him accordingly, but was informed by him that the contract had already been signed by at least the San Francisco papers [in the Associated Press] and that the thing was past remedy. I nevertheless protested with all my force, minced no words, but denounced the whole thing as a most outrageous breach of faith which had been procured by the underhand workings of a ring. I told him in very plain terms what I thought of his company and how this operation would appear to the public; that it was meant to crush the 'Herald' and would crush the 'Herald'; was meant to prevent any future opposition to the Associated Press and would do so until a new line was built; that they had virtually agreed to give a monopoly of the news business to the Association for $40,000 a year—less than they were now getting; that I could not say what you would do, but that if it was my paper I would issue my last number on the 1st of May, declare that it was killed by the Western Union Telegraph Company, who had sold a monopoly to the other papers, fill it with the history of the whole transaction and print an immense edition, which I would circulate all over the Union.

"He appeared much moved by what I said, declared that there was great force in it, but that he did not see what could be done; that he had opposed this thing from the beginning; that he had been overruled; and that though he was sorry for it, there was no use of protesting or appealing.

"Afterwards I made a written request to be heard before a full executive board. Pondering over the matter, I came to the conclusion that the case was very desperate, that the only hope of inducing them to go back was by appealing to their sense of shame and dislike of being stigmatised as a monopoly; that nothing could be hoped from their favour; and that it was useless to mince words. I, therefore, abandoned my pur-

pose of making a verbal protest, and during that night
wrote out a lengthy protest with the idea of printing it
if my other efforts seemed ineffectual; and that if the
instructions I expected immediately from you did not
direct another course.

"By one next day (Wednesday) I got several copies
and sent them in, calling upon Mr. McAlpine about 2.30
P.M. . . . He was anxious for me to see President
Orton. . . . I got an interview with Mr. Orton this
morning, who read the protest in my presence and
seemed unable to say anything in justification. . . .
He did not seem disposed to defend it, but said that he
was sick of the whole matter; that the Associated Press
had been urging this for a long time, and had been
growing ugly, threatening to stop their arrangement."

But John Nugent at this crisis was as silent as the
grave and gave no instructions. Indeed, he cannot be said
to have given any instructions at any time since his paper
started, except to get the news as cheaply as possible. The
New York agent was left to act entirely upon his own re-
sponsibility. And it might have been supposed that having done all that was possible for his paper, he would consult self-interest and avoid aggressiveness, for otherwise
he ran the risk of embittering all the papers in the California Associated Press against him and of winning the
active and lasting hostility of the great telegraph company.
But what he had in mind could be realised only by aggressive action. He wished to make the subject of telegraph
service a political question. In other words, this unknown
newspaper correspondent from the far Pacific Coast, un-
backed by even his own struggling little newspaper, had
chosen, like David, to go out and contend with the gigantic
telegraph Goliath. What added to the daring of the performance was that the Associated Press people were circu-
lating the report that the San Francisco "Herald" was on

its last legs, which the silence to his private despatches seemed to confirm. But counting costs no more now than when two months before he had in the "New York Tribune" openly attacked the California railroad and express corporations, he held to his resolution to strike publicly at the Western Union. He sent his printed protest out to such of the newspapers in New York and other cities in the East as he thought would notice it, and also to Senator Sprague of Rhode Island with a letter, because of his anti-monopoly views; and to the California representatives in Congress—at the same time writing to his friend Sumner, the managing editor of the San Francisco "Herald": "You will hear thunder all around the sky notwithstanding the influence of the Western Union and the Associated Press."

The "New York Herald" was about the only newspaper of influence that published the protest, and whether or not the Western Union directors cared about it, the axe fell, and the San Francisco "Herald's" telegraph news service, so long as that paper could continue to struggle on, had to be reduced to a mere skeleton.

Almost from the beginning John Nugent had been slow to make remittances, and now nearly a thousand dollars was due in New York on salaries and rent and other bills. Confident that he could be of no further use to the paper there, and leaving John Hasson as New York agent, Henry George went to Philadelphia, took leave of his family and relatives, and on May 20 started west over the Erie railroad for California. Under a contract through John Russell Young, its managing editor, he wrote several letters for the "New York Tribune," descriptive of the new transcontinental railroad, and the country through which the road passed. But though paid for, none of these articles were published, for John Russell Young left the paper soon after Mr. George had left New York, and Whitelaw Reid, succeeding as managing editor, not only withheld them, but annulled the contract, to which Mr. George, not wishing to put Mr. Young at the slightest disadvantage for his act of friendship, made no further objection than a mild and formal dissent.

SECOND PERIOD

FORMULATION OF THE PHILOSOPHY

One sole God ;

One sole ruler—his Law ;

One sole interpreter of that law—Humanity.

—Mazzini

CHAPTER I.

COMMENCES THE GREAT INQUIRY.

1869.   AGE, 30.

IT is said that what put the iron into Abraham Lincoln's soul against chattel slavery was an auction sale of negroes—men, women and children, husbands and wives, parents and infants—which he witnessed while a young man at New Orleans, to which place he had gone down the Mississippi on a flat boat.

Likewise, what put the iron into Henry George's soul against industrial slavery was the contrast of poverty with wealth that he witnessed in the greatest city in the new world, when on the visit to New York in the winter of 1868-69. Apparently fully occupied with the difficulties of establishing a telegraphic news service for the western newspaper, there were in reality pauses when the mind, swinging clear of all personal affairs, leaped into the realm of problems that beset mankind. For in the idle hours, when another might have sought amusement, this young man, as by a kind of fascination, walked the streets of the great city, thinking how here, at the centre of civilisation, should be realised the dream of the pioneer—the hard conditions of life softened, and society, preserving the general relations of equality, raised as a mass from the bottom into a state of peace and plenty. How different the view

191

that met his gaze! On every hand he beheld evidences
of advanced and advancing civilisation, but of a civilisation that was one-sided; that piled up riches for the few
and huddled the many in filth and poverty. And just as
in assailing the great telegraph and press monopolies he
did not wait to be supported, but boldly and alone stepped
forth to the contest, so now this unknown man, not yet
quite thirty, of small schooling and scarcely tried abilities,
whose past had led through poverty and adversity, and
whose future was shrouded in uncertainty, audaciously refused to accept the edict of the House of Have—the edict
sanctioned by the teachers of learning and preachers of
religion, that all this want and suffering was in the nature
of things and unalterable. His heart and mind denied it.
Everywhere else in creation was order, design. Could they
fail on reaching man, "the roof and crown of things?"
He could not believe it. Silently, without telling any man
of what he did, he set himself the task of finding the
natural order. In his speech of acceptance of the first
New York mayoralty nomination seventeen years afterwards he said:

> "Years ago I came to this city from the West,
> unknown, knowing nobody, and I saw and recognised
> for the first time the shocking contrast between mon-
> strous wealth and debasing want. And here I made a
> vow from which I have never faltered, to seek out, and
> remedy, if I could, the cause that condemned little chil-
> dren to lead such a life as you know them to lead in the
> squalid districts."[1]

This was not a vague resolution without backing of
thought. It was rather a sudden crystallisation of pro-

---

[1] Also see "Progress and Poverty," Conclusion; and "The Science of
Political Economy," Book II, Chap. viii, p. 201.

tracted meditations; a flashing conviction and passionate
resolve.   For him all at once the bush burned, and the
voice spake: "The people suffer; who will lead them
forth?"   In a letter to Rev. Thomas Dawson of Glencree,
Ireland (February 1, 1883), he wrote:

> "Because you are not only my friend, but a priest
> and a religious, I shall say something that I don't like
> to speak of—that I never before have told any one.
> Once, in daylight, and in a city street, there came to
> me a thought, a vision, a call—give it what name you
> please.   But every nerve quivered.   And there and then
> I made a vow.   Through evil and through good, what-
> ever I have done and whatever I have left undone, to
> that I have been true."

Now while the young philosopher's mind was to work
gradually towards the solution of the problem of deepening
poverty in the midst of advancing wealth, he did something in the East in the early part of 1869 that attracted
more attention than anything he had before accomplished.
As he has said in "The Science of Political Economy," [1]
"John Russell Young was at that time managing editor of
the 'New York Tribune,' and I wrote for him an article on
'The Chinese on the Pacific Coast,' a question that had
begun to arouse attention there; taking the side popular
among the working classes of the Coast, in opposition to
the unrestricted immigration of that people."   The article
appeared on May 1, filled several columns of the "Tribune,"
and was signed.[2]

The immigation of the Chinese in considerable numbers

[1] Book II, Chap. viii, p. 200.

[2] Horace Greeley was the editor-in-chief of the "Tribune," and in the
same issue with Henry George's Chinese article appeared the first instal-
ment of Greeley's essays on political economy.

commenced soon after the discovery of gold in California. They spread over the Pacific Coast and crept into many of the more common fields of labour, soon incurring general and active opposition, being regarded as an alien and non-assimilable race. In this "Tribune" article, Mr. George explained and justified this hostile feeling—the first time, probably, that such views were published on the Atlantic Coast. The kernel of his presentation was this:

"The population of our country has been drawn from many different sources; but hitherto, with but one exception, these accessions have been of the same race, and though widely differing in language, customs and national characteristics, have been capable of being welded into a homogeneous people. The mongolians, who are now coming among us on the other side of the continent, differ from our race by as strongly marked characteristics as do the negroes, while they will not as readily fall into our ways as the negroes. The difference between the two races in this respect is as the difference between an ignorant but docile child, and a grown man, sharp but narrow minded, opinionated and set in character. The negro when brought to this country was a simple barbarian with nothing to unlearn; the Chinese have a civilisation and history of their own, a vanity which causes them to look down on all other races, habits of thought rendered permanent by being stamped upon countless generations. From present appearances we shall have a permanent Chinese population; but a population whose individual components will be constantly changing, at least for a long time to come—a population born in China, reared in China, expecting to return to China, living while here in a little China of its own, and without the slightest attachment to the country—utter heathens, treacherous, sensual, cowardly and cruel. They bring no women with them (and probably will not for a little while yet). . . .

"Their moral standard is as low as their standard of comfort, and though honest in the payment of debts to each other, lying, stealing and false swearing are with the Chinamen venial sins—if sins at all. They practise all the unnamable vices of the East, and are as cruel as they are cowardly. Infanticide is common among them; so is abduction and assassination. Their bravos may be hired to take life for a sum proportionate to the risk, to be paid to their relatives in case of death. In person the Chinese are generally apparently cleanly, but filthy in their habits. Their quarters reek with noisesome odours, and are fit breeding-places for pestilence. They have a great capacity for secret organisations, forming a State within a State, governed by their own laws; and there is little doubt that our courts are frequently used by them to punish their own countrymen, though more summary methods are oftentimes resorted to. The administration of justice among them is attended with great difficulty. No plan for making them tell the truth seems to be effective. That of compelling them to behead a cock and burn yellow paper is generally resorted to in the courts. . . .

"The Chinese seem to be incapable of understanding our religion; but still less are they capable of understanding our political institutions. To confer the franchise upon them would be to put the balance of power on the Pacific in the hands of a people who have no conception of the trust involved, and who would have no wish to use it rightly, if they had—would be to give so many additional votes to employers of Chinese, or ·put them up for sale by the Chinese head centres in San Francisco."

Almost twenty-five years later (November 30, 1893), in a letter to William Lloyd Garrison, the younger, Henry George spoke of the "Tribune" article as "crude," insomuch as he "had not then come to clear economic views." He referred to his exposition of the wages question, which he was led to discuss by the contention of the great California railroad corporation and other large employers of Chinese labour that such employment inured to the benefit of other labourers by liberating the latter for engagement in other fields of industry, at the same time cheapening the cost of production in the primary fields that they had left and thereby cheapening all those primary commodities that all must buy. "Wishing to know what political economy had to say about the causes of wages," he wrote in "The Science of Political Economy" [1] relative to this point: "I went to the Philadelphia Library, looked over John Stuart Mill's 'Political Economy,' and accepting his views without question, based my article upon it." In a conversation at another time he said,[2] "It was the first time I had made any investigation of what political economy had to say on the subject of wages, and I adopted unquestioningly the doctrine of the relation between wages and capital laid down by Mill."

That is to say, doing now as he once had done in embracing the protective principle, and "accepting the belief on the authority of others," he abandoned the suggestion of his own spontaneous thought when writing the article "What the Railroad Will Bring Us," namely, that wages in California had a relation to "the natural wealth of the country. . . . not yet monopolised"—and "adopted unquestioningly" the explanation made by the man famous as the great master of political economy, that wages depend upon the ratio of labourers to the so-called wages fund— to the capital devoted to the payment of wages. How completely this was so is shown by a passage in the "Tribune" article.

"There is a tendency of wages in different industries to an equilibrium, and of wages in general to a level which is determined by the relative proportions of capi-

---

[1] Book II, Chap. viii, pp. 200, 201.
[2] Meeker notes, October, 1897.

tal and labour. . . . Plainly when we speak of a
reduction of wages in any general and permanent sense,
we mean this, if we mean anything—that in the division of the joint production of labour and capital, the
share of labour is to be smaller, that of capital larger.
This is precisely what the reduction of wages consequent
upon the introduction of Chinese labour means."

"This article attracted attention especially in California," Mr. George wrote in his last book. While just beginning to rise to attention on the Atlantic side of the
country, the Chinese question was a burning one on the
Pacific side. Some of the California newspapers reprinted
parts of the "Tribune" article and commended it. The
workingmen's organisations hailed it with particular satisfaction, in the early part of 1871 it being reprinted in full
and circulated by the Mechanics' State Council of California. This organisation, though intended primarily
for the protection of workingmen's interests, at that time
had considerable influence in California politics.

But long before this action of the Mechanics' State
Council the chief San Francisco newspapers were drawn,
into a renewed discussion of the "Tribune" article by a
letter from a high outside source. Mr. George says in
"The Science of Political Economy" that a copy of the
"Tribune" article he sent from California to John Stuart
Mill brought a letter of commendation. The letter was
received in November, 1869, at Oakland, an over-bay sub-
urb of San Francisco, where George had just begun the
editing of a little daily called the "Transcript," of which
more will he learned later. On Saturday, November 20,
he published a long editorial and in it printed the Mill
letter in full, saying by way of explanation:

"It is frequently asserted here that the opposition
upon the part of the labouring classes to the immigra-

tion of Chinese arises from ignorance of the laws of
political economy, and that so far from having a tendency to reduce them to a lower condition, the effect of
Chinese labour will be to elevate them.   Conceiving that
the views of so distinguished an authority would be of
much value, the gentleman to whom this letter is addressed wrote to Mr. Mill, requesting an opinion upon
this point, as well as upon the general subject."

Then came the Mill letter:

Avignon, France, Oct. 23, 1869.

"DEAR SIR: The subject on which you have asked my
opinion involves two of the most difficult and embarrassing questions of political morality—the extent and lim-
its of the right of those who have first taken possession
of the unoccupied portion of the earth's surface to
exclude the remainder of mankind from inhabiting it,
and the means which can be legitimately used by the
more improved branches of the human species to protect
themselves from being hurtfully encroached upon by
those of a lower grade in civilisation.   The Chinese
immigration into America raises both of these questions.
To furnish a general answer to either of them would be
a most arduous undertaking.

"Concerning the purely economic view of the subject,
I entirely agree with you; and it could be hardly better
stated and argued than it is in your article in the 'New
York Tribune.'   That the Chinese immigration, if it
attains great dimensions, must be economically inju-
rious to the mass of the present population; that it
must diminish their wages, and reduce them to a lower
stage of physical comfort and well-being, I have no
manner of doubt.   Nothing can be more fallacious than
the attempts to make out that thus to lower wages is
the way to raise them, or that there is any compensation,
in an economical point of view, to those whose labour is
displaced, or who are obliged to work for a greatly reduced remuneration.   On general principles this state
of things, were it sure to continue, would justify the

exclusion of the immigrants, on the ground that, with their habits in respect to population, only a temporary good is done to the Chinese people by admitting part of their surplus numbers, while a permanent harm is done to a more civilised and improved portion of mankind.

"But there is much also to be said on the other side. Is it justifiable to assume that the character and habits of the Chinese are insusceptible of improvement? The institutions of the United States are the most potent means that have yet existed for spreading the most important elements of civilisation down to the poorest and most ignorant of the labouring masses. If every Chinese child were compulsorily brought under your school system, or under a still more effective one if possible, and kept under it for a sufficient number of years, would not the Chinese population be in time raised to the level of the American? I believe, indeed, that hitherto the number of Chinese born in America has not been very great; but so long as this is the case—so long (that is) as the Chinese do not come in families and settle, but those who come are mostly men, and return to their native country, the evil can hardly reach so great a magnitude as to require that it should be put a stop to by force.

"One kind of restrictive measure seems to me not only desirable, but absolutely called for; the most stringent laws against introducing Chinese immigrants as coolies, i. e., under contract binding them to the service of particular persons. All such obligations are a form of compulsory labour, that is, of slavery; and though I know the legal invalidity of such contracts does not prevent them being made, I cannot but think that if pains were taken to make it known to the immigrants that such engagements are not legally binding, and especially if it were made a penal offence to enter into them, that mode at least of immigration would receive a considerable check; and it does not seem probable that any mode, among so poor a population as the Chinese, can attain such dimensions as to compete very injuriously with American labour. Short of that point, the oppor-

tunity given to numerous Chinese of becoming familiar
with better and more civilised habits of life, is one of
the best chances that can be opened up for the improvement of the Chinese in their own country, and
one which it does not seem to me that it would be right
to withhold from them. I am, dear sir,
            "Yours very sincerely,
"Henry George, Esq.,   "J. S. MILL."
"San Francisco, Cal."

Commenting on this, the "Transcript" editorial said:
"With all its qualifications, Mr. Mill's opinion entirely jus-
tifies the position of those who take ground in favour
of restrictions upon the immigration of these people," for
"Chinese labour has already begun to compete injuriously
with white labour, and that it will soon be competing
very injuriously, no one who has noticed how rapidly these
people are entering and monopolising one branch of business after another, can have any doubt." Moreover, nine-
tenths of the Chinese immigrants are contract labourers
and it would be useless to pass laws against such contracts;
while as for slavery, "Chinese women are sold and staked
at the gambling table in San Francisco every day of the
week." The editorial concluded with this tribute to the
eminent English economist:

"Yet, whether we agree or disagree with his opinions;
whether we adopt or dissent from his conclusions, no
American can fail to have for this great Englishman
the profoundest respect. It is not merely the rank he
has won in the republic of letters; not merely the service
he has rendered to one of the most beneficial, if not
the noblest, of sciences; not merely the courage and devotion with which he has laboured for the cause of
popular rights in his own country; not merely his high
private character and pure life, which set off his great

talents and public virtues, that entitle John Stuart Mill to the respect of Americans. Beyond all this, they can never forget that he stood the true friend to their country in its darkest day; devoting his great talents and lending his great reputation to the support of the Republic when she had closed in what seemed there her death grapple; that it was he more than any other man who turned the tide of English opinion and sympathy in our favour, and by exhibiting the true character of the struggle, gave us the moral support of the middle class of Great Britain. Services such as these entitle John Stuart Mill to something more from us than even the respect which is due him as a writer, statesman or philosopher—to our affection as well as our admiration."

The "Transcript" editorial with the Mill letter made something like a sensation throughout California. Some of the pro-Chinese papers republished both in garbled form, and in such form the letter may have got back to Mill. At any rate, an editorial on the subject in the Chicago "Tribune" drew from Mill a communication to Horace White of that paper, saying that judging from the comments, the published copy of his letter must have been a mutilated one. White published this. Mr. George had meanwhile become editor of the "Sacramento Reporter." Seeing the Mill letter to White, he promptly republished it and also the earlier Mill letter to himself, putting both in a signed editorial explaining that there had been no garbling at any time on his part. This article he sent to Mill, who made reply that he was "perfectly satisfied."

. Some of the pro-Chinese papers in California, while not attempting to garble the original Mill letter, took to abusing Henry George; one of them, the San Francisco "Bulletin," saying that Mill had been misled by George in the "New York Tribune" article, as that was "written from the exaggerated standpoint of a certain class of political alarmists who either have not carefully studied the facts or who use the question as a good demagogue card to win ignorant votes." But notwithstanding such utterances, George's "New York Tribune" article expressed a strong and strengthening sentiment that soon dominated State politics, inspired a long series of legislative acts, and eventuated in 1892, twenty-three years afterwards, in the passage by Congress of the Geary law, prohibiting "the coming of Chinese persons into the United States" and providing for deportation under certain conditions.

To the end of his life Mr. George held to the views against free entrance of the Chinese set forth in his "Tribune" article in 1869. They appear in many of his subsequent California speeches and writings, and in 1881 were set out fully in a signed article published in Lalor's "Cyclopedia of Political Science, Political Economy and of the Political History of the United States."

And when in the fall of 1893, William Lloyd Garrison of Boston addressed a letter to James G. Maguire, who represented the Fourth California District in Congress, upbraiding the congressman with being false to his single tax principles of equal rights, in supporting and voting for an amendment extending the Geary Chinese Exclusion Act, Mr. George replied (New York November 30), a copy of the letter to Maguire having been sent to him by Garrison:

"To your proposition that the right to the use of the earth is not confined to the inhabitants of the United States, I most cordially assent. But what you seem to think follows from that, 'The humblest Chinaman has as much natural right to use the earth of California as yourself, and it is your inalienable right to change your residence to any land under the sun,' I most emphatically deny. Are men merely individuals? Is there no such thing as family, nation, race? Is there not the right of association, and the correlative right of exclusion? . . .

"Your parallel between those who supported slavery and those who oppose Chinese immigration is not a true one. The first of the evils wrought by African slavery in the United States was the bringing hither of large numbers of the blacks, an evil which still remains a source of weakness and danger, though slavery is gone. Let me ask you: If to-day there was the same possibility of a great coming of African negroes to this country as there would be of Chinamen if all restriction were removed, would you consider it a wise thing to permit it under present conditions? And would you consider it at all inconsistent with your anti-slavery principles or with your recognition of human equality to try to prevent it? I certainly would not. . . .

"I have written to you frankly, but I trust not unkindly. I have for you too much respect and affection to wantonly accentuate any difference there may be in our ways of looking at things."

But while approving of Chinese exclusion "under present conditions," Henry George could conceive of a state of things under which such a policy would not be necessary. In a lecture in San Francisco [1] while writing "Progress and Poverty," he said: "Ladies and gentlemen, it is not only more important to abolish land monopoly than to get rid of the Chinese; but to abolish land monopoly will be to make short work of the Chinese question. Clear out the land-grabber and the Chinaman must go. Root the white race in the soil, and all the millions of Asia cannot dispossess it."

---

[1] "Why Work is Scarce, Wages Low, and Labour Restless," Metropolitan Temple, March 26, 1878.

CHAPTER II.

STRIPE AND THE NATURAL ORDER.

1869-1871.   AGE, 30-32.

WHEN Œdipus, in Greek mythology, travelled towards the city of Thebes he found widespread distress from deaths wrought by the monster Sphinx, who had the body of a lion, and the head, breast and arms of a woman, and who put a riddle to all approaching, which not to answer meant to be hurled headlong from the rock where she abode. Many had tried, but all had failed; and through the country as Œdipus moved on came constant lamentation and constant warning.

Henry George walking through the streets of New York, had seen the want and misery wrought by the Sphinx of modern civilisation, and as if to keep him strung to nervous tension and ever mindful of his vow to charge the monster and solve the problem, Adversity kept close to his heels. For when he got back to San Francisco, the pressing personal question was, what was he to do?

But he was not one to wait for something to come to him. He at once got an anti-telegraph monopoly resolution introduced into the legislature, and this being popular, was easily passed. Next he sketched out several magazine articles on the Chinese question, (though none of these were ever finished); and wrote several editorials for the "Evening Bulletin," for which he was twice urged to go East as special correspondent, but refused. For awhile, hard pressed for money, he went into the composing room of the "Herald" and set type. Something over $700 was still owing from that paper on his back salary and various accounts in New York. Nugent getting into a rage when the money was demanded, George retaliated by wiring Hasson to stop the news service. Small though that service then was, its absence was a great loss to the paper, and Nugent came partially to terms, yet did not settle entirely until George sued out an attachment. In the middle of August (19) George wrote to Philadelphia:

"As for me, I am doing various miscellaneous work; just now for a few days editing an Irish Catholic paper for a friend.[1]

"I go around very little—not as much as would be wise, I presume, and pass most of my evenings in reading, something I have not done much of for some years —not a tenth part as much as I would like to."

One of the books he read, and was "much impressed" with, was "Lord Chesterfield's Letters," entering in his pocket diary: *"Suaviter in modo; fortiter in re."* The diary also announces that on July 30 after dinner, he went to his room to read, "fell asleep, and was nearly suffocated by gas"; for the supply, cut off at the meter during the day, was turned on as night approached, and the cock in the room having by some chance been left open, allowed free escape. This was in the old Federal building on Washington Street, where Mr. George at the time was rooming. His wife heard nothing of the matter until long afterwards. But she did hear something from him that gave her deep pleasure.

---

[1] The paper was the "Monitor," and the friend, its editor, John Barry.

Acting upon an idea thrown out in a letter from New York to Sumner, Mr. George had got his friends to work for his nomination on the Democratic ticket for the Assembly. Presently he wrote to his wife that her uncle, Matthew McCloskey, who had not exchanged a word with them since the runaway marriage, was showing active hostility by working against the nomination. Next day the husband wrote that he had been misinformed; that Mr. McCloskey was working for him, not against him, and singing his praises for character and ability; and that they had become reconciled. The friendship thus renewed was of the strongest kind, Matthew McCloskey on his death-bed six or eight years later commending his family to Henry George for counsel.

Mr. George's desire for election to the legislature was more than a vague ambition to get forward in the world. For the young man, though he had not yet come to clear ideas on the social problem, had in his mind's eye, as may be judged from his editorial and correspondence experience, a mass of matters to press for legislative attention; and as for big things, there were the anti-telegraph, anti-express company and anti-railroad fights to make, and it was also quite evident that something should be done to discourage the massing of land in California into great estates. But disappointment was in store. He failed to get nominated, or rather, he could have been nominated but refused to pay the assessment asked by the party managers, and that ended his hope for the candidature.

The disappointment was all the harder to bear because it came at the end of a line of failures since his return from the East. He had succeeded neither in making any permanent newspaper connection, nor in getting started in a higher literary field. He had not even contrived to make a good living, getting a mere hand-to-mouth subsistence.

And now the political view had been cut off.   The future looked dark, indeed.   The one chance seemed to be in the East, where a place on John Russell Young's proposed paper was held out, Mrs. George, who was beginning to develop a lively interest in public questions and to enter understandingly into her husband's ambitions, having written in August (15):

> "Mr. Hasson spent two or three hours with us this afternoon.   He is a firm friend and ardent admirer of yours. . . .   He says that John Russell Young is going to start a hundred thousand dollar paper in the fall, and will want your services, as he thinks there is no one like you.   Hasson says that Young told Greeley that when he let you go he let go the very man he had been looking for for two years."

This newspaper project of Young's seemed the only but yet very slender hope, for New York was very far away and the plan a thing nebulous and uncertain.   He was greatly dejected.   His plight, as he said afterwards, was like that of a traveller on the plains, a mountain range in front.   The mountains rose wall-like against the distant sky—unbroken and too high to scale.   But as he advanced, a cleft appeared and then deepened and widened into a pass.   For in the midst of his depression came a call to him from an unthought of quarter.

Through the organisation in San Francisco of a branch of the American Free Trade League, whose headquarters were in New York, Mr. George came into touch with the Governor of California, Henry H. Haight, regarded by many as the ablest executive the State has ever had.   During the war Haight had been a strong Republican, but he revolted against the policy of centralisation and special legislation that followed.   He espoused the principles of

Thomas Jefferson and became an avowed Democrat and an out-spoken free trader. Henry George had gone through precisely the same kind of political change. While on the "Times" he wrote many editorials supporting principles and measures leading away from the Republican strict party policy, and as a consequence even then was "rapidly becoming disgusted" with that party. He voted for Grant for the Presidency in the fall of 1868, only to see the soldier, as he expressed it, give himself up to his political friends, so that Mr. George concluded that "the Republican party had served its purpose," that it had become chiefly a party for special interests.

Now, across San Francisco Bay at Oakland was a little Democratic paper called the "Transcript," owned by two men, Hiram Tubbs, proprietor of the leading hotel and much real estate there, and John Scott, a prosperous carpenter and builder and prominent as a politician. Scott was a colonel on the staff of the governor, who thereby was indirectly interested in the paper. Indeed, he and Scott had looked about for a good Democratic editor, and judging of George's principles and abilities by his Chinese article and his editorials in the "Times," and coming in contact with him through the organisation of the Free Trade League, concluded that he was the man they sought, and the position was offered him. He accepted and his name appeared at the head of its editorial columns.

Henry George's connection with the "Transcript" was short, but was marked by three important events. It was then that the John Stuart Mill letter came. Mill was at the zenith of his reputation, so that it was with keen pride that this young country editor published in the columns of his paper a letter that set all the papers of the State to buzzing.

It was also at this time that Mr. George made the acquaintance of William Swinton, brother of John Swinton, the well-known radical of New York. William Swinton was born in Scotland in 1833, was well educated, finishing at Amherst College, Mass.; at twenty wrote a large part of a book, "Rambles Among Words"; later held a professorship of ancient and modern languages; during the war made a brilliant field correspondent for the "New York Times"; afterwards wrote two authoritative works, "Campaigns of the Army of the Potomac" and "The Twelve Decisive Battles of the War"; and in 1869 had come to California to accept the chair of English language and literature, rhetoric, logic and history in the University of California, then just being founded at Oakland. He was a man of wide reading in the field of *belles-lettres*, of quick mind, fine taste and copious suggestiveness; and though sprung from, and following the schools, formed a close affinity with this young editor, who could not boast of ever having had any college connections. Then and in the years following Swinton drew George out and encouraged him to aim at the higher domain of literature.

But more important for the young editor than anything else that occurred during the "Transcript" period was the solution of the Sphinx's question, the discovery of the natural order; the answer to the quest he had set himself in the streets of New York—why poverty accompanies wealth in advancing civilisation. It came about through a trifling incident. Mr. George had now commenced the habit of horseback riding—a habit that continued intermittently for nearly ten years. At any hour that he was free and had the inclination he would hire a horse and find mental change in a lope into the open country of the foot-hills. But wherever he rode, one thing faced him. The trans-continental railroad system had been completed, only a few months before the last spike, made of gold, having been driven. The California terminal was at Sacramento, and there was a ferment over the proposal to extend the line to Oakland. A very general belief was that the advantages from the railroad would be so important as rapidly to attract population and form a great city in and about Oakland to compete with San Francisco. Land at even far-removed points therefore rose to extravagant figures. Men made themselves "land poor" in order to get and to hold as many feet or acres as possible in anticipation of the rise in value that a swelling population would make. Speculation in land ran far in advance of its use.

Amid these circumstances Henry George went for a ride one afternoon. Of this he has said.[1]

> "Absorbed in my own thoughts, I had driven the horse into the hills until he panted. Stopping for breath, I asked a passing teamster, for want of something better to say, what land was worth there. He pointed to some cows grazing off so far that they looked like mice and said: 'I don't know exactly, but there is a man over there who will sell some land for a thousand dollars an acre.' Like a flash it came upon me that there was the reason of advancing poverty with advancing wealth. With the growth of population, land grows in value, and the men who work it must pay more for the privilege. I turned back, amidst quiet thought, to the perception that then came to me and has been with me ever since."

This truth was to dwell in his thoughts and slowly develop for a year and a half, when it should burst into expression. Meanwhile Governor Haight's political plans matured. He determined to broaden out his fight against the Central Pacific Railroad which now, like a monster of fairy lore, had swallowed, or was about to swallow,

---

[1] Meeker notes, October, 1897. Also see "The Science of Political Economy," Book II, Chap. v, p. 163.

great and small competitors, and all things else that could be useful or that got in its way.   Public feeling expressive of resentment at the encroachment on popular rights began to appear, and Haight, sharing this feeling, gave definite form and direction to it by attacking the railroad's subsidy policy.   The railroad was gulping down lands, bonds and money showered upon it, all the while like a weakling pleading for more.   The plain and palpable fact was that leaving out of consideration the imperial endowment in lands, it had already received several times more money, or what could immediately be turned into money, than was necessary to build the system, and that contemporary with the work of railroad construction had arisen the private fortunes of the big four manipulating the corporation—Stanford, Crocker, Huntington and Hopkins, who, from comparative poverty, had quickly risen to the class of multi-millionaires.

Aside from the principle of subsidies, these private fortunes were a proof to such men as Haight that the policy was wrong for California as a State to pursue, or to authorise its municipalities to pursue.   He, therefore, prepared for war on the "Great Absorber," and invited Mr. George to take the management of the chief party paper at the capital, the "Sacramento Reporter," which, under the name of the "State Capital Reporter," had been edited by Ex-Governor Bigler, who now retired.   The State Publishing Company was organised to publish the paper, and besides a fair salary, Mr. George was offered a fourth of the stock.   The rest was to be held by some of the Governor's political friends.   Mr. George was ready to leave the "Transcript," as his relations with Colonel Scott were no longer pleasant.   He accepted the "Reporter" offer and in February, 1870, moved to Sacramento and commenced work in his new field.

Soon after Mr. George took charge of the Sacramento paper a press war opened and he got into the middle of it. It was nothing less than a resumption of the fight against the Western Union Telegraph Company and the Associated Press. A new telegraph system, the Atlantic and Pacific, had entered the field against the Western Union Company. Discontent among the old newspapers and needs of the new ones seized this channel for news competition by the organisation of the American Press Association as a rival to the Associated Press. It was made up of a lot of strong journals in the East and started off under favourable auspices, with John Russell Young, who had just started his New York "Standard," as president, and John Hasson, as general agent. Indeed, Hasson had largely, if not chiefly, to do with the organisation of the association, and in turn acknowledged that he had got much of his experience and preparation under George, when they were warring with the Associated Press and the Western Union Telegraph Company for the San Francisco "Herald." Young and Hasson at once chose George for their California agent.

Mr. George drew a number of papers into the new association, starting with his own, the "Reporter," and including Charles DeYoung's paper, the "San Francisco Chronicle." The Franco-Prussian war being on, foreign news was heavy; accordingly, the expense high. The price of the service for the California papers was advanced and the agent put the increase upon the "Chronicle," the paper which could best bear it and which got most advantage from it. But DeYoung made such an ado that George called a meeting of the papers' representatives. In one of his books, "The Land Question," to illustrate another matter, he in a veiled way told of what occurred at this meeting:

"Once upon a time I was a Pacific Coast agent of an Eastern news association, which took advantage of an opposition telegraph company to run against the Associated Press monopoly. The Association in California consisted of one strong San Francisco paper, to which telegraphic news was of much importance, and a number of interior papers, to which it was of minor importance, if of any importance at all. It became necessary to raise more money for the expenses of collecting and transmitting these despatches, and thinking it only fair, I assessed the increased cost to the strong metropolitan paper. The proprietor of this paper was very indignant. He appealed to the proprietors of all the other papers and they all joined in his protest. I replied by calling a meeting. At this meeting the proprietor of the San Francisco paper led off with an indignant speech. He was seconded by several others, and evidently had the sympathy of the whole crowd. Then came my turn. I said, in effect: 'Gentlemen, you can do what you please about this matter. Whatever satisfies you satisfies me. The only thing fixed is that more money has to be raised. As this San Francisco paper pays now a much lower relative rate than you do, I thought it only fair that it should pay the increased cost. But, if you think otherwise, there is no reason in the world why you should not pay it yourselves.' The debate immediately took another turn, and in a few minutes my action was indorsed by a unanimous vote, for the San Francisco man was so disgusted by the way his supporters left him that he would not vote at all."[1]

This fight on the Associated Press and the Western Union Telegraph Company was kept up, so far as Mr. George was concerned, until the following spring, when he was out of the "Sacramento Reporter" and back in San Francisco.

---

[1] "The Land Question," Chap. XI; (Memorial Edition, pp. 69–70).

Meanwhile he had brought his family to Sacramento from the East, and with them his brother Vallence, and settled down at housekeeping. But now he narrowly escaped losing his life, for one day just as he was about to mount a horse for a ride, the animal jumped, and throwing him, dragged him for some distance before he could free his foot from the stirrup. He received a slight blow on the head and other injuries that were only temporary. That accident made him realise how uncertain life is, so that at once he got out an insurance, a thing that before this he had thought of but lightly. All through this period he was in regular and loving communication with his folks at Philadelphia, his father for instance writing June 2: "Your papers, after I have read them, I give to some good old Jackson Democrats, and many warm congratulations I have received that I have a son so bold and firm and consistent for the old Democratic principles."

The father truly characterised his son's paper. While it vigorously denounced "carpet-bag" rule in the so-called "reconstructed" South, it took high Jeffersonian ground on questions raising local issues. Of necessity the young editor was brought into close touch with Governor Haight, and through this intercourse became acquainted with Haight's private secretary, a young man named Edward R. Taylor, with whom he afterwards grew intimate, until, when "Progress and Poverty" was being written, Taylor was chief friend, critic and adviser.

First of all matters of interest at this period was the anti-railroad war. The Central Pacific had set its heart on a further era of subsidies. Haight set himself to kill the scheme, and with the scheme to destroy the principle in public estimation; for it was a generally approved principle prior to this, the Governor himself, having given his sanction to several subsidy bills in behalf of other corporations.　Under his direction public thought became roused, the question entered politics and the railroad was suddenly conscious of formidable opposition—an opposition which had been awakened, aside from the Governor's official and personal efforts, largely through the columns of the"Sacramento Reporter."

The Central Pacific had become the overshadowing influence in California.　It owned or controlled most of the press, swayed the legislature, bent the courts, governed banks and moved as a mighty force in politics.　It was quick to recognise talent and as quick to engage or reward it.[1]　Out of imperial coffers it had fortunes to bestow. With a word it could make men, and so far as the masses were concerned, could as easily break men.　Of those who could not, or would not serve, it asked only silence, merely immunity from attack.　Henry George had now come to have a recognised influence with his pen.　What more easy

---

[1] "Among the most prominent figures in the Republican national convention (1888) was Creed Haymond, chairman of the California delegation, and foremost among the 'boomers' of 'Blaine and Protection.'　To those who knew him years ago it seemed a queer place for him to be.　Creed Haymond is a Virginian by birth, and a Democrat by instinct and tradition. During the War. he was in California, a strong secessionist and afterwards was prominent and useful as an anti-monopoly, free-trade Democrat. He is a fine lawyer, a man of exceedingly quick and nimble mind, and like most Southern men of his class, a born politician.　He rendered very efficient aid to Governor Haight in his struggle with the Pacific Railroad monopoly, and no one in the country could have better startled the Chicago convention with a Jeffersonian speech.　But like many other men in California, Creed Haymond at length grew tired of what seemed an utterly hopeless fight, and the railroad octopus, true to its policy of taking into its service men of ability who might be dangerous to it outside, made him head of its law bureau with a salary of $25,000 a year.　Thus it comes that Creed Haymond makes his appearance in a national Republican convention at the head of a delegation representing the Central Pacific railroad ring."— Signed editorial by Henry George, "The Standard," New York, June 30, 1888.

than for him to be at peace with the great corporation,
and obtaining some dignified place within its giving, as
some of his acquaintances had already done, enjoy tranquil
days, during which to develop his philosophy of the natural
order to a readiness for launching when the favourable
moment should come! But the young man was not to be
tempted. The one course, then open for the railroad people was to buy control of the "Reporter," which they
quietly did. George thereupon found himself to be editor
of a newspaper whose policy he could no longer direct—a
paper which by reason of its new ownership must favour
the very interest which he had been so vigourously opposing. He at once resigned, sold out his fourth interest,[1]
moved with his family to San Francisco, and took a little
house on Stevenson Street, on the site since occupied by
the Odd Fellows' building. This was in the beginning of
October, 1870, nine months after going on the paper.

But if the railroad management expected in this way to
silence the trenchant pen they made a mistake, for it
was Haight's plan, as well as George's desire, to make the
subsidy question the chief issue at the State election in the
fall. Mr. George therefore wrote a sixteen paged, closely
printed pamphlet under the title of "The Subsidy Question and the Democratic Party." The nature and tone of
the pamphlet may be judged by the concluding paragraphs:

"Let us recapitulate:
"Railroad subsidies, like protective duties, are condemned by the economic principle that the development
of industry should be left free to take its natural
direction.
"They are condemned by the political principle that
government should be reduced to its minimum—that it

---

[1] The "Reporter" not long afterwards was merged in the "Sacramento
Record Union," a strong railroad paper.

becomes more corrupt and more tyrannical, and less under the control of the people, with every extension of its powers and duties.

"They are condemned by the Democratic principle which forbids the enrichment of one citizen at the expense of another; and the giving to one citizen of advantages denied to another.

"They are condemned by the experience of the whole country which shows that they have invariably led to waste, extravagance and rascality; that they inevitably become a source of corruption and a means of plundering the people.

"The only method of preventing the abuse of subsidies is by prohibiting them altogether. This is absolutely required by the lengths to which the subsidy system in its various shapes has been carried—by the effects which it is producing in lessening the comforts of the masses, stifling industry with taxation, monopolising land and corrupting the public service in all its branches. . . .

"But it will be said that the Democratic party is opposed to the building of railroads? On the contrary, should the Democratic party carry out its programme of free trade and no subsidies, it will stimulate the building of railroads more than could be done by all the subsidies it is possible to vote. It will at once reduce the cost of building railroads many thousand dollars per mile, by taking off the protective duty now imposed on the iron used; and the stimulus which the reduction of taxation will give to the industry of the whole country will create a new demand for railroads and vastly increase the amount of their business."

Haight so thoroughly appreciated the value of this pamphlet that he had a large edition circulated throughout the State as a campaign document. Bearing Henry George's name, it did much to extend and strengthen the reputation the young man had already won as newspaper editor and author of the Chinese article.

In June, 1871, the Democratic State convention met in San Francisco, and installing Henry George as secretary. nominated Haight for re-election as governor. There was some friction among Democrats over the radical issue, but the party generally being lined up squarely for a big fight on a straight principle, and he himself beginning to think clearly on the great social as well as the great political questions, Mr. George was even more desirous than he had been two years before to run for the legislature. On August 10 he secured a nomination for the Assembly in a San Francisco district and he made several speeches there and elsewhere. Again his hopes were to be dashed. At dinner time on election day he announced to his wife that the indications were that the Democrats were carrying everything, but late that evening he came home again in laughing humour. "Why," he almost shouted, "we haven't elected a constable!"

Haight had opened and pressed the fight—and George had taken an important part in it—that had stamped out the policy of subsidies in California; but the great railroad corporation had in turn thrown its gigantic power into the election and had cast Haight and his entire party into the dust of defeat. Henry George, whose pen had been so active, was a shining mark for the powerful company, and his vote did not rise to the average of the party Assembly candidates in San Francisco. His one personal satisfaction in that hour of defeat was that he had fought and lost on a principle.

CHAPTER III.

ANSWERS THE RIDDLE OF THE SPHINX.

1871.   AGE, 32.

"I CANNOT play upon any stringed instrument, but I can tell you how of a little village to make a great and glorious city." Thus spake Themistocles, the Athenian, when asked if he could play the lyre. It was a reply seemingly arrogant enough; for was this not beyond the powers of any mortal man? Do not communities have their birth, their thriving to maturity, their decline and death, as regularly and immutably as the individual man himself?

Yet there have arisen those in the history of the world who have dreamed of a reign of justice and of the prolonged, if not indeed continuous life of the community. Such a dreamer was this Californian—this small, erect young man; with full, sandy beard; fresh, alert face; shining blue eyes; who, careless of dress, and wrapped in thought, rode a mustang pony about San Francisco. In the streets of the great Eastern city he had seen the want and suffering that accompany civilisation. It had made him who came "from the open West sick at heart." He knew nothing of the schools, but this that he saw he could not believe was the natural order. What was that order?

219

He vowed that he would find it. And afterwards as he
rode in the Oakland foothills came the flash-like revelation
—the monopoly of the land, the locking up of the storehouse of nature! There was the seat of the evil. He
asked no one if he was right: he *knew* he was right. Had
he not come into the new country and grown up with the
phases of change? Had he not seen this young community develop the ills from which the older communities
suffered? He did not need to go to books or to consult
the sages. There the thing lay plainly to view for any
who would see.

On Sunday night, March 26, in his work-room in the
second story of the Stevenson Street house, Henry George
sat down to write but the simple answer to the riddle of
the Sphinx. When ultimately finished it made a pamphlet
of forty-eight closely printed pages, equivalent to one hundred and fifty pages of an ordinary book. To it he gave
the title, "Our Land and Land Policy, National and
State." He divided his subject into five parts, which we
shall briefly review, following the author's language wherever possible.

I.

THE LANDS OF THE UNITED STATES.

The secret of the confidence of Americans in their own
destiny and the reason of their cheerful welcome to the
down-trodden of every nation, lay in the knowledge of the
"practically inexhaustible" public domain spreading over
the great Western country that would provide farms and
homes for all. But beginning with the Civil War period,
a policy of dissipation of the public lands commenced, and

From photograph taken in 1871, showing Mr. George at 32,
when he wrote " Our Land and Land Policy."

so great have been the various kinds of grants, especially to the railroads, up to 1870, that continuing at the same rate, all the available arable land will be given away by 1890.[1] To a single railroad—the Northern Pacific— 25,600 acres have been given for the building of each mile of road[2]—land enough to make 256 good sized American farms or 4,400 such as in Belgium support families in independence and comfort. Nor was this given to the corporation for building a railroad for the government or for the people, but for building it for itself.

II.

The Lands of California.

In California, twenty-four times as large as Massachusetts and with but 600,000 inhabitants, free land should be plentiful; yet the notorious fact is that so reckless has been the land policy that the immigrant in 1871, has, as a general thing, to pay a charge to middlemen before he can begin to cultivate the soil. Already individuals hold thousands and hundred of thousands of acres apiece. Across many of these vast estates a strong horse cannot gallop in a day, and one might travel for miles and miles over fertile ground where no plow has ever struck, but which is all owned, and on which no settler can come to make himself a home, unless he pay such a tribute as the lord of the domain may choose to exact.

---

[1] This was verified, resort being made at about 1890 to lands (since Oklahoma Territory) which in Indian Territory had been set apart for the Indian tribes.

[2] Twenty sections in the States and forty sections in the Territories.

LAND AND LABOUR.

Land, that part of the globe's surface habitable by man, is the storehouse from which he must draw the material to which his labour must be applied for the satisfaction of his desires. It is not wealth, since wealth is the product of human labour. It is valuable only as it is scarce. Its value differs from that of, say a keg of nails, for the nails are the result of labour, and when labour is given in return for them the transaction is an exchange; whereas, land is not the result of labour, but the creation of God, and when labour must be given for it, the result is an appropriation.

The value of land is not an element in the wealth of a community. It indicates the distribution of wealth. The value of land and the value of labour must bear to each other an inverse ratio. These two are the "terms" of production, and while production remains the same, to give more to the one is to give less to the other. The wealth of a community depends upon the product of the community. But the productive powers of land are precisely the same whether its price is low or high. In other words, the price of land indicates the distribution of wealth, not the production. The value of land is the power which its ownership gives to appropriate the product of labour, and as a sequence, where rents (the share of the land-owner) are high, wages (the share of the labourer) are low. And thus we see it all over the world: in the countries where land is high, wages are low, and where land is low, wages are high. In a new country the value of labour is at its maximum, the value of land at its minimum. As population grows and land becomes monopolised and increases in value, the value of labour steadily decreases. And the higher land and the lower wages, the stronger the tendency towards still lower wages, until this tendency is met by the very necessities of existence. For the higher land and the lower wages, the more difficult is it for the man who starts with nothing but his labour to become his own employer, and the more he is at the mercy of the land-owner and the capitalist.

According to the doctrine of rent advanced by Ricardo and Malthus, the value of land should be determined by the advantage which it possesses over the least advantageous land in use. Where use determines occupancy, this may be called the *necessary* or real value of land, in contradistinction to the *unnecessary* or fictitious value which results from speculation in land.

The difference between the *necessary* value of the land of the United States and the aggregate value at which it is held is enormous and represents the unnecessary tax which land monopolisation levies upon labour.

Now the right of every human being to himself is the foundation of the right of property. That which a man produces is rightfully his own, to keep, to sell, to give or to bequeath, and upon this sure title alone can ownership of anything rightfully rest. But man has also another right, declared by the fact of his existence—the right to the use of so much of the free gifts of nature as may be necessary to supply all the wants of that existence, and which he may use without interfering with the equal rights of anyone else; and to this he has a title as against all the world.

To permit one man to monopolise the land from which the support of others is to be drawn, is to permit him to appropriate their labour.

The Tendency of Our Present Land Policy.

The same causes which have reduced 374,000 land-holders of England in the middle of the last century to 30,000 now are working in this country. Not only are large bodies of new lands being put in the hands of the few, but a policy is pursued causing the absorption of the small farms into large estates.

The whole present system, National and State, tends to the concentration of wealth and the monopolisation of land. A hundred thousand dollars in the hands of one man pays but a slight proportion of the taxes that are paid by the same sum distributed among fifty; a hundred thousand acres held by a single landholder is assessed for but a fraction of the amount assessed upon the hundred thousand acres of six hundred farms.

Concentration is the law of the time. The great city is swallowing up the little towns; the great merchant is driving his poorer rivals out of business; a thousand little dealers become the clerks and shopmen of the proprietor of the marble fronted palace; a thousand master workmen, the employees of one rich manufacturer; and the gigantic corporations, the alarming product of the new social forces which Watt and Stephenson introduced to the world, are themselves being welded into still more titanic corporations.

In the new condition of things what chance will there be for a poor man if the land also is monopolised? To say that the land of a country shall be owned by a small class, is to say that that class shall rule it; to say that the people of a country shall consist of the very rich and the very poor, is to say that republicanism is impossible.

V.

WHAT OUR LAND POLICY SHOULD BE.

When we consider what land is; the relations between it and labour; that to own the land upon which a man *must* gain his subsistence is practically to own the man himself, we cannot remain in doubt as to what should be our policy in disposing of our public lands.

They should be given to actual settlers, in small quantities without charge.

But this policy would affect only the land that is left. It would still leave the great belts granted to railroads, the vast estates—the large bodies of land everywhere the subject of speculation. Still would continue the tendency that is concentrating ownership in the older settled States.

When our 40,000,000 of people have to raise $800,000,000 per year for public purposes [1] we cannot have any difficulty in discovering the remedy in the adjustment of taxation.

The feudal system annexed duties to privileges. One portion of the land defrayed the expenses of the State; another portion, those of the army; a third, those of the Church, and also relieved the sick, the indigent and the wayworn; while a fourth portion, the commons, was free to all the people. The great debts, the grinding taxation, are results of a departure from this system. A recent English writer [2] has estimated that had the feudal tenures been continued, England would now have had at her command a completely appointed army of six hundred thousand men, without the cost of a penny to the public treasury.

---

[1] Estimate of Commissioner David A. Wells.
[2] "The Strength of Nations," by Andrew Bisset.

Why should *we* not go back to the old system, and charge the expense of government upon our lands?

Land taxation does not bèar at all upon production; it adds nothing to prices, and does not affect the cost of living. As it does not add to prices, it costs the people nothing in addition to what it yields the Government; while as land cannot be hid or moved, this tax can be collected with more ease and certainty, and with less expense than any other tax; and the land-owner cannot shift it to any one else.

A tax upon the value of land is the most equal of all taxes, because the value of land is something that belongs to all, and in taxing land values we are merely taking for the use of the community something which belongs to the community. By the value of land is meant the value of the land itself, not the value of any improvement which has been made upon it—what is sometimes called in England the *unearned* value.

The mere holder would be called on to pay just as much taxes as the user of land. The owner of a vacant lot would have to pay as much as his neighbour who is using his. The monopoliser of agricultural land would be taxed as much as though his land were covered with improvements, with crops and with stock.

Land prices would fall; land speculation would receive its death-blow; land monopolisation would no longer pay. Millions and millions of acres from which settlers are now shut out, would be abandoned by their present owners, or sold to settlers on nominal terms.

The whole weight of taxation would be lifted from productive industry. The million dollar manufactory and needle of the seamstress, the mechanic's cottage and the grand hotel, the farmer's plow and the ocean steamship, would be alike untaxed. All would be free to buy or sell, to make or save, unannoyed by the tax-gatherer.

Imagine this country with all taxes removed from production and exchange! How demand would spring up; how trade would increase; what a powerful stimulus would be applied to every branch of industry; what an enormous development of wealth would take place. Imagine this country free of taxation, with its unused land free to those who would use it! Would there be many industrious men walking the streets, or tramping over our roads in the vain search for employment? Would there be in such a city as New York a hundred thousand men looking for work; such festering poverty and breeding vice as make the man from the open West sick at heart?

This was the nature of the little book to the writing of which this Californian, not yet thirty-two, devoted himself during the four months and three days between March 26 and July 29, 1871, though in the meantime came the Haight convention and other interruptions. He printed it in small type and in pamphlet form, for he had no money to present it in a better way. At first it made only thirty-one pages and in that form was printed; but when only a few copies were off, he stopped the press and expanded the last part, so that as published the pamphlet made forty-eight pages and had attached to it a folding map of California showing the extent of the railroad land grants.

Perhaps the first question to arise is, how much was Henry George indebted to others for the comprehensive views of political economy as set down in his little book? He answered this himself in later years:[1]

"When I first came to see what is the root of our social difficulties, and how this fundamental wrong might be cured in the easiest way, by concentrating taxes

---

[1] "The Standard," New York, October 19, 1889.

on land values, I had worked out the whole thing for myself without conscious aid that I can remember, unless it might have been the light I got from Bisset's 'Strength of Nations' as to the economic character of the feudal system. When I published 'Our Land and Land Policy,' I had not even heard of the Physiocrats and the *impot unique.* But I knew that if it was really a star I had seen, others must have seen it too."

While Ricardo and Malthus are credited with the formulation of the law of rent; while John Stuart Mill's proposal to compensate land-owners is deprecated, and his phrase "unearned increment," is spoken of as "the unearned value of land," it is not necessary to assume that Henry George was indebted to others further than this, even at points where there chanced to be a similarity of thought. In his last book,[1] discussing the concurrent writings of Adam Smith and the French Physiocrats and the probably independent thought of Smith, where his utterances closely resembled that of the latter, Mr. George has drawn the instance of his own case.

"It is a mistake to which the critics who are themselves mere compilers are liable, to think that men must draw from one another to see the same truths or to fall into the same errors. Truth is, in fact, a relation of things, which is to be seen independently because it exists independently. Error is perhaps more likely to indicate transmission from mind to mind; yet even that usually gains its strength and permanence from misapprehensions that in themselves have independent plausibility. Such relations of the stars as that appearance in the North which we call the Dipper or Great Bear, or as that in the South which we call the Southern Cross, are seen by all who scan the starry heavens, though the names by which men know them are various. And to think that the sun revolves around the earth is an error into which the testimony of their senses must cause all men independently to fall, until the first testimony of the senses is corrected by reason applied to wider observations.

"In what is most important, I have come closer to the views of Quesnay and his followers than did Adam Smith, who knew the men personally. But in my case there was certainly no derivation from them. I well recall the day when, checking my horse on a rise that overlooks San Francisco Bay, the commonplace reply of a passing teamster to a commonplace question, crystallised, as by lightning-flash, my brooding thoughts into coherency, and I there and then recognised the natural order—one of those experiences that make those who have had them feel thereafter that they can vaguely appreciate what mystics and poets have called the 'ecstatic vision.' Yet at that time I had never heard of the Physiocrats, or even read a line of Adam Smith.

"Afterwards, with the great idea of the natural order in my head, I printed a little book, 'Our Land and Land Policy,' in which I urged that all taxes should be laid on the value of land, irrespective of improvements. Casually meeting on a San Francisco street a scholarly lawyer, A. B. Douthitt, we stopped to chat, and he told me that what I had in my little book proposed was what the French 'Economists' a hundred years before had proposed.

"I forget many things, but the place where I heard this, and the tones and attitude of the man who told me of it, are photographed on my memory. For, when you have seen a truth that those around you do not see, it is one of the deepest of pleasures to hear of others who have seen it. This is true, even though these others were dead years before you were born. For the stars that we of to-day see when we look were here to be seen hundreds and thousands of years ago. They shine on. Men come and go, in their generations, like the generations of the ants."

Ex-State Senator John M. Days of California became acquainted with Mr. George soon after the pamphlet was written and bears testimony on the subject:

"In 1871 I was elected a member of the Legislature and introduced a set of resolutions in favour of the land of the United States being held for the people thereof. In preparing my speech I came across Henry George's pamphlet 'Our Land and Land Policy' and I quoted two whole pages. I first met Henry George personally in the month of May, 1872, and I loaned him all the writings of Bronterre O'Brien,· together with Gamage's history of chartism. He returned them within so short a time that he could not have had time to read them carefully, let alone study them. He told me that when he wrote the pamphlet he had never read or seen any work on the land question."

But without direct or indirect statements from Mr. George or any one else as to the independence of his thought, a striking proof of it might be found in his writings themselves. He has frankly stated [1] that in the spring of 1869, when writing the Chinese article, "wishing to know what political economy had to say about the causes of wages," he "went to the Philadelphia Library, looked over John Stuart Mill's 'Political Economy,' and accepting Mill's view without question," based his article upon it. Yet in "Our Land and Land Policy," in dealing with the cause of wages, he rejected Mill's view and gave a different explanation to the one assumed in the Chinese article. He, in fact, took up and developed something he had perceived months before the Chinese article was thought of and which he had set forth in his "Overland Monthly" article, "What the Railroad Will Bring Us," in the fall of

[1] "The Science of Political Economy."   Book II, Chap. viii, pp. 200, 201.

1868. Passages from his former and his later work set side by side, show the development of his thought:

"Overland" Article, 1868.	"Land Policy," 1871.
"For years the high rate of interest and the high rate of wages prevailing in California have been special subjects for the lamentation of a certain school of political economists, who could not see that high wages and high interest were indications that the natural wealth of the country was not yet monopolised, that great opportunities were open to all."	"The value of land and of labour must bear to each other an inverse ratio. These two are the 'terms' of production, and while production remains the same, to give more to the one, is to give less to the other. The value of land is the power which its ownership gives to appropriate the product of labour, and, as a sequence, where rents (the share of the landowner) are high, wages (the share of the labourer) are low. And thus we see it all over the world, in the countries where land is high, wages are low, and where land is low, wages are high. In a new country the value of labour is at first at its maximum, the value of land at its minimum. As population grows and land becomes monopolised and increases in value, the value of labour steadily decreases."

The truth is that primitive conditions were all about Henry George. The miners throughout the early California placers commonly spoke of washing their "wages" out of the soil, and there was a universal if unwritten law among them that "claims" should be limited in size and that ownership should be conditioned upon use. In the agricultural regions, and even in some of the towns, "squatters" had constantly asserted the principle commonly recognised through the whole frontier country that any man was free to use land that was not already actually in use. The passage of statutes permitting the adding of mining claim to claim and promoting monopolisation in the agricultural regions, accompanied by enormous grants to comparatively few individuals, brought a keen sense of scarcity of land to a people who had been accustomed to think of practically "all out-doors" as being free.

With a fresh young people, full of self-confidence and free from restraints and traditions, here were all the conditions needed to quicken original thought—thought that should go back to first principles. Henry George did not therefore have to go to books for his political economy. His keen perception, and active, analytical mind found what he hailed as the fundamental and eternal truths of social order written so that all might read them in the primary conditions of the new country. His political economy he got from nature herself.

But there was one small passage in the pamphlet which should not be overlooked. Of this Ex-Senator Days has since said:

"In 'Our Land and Land Policy' Henry George made a plea for private property in land. In August, 1872, I became president of a Lyceum in San Francisco which discussed various questions every Sunday afternoon. I invited him to open on the land question. In his speech he still favoured private property in land. In closing the meeting I made a few remarks in which I observed that Mr. George said that he favoured private property in land, but that he .made a mistake in so saying, for every argument he made on the question showed that he was opposed to it.   From that day to the day of his death Mr. George openly opposed by word as well as argument private property in land."

The passage of the pamphlet to which the Senator refers runs:

"It by no means follows that there should be no such thing as property in land, but merely that there should be no monopolisation—no standing between the man who is willing to work and the field which nature offers for his labour.   For while it is true that the land of a country is the free gift of the Creator to all the people of that country, to the enjoyment of which each has an equal natural right, it is also true that the recognition of private ownership in land is necessary to its proper use—is, in fact, a condition of civilisation.   When the millennium comes, and the old savage, selfish instincts have died out of men, land may perhaps be held in common; but not till then."

The idea that Mr. George wished to convey was the necessity of securing improvements, which could not be the case if titles were to be confiscated and the State were to resume actual possession of all the land.   But seeing in the instance of Senator Days the wrong idea his language expressed, when writing "Progress and Poverty" he changed it materially, to wit:

"What is necessary for the use of land is not its private ownership, but the security of improvements. . . .   The complete recognition of common rights to land need in no way interfere with the complete recognition of individual right to improvements or produce. . . .   I do not propose either to purchase or to coufiscate private property in land. The first would be unjust; the second, needless. Let the individuals who now hold it still retain, if they want to, possession of what they are pleased to call *their* land. Let them continue to call it *their* land. Let them buy and sell, and bequeath and devise it. We may safely leave them the shell, if we take the kernel. *It is not necessary to confiscate land; it is only necessary to confiscate rent.*"[1]

This Days incident and others like it bringing to **Mr.** George a realisation of obscurities of his language in some instances and of his thoughts in others, made him henceforward most patient with those who, sincerely striving to comprehend his ideas, floundered around in self-made confusions; for with all his powers, no one more fully appreciated the difficulty of clear expression, and before that, of clear thinking, than **Mr.** George himself.

If "Our Land and Land Policy" was sent to John Stuart Mill, the acknowledged master political economist of the day, there is nothing to show it. But E. T. Peters, of the Bureau of Statistics at Washington, whom George had quoted and to whom he presented a copy, wrote strongly commending it; Horace White of the "Chicago Tribune" wrote that George was "entitled to be ranked as an economist"; while David A. Wells, New York Commissioner for the Revision of the Revenue Laws, whose report had been cited, said, "I see you have enunciated a principle relative to value of land and pauperism which strikes me as original and well put." But beyond a few such letters as these, the pamphlet got little attention. Nor even in California did it awaken the public recognition for which he may have looked. "Something like a thousand

---

[1] "Progress and Poverty." Book VIII, Chaps. i and ii, (Memorial Edition, pp. 396, 397 and 403).

copies were sold," he said towards the end of his life,[1] "but I saw that to command attention the work must be done more thoroughly." The work was done more thoroughly eight years later when "Progress and Poverty" was written.

Two articles by Henry George appeared in the "Overland Monthly" during this year of 1871, one in February entitled, "How Jack Breeze Missed Being a Pasha," and the other in December entitled, "Bribery in Elections," in which, pointing at the shameless corruption at the polls in the fall election when Haight was overwhelmed by railroad money, George advocated the adoption in California of the Australian ballot system. But these efforts were trifling compared with the pamphlet, "Our Land and Land Policy." This latter was set aside for a time in a new era of newspaper activity.

---

[1] "The Science of Political Economy." Book II, Chap. viii, p. 201.

CHAPTER IV.

THE "SAN FRANCISCO EVENING POST."

1871-1875.   AGE, 32-36.

IT was in 1859, before he came of age and while setting type on the "Home Journal," that, on an alarm of fire one day which brought most of the people of the neighbourhood into the street, Henry George found himself wedged in a doorway with a strange printer from another part of the building, both trying to pass through at the same moment. Seven years later on meeting him again, George learned that this man was William M. Hinton. George was then about to set off on the Mexican filibustering expedition and Hinton deprecated his going, because George would imperil his life and most likely cut off the means of his family's support. That commenced the friendship, and when "Our Land and Land Policy" had been published, Hinton was one of those to whom the author gave a copy. Born in England, in 1830, nearly ten years before George's birth, he was brought to the United States as a child, his father, I. T. Hinton, coming to Philadelphia in 1832 to sell a history of the United States written by himself and his brother, John Howard Hinton. George wavered during the summer of 1871 between remaining in California and going to New York or Philadelphia to establish himself, when he chanced one day to talk with Hinton, of which conversation the latter says:

> "Mr. George was talking of going East to settle. I had read his pamphlet, 'Our Land and Land Policy,' and was taken with it, believing its author showed marked ability. In talking with him about it and other things, I asked him why he did not start a newspaper. He replied that he had no money; to which I said that anybody could start one with money, but that the difficult and commendable achievement was to start one without it. I had no thought about entering upon such an enterprise myself, as I was getting a good living out of the job-printing establishment of Mahan & Co., of which firm I was a partner. I made the suggestion to Mr. George simply because at the time he had no employment. Yet as a result of this casual conversation, the idea catching fire in his mind, I found myself before long getting into the thing, though even then I purposed to stay only until it should be set on its feet, planning then to withdraw. Three of us entered into an equal partnership—George, who was to be editor; myself, who was to superintend the printing; and A. H. Rapp, a member of my job-printing firm, who was to be business manager. We got together about $1,800 and this and some more that we got in by the sale in advance of delivery routes, constituted all the capital we had with which to start a daily newspaper. We lost no time, and on Monday, December 4, 1871, the first copy of the 'Daily Evening Post' appeared, with Hinton, Rapp & Co. as publishers, and Henry George as editor. Our office was at 605 Montgomery Street, west side, a few doors north of Clay."

Following the example of very successful newspapers in the East, the price was set at one cent a copy, it being the first penny paper west of the Rocky Mountains. Indeed, the cent piece was not in commercial use on the Pacific Coast, so that it had to be introduced specially;

which was accomplished by inducing the largest financial institution in the Western country—the Bank of California—to import a thousand dollars' worth of pennies on the presumption of their usefulness in a multitude of minor commercial transactions. Then San Francisco was astonished by the spectacle of newsboys crying the new paper on the streets for a cent a copy, and ready with a large supply of pennies to make change. The novelty of the thing caused people to buy the little "Post." For the paper, consisting of four pages, was only eleven by fourteen inches, and the type very small. The early numbers contained little advertising and telegraphic, the space being filled with local news and editorials, written in short, sharp, direct style. In its salutatory it said: "In the higher, wider sense the 'Post' will be Democratic; that is, it will oppose centralisation and monopolies of all kinds. But it will be the organ of no faction, clique or party. It will endeavour to deal with all questions without cowardly reserve, but with firmness and candour; and whether it praises or censures, it will be without reference to party lines or party affiliations."

Towards the end of his life Henry George told of the early history of the "Post."[1]

"The vigour of the little paper attracted attention and it began to run to as large a circulation as could be obtained with our press facilities. We could get only one double flat-bed press. An offer soon came from another newspaper man, H. W. Thomson, now dead, to buy at a good price a fourth interest. The third partner, Rapp, wanted to sell his share, and he did sell it for about $2,500. Mr. Hinton and I concluded that we had better withdraw, and we sold our interests, each getting $2,700. All three of the original

_____
[1] Meeker notes, October, 1897.

partners had thus sold to Thomson. This happened within four months and a half after the first issue appeared. But no sooner was the policy changed than the circulation of the 'Post' dropped, and in less than sixty days Thomson offered the paper to us for a merely nominal sum. This Mr. Hinton and I accepted, and Frank Mahan, another printer, was given a small interest. I went along editing the paper, which immediately started to grow."

A feature that was quickly recognised by the public as indicating the independence of the new journal was its treatment of the land and taxation questions. Frequently quotations were made from "Our Land and Land Policy" and more frequently there were editorials favouring the taxation of land values to the exclusion of all other things. These editorials were always short and direct. This feature grew strong enough to become the objective point with the opposition press, which ridiculed "George's fad." But fad or no fad, the editor kept persistently talking of it and snapped up every challenge to discuss it with other papers. When in May, 1873, John Stuart Mill died at Avignon, France, the "Post" paid a fine editorial tribute to the passing of this "greatest living master of political economy," making commendation of the decision of those having the matter in hand that instead of raising a statue to him in America, they should publish a memorial edition of his writings—"his best monument."

In national politics the paper was strongly opposed to Grant, "carpet-bag reconstruction" and centralisation, and warmly advocated the nomination for the Presidency of Horace Greeley, editor of the "New York Tribune," who, although formerly a zealous supporter of war measures, now wished to ignore sectionalism and bind up the nation's wounds. Mr. George was elected a delegate to the

Democratic National Convention to meet in Baltimore, Maryland, early in July, 1872. He went East by way of Philadelphia, where he had sent his family just before starting the "Post," on account of his wife's ill health. Thence, accompanied by his wife, he went to Baltimore, where he was elected secretary of the California delegation, Ex-Governor Downey being chairman. On July 10, 1872, Greeley was nominated unanimously and a few days later the California delegation visited the candidate on his estate at Chappaqua, Westchester County, N. Y., George writing to his paper a long signed description of the occasion, closing with the words: "We all felt . . . that in this sturdy, benignant old man we had a candidate round whom we could all rally, and who fittingly represented the grandest idea of the time—the idea of reconciliation."

Then Mr. George hastened back to San Francisco to plunge editorially into the campaign. In this, as in all his fights, he grew more and more hopeful as his blood warmed in the conflict; but his wife, who now was growing to understand public affairs and therefore becoming more his counsellor in such matters, was not so sure, writing October 8, on the day of the Pennsylvania State election: "This is the day that in a measure determines Greeley's fate. I am not at all sanguine, but I won't give up even if the Republicans win this contest." Greeley was badly beaten; and George was sorely disappointed. But he was not the man to repine. At once he was up and doing on another line.

Meanwhile in August, when less than eight and a half months old, the "Post" had been increased in size and its price advanced to two cents; and a month and a half later, enlarged to the size of the ordinary newspaper and the charge for single copies made five cents, "to accommodate the price to the currency," the attempt to introduce the one cent piece proving after a long trial a failure.

As might be imagined, a newspaper that saw evils to oppose and did not hesitate to oppose them, could find plenty of work to do. As a matter of fact, the "Post" was kept busy with fights of one kind or another. One of these attracted wide attention. It was the case of the ship *Sunrise*, which sailing from New York harbour in May, 1873, had a passage to San Francisco marked by such cruelty towards the crew by the captain and first mate that three of the men jumped overboard and were drowned. Attempts were made to hush up the matter when the ship reached the Golden Gate, but Mr. George learned of it and at once demanded a prosecution. The captain and first mate fled, but upon the "Post's" offering a reward, were apprehended and brought to trial, the newspaper engaging special counsel. The officers were convicted to long terms of imprisonment. The "Post" subsequently took up some less flagrant cases of maritime brutality and established itself as a champion of sailor's rights.

That personal danger attended the editing of an aggressive Western newspaper has been often attested, and Mr. George had his share. Ex-Judge Robert Ferral, then one of the editorial writers on the "Post," says of one of these cases:

"I went with Henry George to attend an investigation of the House of Correction, or Industrial School, which was in charge of a brute named George F. Harris. At the gate stood the redoubtable Harris, with his hand on his pistol, looking more like a pirate than the superintendent of a public institution. Without the least hesitation Mr. George walked right up to him, looked the burly ruffian straight in the eyes, and passed into the yard without a word. All through that investigation Harris avoided the steady, indignant gaze of the brave little man who pressed his charges of brutality and drove him from his position and out of the city."

Another instance of personal danger arose out of the Tarpey case in the beginning of 1873. Matthew Tarpey, a brutal but affluent land-owner in Monterey County, quarrelled with an unoffending woman named Nicholson about a tract of land. He dug a pit, lay in it for hours waiting for her, 'and shot her in the back and killed her when she took alarm and tried to run away. The country around became fiercely excited, and more so when it was rumoured that Tarpey's wealth would clear him as others had been cleared of late, and that the first step would be to move him to another locality for trial. Word went out at once that the citizens would stop that and take the matter in hand themselves, and despatches came to San Francisco that Tarpey would be lynched. John V. George, Henry's brother, was engaged in the business office of the "Post" and was a witness of what followed.

"Tarpey money and political influence were strong enough to hush the matter up in the other newspapers, but the 'Post' published the news of the intended lynching, and an editorial saying that there would be no regrets if the people should deal out to him the same measure he had meted out to others, and hang him to the nearest tree, as a 'ghastly evidence' that there was 'still a sense of justice in California.' Tarpey's relatives in San Francisco and others of influence came to the office to implore the editor to say no more, and several anonymous letters were received threatening violence if he did not stop, but he would not change his course, and next day, following news of Tarpey's death, he published as a leader an editorial a column and a quarter long de-

nouncing Tarpey's deed and justifying the lynching.[1]
The effect of this was lost by the buying up of a large
part of the edition of the paper by the Tarpey partisans.

"Next day a man, I think named Donally, came to
the office inquiring for the editor. My brother was out
and Donally hung around on the sidewalk. When my
brother returned Donally approached and asked him if
the article of the day represented his sentiments. My
brother answered that it not only represented his sentiments, but that he himself wrote it, whereupon Donally
impeached the article and called its author a liar. My
brother struck him in the face, though Donally was a
much larger and heavier man. The bystanders inter-
fered and Donally left. Nothing came of this, although
there was talk for a time of violence to the editor of the
'Post.' But the paper did not change its front and
short editorials on the Tarpey matter kept appearing."

John V. George tells of another occurrence that almost
resulted in the shooting of the aggressive editor. It grew

---

[1] Touching this method of effecting justice, the editorial said : "Lynch
law is a fearful thing. It is only better than the crime it is invoked to
repress in that the impulses of the many are generally truer and purer
than the passions of the individual. It is liable to terrible mistakes, and
it strikes at the very foundations upon which society is organised. To
say that even in a case like this Lynch law is justified is to admit that
the regular and legal methods by which society protects itself have failed,
that our laws in their practical workings are but a snare and a delusion,
and that justice in our courts is but a matter of chance. . . . The people
of Monterey hung Tarpey themselves because they could not trust the
law to do it. But it will not do to dismiss the case with the simple reflection that justice has been done. There is a deep moral in it, which
we must heed, unless we are willing to drift back to a condition little
short of anarchy. And there is a moral in it, too, for law breakers as
well as law makers — not for murderers alone, but for thieving officials,
corrupt representatives, and the robbers of all grades who make of law a
protection and means of escape. Our society is not too highly organised
to revert upon great provocation to first principles, and to do for itself,
what its ministers and administrators refuse to do."—"Evening Post,"
March 18, 1873.

out of the paper's arraignment of city Chief of Police
Crowley, whom it had helped to office, but now hotly denounced for not closing the gambling hells and clearing
out the crime-infested Chinese quarter, as commanded by
city ordinances.

"It was in May, 1873, two months after the Tarpey
case. Accompanied by Mr. Hinton, his partner, and by
City Supervisor Stuart Menzies, Port Warden Joseph
Austin, and Daniel O'Connell of the 'Post' staff, my
brother, one afternoon after the paper had gone to press
went to the Mint saloon and restaurant, on Commercial
Street, a resort for lawyers and politicians. As they
entered, James Gannon, an ex-detective and supporter
of Crowley, tapped my brother on the shoulder, saying
that he wanted to speak with him privately. My brother
stepped aside with him, when Gannon said, 'Let up on
Crowley or there will be trouble,' and when asked what
he meant, the ex-detective seized my brother by the
neck with one hand and struck him in the face with
the other. My brother tried to strike back, when Gannon reached down and drew a revolver. But before he
could fire, Menzies, a very strong man, caught his wrist
and held the weapon down, while he and Supervisor
McCarthy, who was in the place at the time, pulled Gannon away. It was proposed at first to bring Gannon to
trial, but the matter was dropped and he afterwards became very sorry for his part in it."

William A. Plunkitt, a school director in the early
seventies and supported by the "Post" in an investigation
into a big scandal in the purchasing of school supplies,
has since said:

"Under Henry George's management the 'Post' was
a bold, fearless, reform paper. The standard of political morality or public morals in San Francisco
at that time was very low. While many good men

held public official positions, quite a number of important places in the municipal government were filled
by characterless and unscrupulous demagogues. Mr.
George neither respected nor feared.that kind of public
functionary. He lashed them as with 'a whip of scor-
pions.' The 'Post' and its editor thus became a power,
esteemed and respected by all thoughtful and worthy
citizens in San Francisco, and feared by all public
malefactors."

A yet fuller picture of the editor is presented by another
contemporary, Mrs. C. F.' McLean, who was then Miss
Sallie Hart, and who says that "while writing his editorials
or correcting proof, Mr. George received any and all who,
with or without excuse, 'dropped in to see the editor.' " [1]

"I was a teacher in the public schools of San Francisco when there arose a question of the reduction of
the salaries of the teachers in the lower grades. Picking up the 'Evening Post,' I noticed an editorial protest, which inspired me to write a communication to the
editor, which I signed with an assumed name. When
the article appeared it was with an editorial request
that 'Susan' call at the office. Saturday came and with
it the first visit of my life to a newspaper office. The
place was up two flights of stairs. . . . To my
knock there came a cheery 'Come in,' and on opening
the door I came face to face with Henry George. He
was seated at a common table piled high with papers,
while all about on the small floor space were other newspapers, all, to my unsophisticated eyes, piled in mournful confusion. . . . I was embarrassed, almost
frightened, but in an instant my breath was fairly taken

---

1 "Henry George : A Study from Life," "The Arena," September, 1898.
Mrs. McLean subsequently became an occasional writer for the "Post."
She is alluded to in "The Science of Political Economy" (pp. 282, 283) as
"the wife of the superintendent of a Western zoological garden, who,
coming to New York with her husband on the annual trip he makes to
buy wild animals, jokingly speaks of 'shopping for menagerie goods.' "

away, for the man in front of me said: 'Come in, my
little girl.' However, I gasped out that I had sent the
article signed 'Susan.' . . . 'Now, come sit down,'
he said. 'You must excuse me, but you are so small,
and you look so young; do sit down.'

"I sat down, and before I knew what I was saying
I had told the editor before me all about myself. Even
then I noticed his large head and bright eyes, and at
once compared them with a picture of Henry Clay that
had been familiar to me from childhood, and thought
the head before me was the finer of the two. I remember now that my first interview with Henry George was
brought to a close by a boy who, I thought, rather im-
peratively demanded 'copy'; therefore I hastily rose to
go, but not before I had promised to call again soon."

Arthur McEwen was a brilliant young contemporary
newspaper worker on the Pacific Coast with Henry George
and testifies that it was the "editorial policy that marked
the 'Post' off from the usual."

"It was as foreign to George to be either a demagogue
or a follower in politics as it was for the 'Post' to keep
subscribers and advertisers by thrifty silence. Women
were appearing at local option elections soliciting votes
and receiving disrespectful treatment. Instantly the
'Post' charged upon the ungallant blackguards, and in a
day had every saloon in California for its enemy. Subscribers withdrew by the thousand and advertisements
were withdrawn by the column, but that made no difference to George."

James V. Coffey, editorial writer on the "Examiner"
at this time, and since Judge of the Superior Court of
San Francisco, says that Mr. George "had apparently an
unsystematic method of work, jotting down a paragraph
here and a paragraph there; yet in the end the writing
was smooth and connected." This apparently "unsys-

tematic method of work" doubtless came from dictating to a stenographer. Having a habit of procrastination, he put off his daily writing until he was cramped for time and had to work under great pressure. To relieve this stress he engaged a stenographer, Edward Lande, the first secretary he ever had. Lande was soon succeeded by Stephen Potter who remained until George left the "Post" and who says that his chief had an original way of working.

"He would dictate for a few minutes, and then leaving me to transcribe, would continue the thread of his thoughts with his own pen. In this way he would dictate and write, and get through an immense amount of work. I ought to say that at this time he had curious habits of abstraction, often even on the street he would stop, walk to the curb and stand there apparently deep in thought and oblivious to the stir about him. I have had to speak several times on such occasions to rouse him."

Henry George's career on the "Evening Post" terminated November 27, 1875. Starting the paper with scarcely any capital, it had from the business point of view a hand to mouth struggle until the close of 1873, when a comparatively large sum of money was obtained for it. We have Mr. George's own story for this.[1]

"John P. Jones, then elected United States Senator from Nevada, sought an interview with me and declared himself interested in such a paper, offering to furnish us on our own notes, money enough to buy the best press that could be obtained.[2] I had seen in the

[1] Meeker notes, October, 1897.

[2] Mr. Hinton, in conversation with Henry George, Jr., in April, 1898, said that Jones put in two sums of money — $30,000, for which he received 30 of the 100 shares of the stock of the paper, and $18,000 for which he received notes. Jones professed to do this solely from motives of friend-

'Sun' office when in New York in 1869, the first perfecting press, the Bullock, and concluding to accept this offer of Jones, Mr. Hinton went East and made an arrangement with the Bullock Company for a press. It was brought out and set up, the first perfecting press on the Pacific Coast.[1]

"Feeling that we now had facilities for larger circulation and that we should be making a mistake not to improve it, we concluded to establish a morning paper, 'The Ledger,' which we did in August, 1875. This was done on an extensive scale. It was a small daily paper, and for the first time in journalism, an illustrated Sunday paper. We disdained asking for advertisements and designed to fill up the whole with reading matter until advertisements should seek us.

"But a few days after it started there was a great fire in Virginia City, Nevada, in which many San Franciscans were interested; a heavy decline in some of the greatest of the mining stocks and the suspension of payment by the Bank of California. Then came an intense local money panic, during which it became impossible to collect money[2] and we had to suspend the 'Ledger.' While we were thus embarrassed John P. Jones demanded the return of the money he had loaned us or that the paper that we had made should be surrendered to him. I felt like fighting, and a short article in the 'Post' would have ended all hopes of his getting anything from it, but my partner, Mr. Hinton, pleaded the duty of our providing for the employees who were friends, and tired out with the fight, I finally suc-

---

liness, but if his real motive was the hope of influencing the paper to change its policy of hostility to President Grant, whom he warmly supported, he was disappointed, as his loan and purchase of stock did not affect the editorial columns.

[1] The paper also moved to new and larger quarters, 504 Montgomery Street, corner of Sacramento, and was supplied with a new dress of type and office fittings.

[2] Mr. Hinton says that he saw a man bring an ingot of gold worth $9,000 into the office of Hickox & Spier, money-brokers, and get only $1,500 on it.

cumbed, and without a cent of compensation, on November 27, almost four years to a day after we started it, gave over the paper to the representative of Jones.

"I thus went out with a dependent family to make a living and not caring to ask or to receive any offer of employment from other papers, I wrote to Governor Irwin, whom I had been instrumental in electing a few months before, and asked him to give me a place where there was little to do and something to get, so that I might devote myself to some important writing. He gave me the office of State Inspector of Gas-Meters, which yielded, though intermittently, a sufficient revenue to live on and which required very little work."

But though Mr. George thus obtained a public offiee that would afford him a living, and though he had the purpose before him of engaging in more permanent writing, the loss of the "Post" seemed to him at the time a great misfortune, for not only was he at a stroke shorn of the fruits of years of labour, but was bereft of his weapon as an active factor in the affairs of the City and State— the keenest of losses to an energetic public man. But this in fact proved another and a momentous turning point in his career.

CHAPTER V.

DOMESTIC LIFE.

1873-1876.   AGE, 34-37.

WE break in on the narrative at this point for a glimpse of the home life.

In the fall of 1873 the wife and children had returned from the East and the family settled down in a cozy two-story house at the Mission—on Valencia Street. There was a small garden, and a climbing rose covered the front of the house with a mass of white blossoms in the early summer. It was there that the editor had what was described as a "tan-coloured mustang," riding down to the "Evening Post" office in the morning and back in the afternoon, and at night putting him up at a near-by stable. The horse was one of the small, wiry, native animals, its shaggy hair at most times looking frowsy and "a lick and a promise" generally doing for grooming. The saddle was of the Mexican pattern commonly used in California at the time, covered with embossed leather, and having big horn pommel and ponderous, leather-enveloped stirrups. Horse and rider had a careless, though not ungraceful appearance, Mr. George with his trim figure, square shoulders, and easy posture moving with a swing as the animal quickened into its natural lope. Sometimes he took up behind him one or the other of his two boys, now getting to be ten and twelve; sometimes he rode in company with friends; but for the most part he took solitary "thinking" rides, the free motion of the body in the open air seeming to exhilarate the action of the mind.

It was on a Sunday afternoon in the spring of 1874 while on one of these solitary rides on the ocean road that his horse shied, threw him from the saddle and dragged him by one stirrup. Fortunately the animal at once slowed down from a gallop or his master must have been dragged to death. But Mr. George disengaged his foot, when the horse ran away and was not recovered until several days afterwards. This was the second accident of the kind. Besides having his right hand badly lacerated, Mr. George's wrist was broken. Holding his injured arm against his body, he made the long walk of five or six miles at nightfall back over the lonely roads to the city. Even when he found a doctor his chief thought was of his wife, and before anything was done he sent a message to her not to hold supper as he had been detained. When he got home he said to her, "That mustang has hurt my wrist, and now you must be doubly my right hand to me."

His great energy and restlessness made him the most impatient of patients. Because he could not go to the office, he insisted on having a stenographer to whom to dictate editorials. But by April he had recovered the full use of his injured member and in May the family moved to a house on Rincon Hill, more convenient to the ofhee.

Domestic life was very dear to the energetic public man. Perhaps the necessities of his exacting vocation made him delight the more to be with his family. While the wife sat beside with her work-basket, he would lie on a lounge in the library and read poetry to the two boys and the girl, or have them in turn read or recite before him or such strangers as he chanced to bring home. Or perhaps, he went swimming with the boys in a bath-house off Long Bridge, or took the family for a row or for a sail in a "plunger." It frequently happened in these trips that they found lying at anchor the little *Shubrick* in which the father had come to California and he would tell of his early seaman's adventures. Frequently there were Sunday cruises about the bay on sloop or schooner, the party made up of friends with their families.

Henry George was not a member of any church, nor did his family attend any regularly, though in his broadness of mind he left his wife entire freedom in this for herself and the children. He attached himself to no sect, yet his nature was strongly reverent. He wished to have his children say night and morning prayers, and often at twilight or before they went to bed he would lie on his lounge in his library and have them and their mother mingle their voices in the old hymns that he had heard as a child in Philadelphia, and again "Praise God from whom all blessings flow" seemed to swell and echo through old St. Paul's. Out of the inquiry, why want goes with plenty, religion had come to have a new meaning. In the conviction that he had discovered that it was not by God's will, but because of violation of God's ordinance that men suffered involuntary poverty in the heart of civilisation, "a faith that was dead revived." He had turned from a religion that taught either of a Special Providence on the one hand or of a merciless fate on the other. Now all the fervour of his spirit went forth in the belief that social progress is governed by unchanging and beneficent law.

His children's training began at this time to engage his earnest attention. They had never attended any but public schools, and travelling and moving had broken even this schooling. His own method broke it more. He discouraged lesson-studying at home, saying that the regular school hours were long enough, and that the hours at home should be spent in recreation and other ways. But if his children, as a consequence, stood low at recitations, they stood high in general information and the independent use of their faculties, for he would talk or read to them on whatever topic arose which could be brought within their understanding; and at dinner table, when the family was alone, he would ask them in turn questions touching history, literature, public matters or elementary science—such things as may have come up in previous conversations. When they could not answer, he himself would do so. Reading was encouraged, and the boys, at least, were directed to such books as the father delighted in when of their age. A copy of "Robinson Crusoe" was the first book he gave to his eldest boy—a tale that all his life fascinated Henry George and is frequently referred to in his writings. Another book-present to his children was the "Arabian Nights," which he sent while they were in Philadelphia, and which, he wrote to his wife, he had, "like a goose, spent the night re-reading." Thus the children might constantly fail in the school lessons they were expected to study at home, but if asked, could recite from Tennyson, Browning or Macaulay, had heard of the buried cities of Egypt and Yucatan, and in their own way, could talk about the rotation of crops, the forms of water or the nebular hypothesis. From either parent a request was a command, with corporal punishment swiftly following delay or delinquency; yet affection blended with obedience.

Visitors added materially to the children's education; for at the table, where the children were brought when old enough and taught to be silent, the guests were drawn towards topics most congenial to themselves, good feeling

was let loose, and anecdotes, strange adventures, curious
bits of information, flashes of wit and tales of humour
poured forth. The host had the habit of politely with-
drawing to the place of questioner. This was most agreeable to his personal modesty. It also gratified a never-
ceasing desire for information—information, apparently,
of any kind and every kind, which, like his miscellaneous
reading, was to be drawn on when needed, many a dinner
talk later serving him with happy illustrations in his
writings. Men from various parts of the world came,
and as it were, poured out their contributions to the
varied and instructive symposium.

Mr. and Mrs. George had now grown closer than ever
before. In the early days of their marriage, when they
were struggling along in poverty, she had refrained from
inquiring into the matters outside of domestic affairs that
interested her husband. Believing her mission to be to
look after his health, his rest and recreation, she avoided
all matters of business and tried to draw his mind into
other channels. But as he advanced as a writer and their
manner of living improved, she entered the council of his
general affairs and came to be his close adviser.

The Georges had a small number of intimate friends.
They never desired to move in the fashionable circles.
Formal social occasions always had their snares and pit-
falls for the husband. On one occasion when he was led
to attend a reception at the Ralston residence alone, his
wife being ill, he returned disgusted. "Such people live
in a frivolous atmosphere," he said. "There was Mrs.
—— for instance. She had nothing to talk about but the
weather." "The weather!" exclaimed Mrs. George, somewhat doubtfully. "Why, yes," answered the husband;
"she asked me what kind of a season we were likely to
have, and I told her the indications were for a wet sea-

son!" Mrs. George broke into merriment. "Your social butterfly," said she, "wanted to know about the outlook for social events—receptions, concerts, balls, weddings, and the like!"

But if Mr. George disliked formal social gatherings, he deferred to his wife in other particulars. He took her to the theatre, even when he himself cared little or nothing for the performance; and to concerts, though he had no taste for any but the simplest music. On ladies' night, when his newspaper friend, Daniel O'Connell, or his actor friend, Henry Edwards, presided over the fun, he took her to "high jinks" at the Bohemian Club, of which he was one of the earliest members.

The dream of wealth, indeed, the desire for it, had long since departed. The dream of increasing the world's happiness and of raising the mass of men out of the slough of poverty had taken its place. But the wish to get beyond the anxieties of a hand-to-mouth way of living drew Mr. George into mining investments now and again, when the atmosphere became surcharged with the mining fever. When in 1872 silver bonanza discoveries occurred on the Comstock lode in the Washoe Mountains, Nevada—principally in the Crown Point and Belcher mines—he was drawn into investments during the general excitement, and came out with losses. His wife's letter to him from Philadelphia (May 17, 1872) touching the matter ran:

"I won't blame you. You feel it as much as I do. It was a risk at any rate, and I'm not surprised. You know I'm far off and can look at these matters coolly, while you have all the excitement. Don't gamble in anything else than newspapers. That is the only way you make anything."

But in 1875 he went in again. There was at the time the wildest and most general excitement that San Fran-

cisco had ever seen. It grew out of the discovery in the
up to that time practically unproductive Consolidated Virginia mine on the Comstock lode of a bonanza that it was
said would yield fifteen hundred millions. The mine was
managed, under the firm name of Flood & O'Brien, by
four men—James C. Flood and William S. O'Brien, who
had kept a drinking saloon on Washington Street, San
Francisco, and themselves served customers; and John
W. Mackay and James G. Fair, who were practical miners
on the Comstock, and who, with some real or fancied
knowledge of conditions, drew the other two men with
them into the purchase of the Consolidated Virginia mine.
They paid for it less than $100,000. During the first half
of 1875 the monthly output was more than a million and
a half of silver, and the shares that had been purchased
for less than one tenth of a million rose towards one hundred and fifty millions. Contagion of speculation "bulled"
the whole market of mining stocks, during which, the managers unloaded their shares, reaction set in and the whole
list fell with a rush. Mr. George's investments were in
Ophir and Consolidated Virginia. He reaped a loss, which
cramped his circumstances.

And as his wife was his counsellor in his mining losses,
so was she when the break came on the "Evening Post"
and he went out penniless. He quickly recovered his self-
poise in the latter disaster, so that he could write from
Sacramento shortly afterwards (March 14, 1876):

> "Mills[1] tells me that they are willing to sell the 'Post,'
> lock, stock and barrel, for $35,000 over its receipts.
> Jones, he says, is heartily disgusted, and the chances are
> that he will soon drop the thing. For my part I would
> not touch it, unless it was given to me outright."

---

[1] William H. Mills, of the Sacramento "Record-Union."

Mr. George received strength from his wife when he needed it, and in return supported her when occasion called, for instance writing to her (February 24) touching the condition of her uncle, Matthew McCloskey, who was on his death bed:

> "I am sorry to hear about Matt. I do not think much of the new doctor that will talk that way—that is if he talks so to his patient, as the most potent thing in medicine is hope. But however it may be, you must not suffer it to make you blue. We must all die, and what, after all, signifies a few years more or less. It is not Christian or reasonable to grieve about what God has appointed, nor is it wise to borrow trouble. I wish when you feel so you would go out somewhere."

They read much from general literature together and discussed what they read; and besides this, Mr. George now read some law, which he thought would be useful to him in understanding and discussing public affairs, even though he should never follow law as a profession. A letter dated Marysville, May 26, 1876, while he was on a meter inspecting trip with his brother Vallance touches on this:

> "I have a good square day to loaf in, as Val is at work, and one can get ahead as well as two. Going to bed at nine o'clock, and right off to sleep, six in the morning at this season of the year seems late. After breakfast I went up-stairs and took a tussle with Kent. I was making fine progress till all of a sudden he threw me, and stretching out on the bed, I snoozed for an hour—very pleasant those sleeps are. . . . It is a nice day here—warm, but yet not oppressive. There is nothing particular though to see or to do and I shall put in my time this morning reading and writing. I feel encouraged by my progress in law, and really interested, though it does put me to sleep, and I think I can

in a year make as much progress as ordinary students do in three or four."

There were times when his over-wrought, highly strung nerves brought a flash of irritability; but this was all—a flash—so that there was never anything like a lasting disagreement. The current of devotion ran even stronger and freer now than when, entering manhood, he went courting the girl who had just come from the convent school. And what affection and the marriage tie were to him only his own words can adequately tell—letters written by him from Sacramento to his wife in San Francisco during a few days' separation in the fifteenth year of wedlock.

Sacramento, March 18, 1876.

"I have been sitting in the Senate listening to a debate on the divorce bill—Pierson's bill to limit cause for divorces to adultery. I think the bill is in the right direction. We have found out, as Pierson said, that it was dangerous to talk of divorces in mixed company. He also said that there was one divorce granted in San Francisco for every three marriages, and that divorces were often got in a single day.

"If I ever had any leaning to the modern doctrine in this matter I have entirely got over it. Marriage is not only the foundation of society; it is the divinely appointed state which confers the highest and purest happiness, and I have no doubt that if people knew that they could not separate from each other, the result would be to make them try harder to live comfortably with each other."

Sunday evening, March 27, 1876.

"I have wanted to write to you all day; but I have been moving around, and though I have thought volumes, I did not have a chance to write them.

"I got at noon to-day your letter of last night. Many thanks. I hardly expected it, but thought it would be so nice if I should get a letter, and when I went down to the 'Record-Union' after the train got in, there it was.

"You are a dutiful little woman, my darling. By my own feelings, I know how hard it was for you to have me stay away; but it pleased me to think you approved of it, and it made the separation lighter. I have felt happy all the afternoon. In all the pauses of the talk the face of the woman I love rose up before me. A man is a bundle of inconsistencies. It delights me to think that you are wholly and absolutely *mine*. There is a pride and pleasure in feeling that I am really your 'lord and master'; and yet your approbation, it seems to me, outweighs that of all the world. What a blessed thing it is to be truly married, as we are married—in body and mind and soul. I often thank God for it, and when I hear, as I often do, how married men sin against their vows, I think what poor fools they are, not to realise how much more real pleasure there is in the love of one virtuous woman. If my darling is mine, I also am hers. If I have the right to her, she also has the right to me. All that I can achieve she must share; my full possession of her involves just as complete a possession on her part of me. The old ideas are right and are founded on the depths of human nature. The 'love, cherish and protect' on one side, and the 'love, honour and obey' on the other, are more than any other contract; and when the binding force of the obligation is felt, the touch of the chain, instead of galling, is a pleasure.

"How much fresh delight there is in our love. From the time I first saw you and was captivated by that something in face and voice and manner, which I never could explain in words, it has gone on increasing and increasing. Husband and father, I am still more lover than when I used to stop in my work to take out your picture and steal a glance at it. Satisfaction only crowns desire, and the love of the mature man is not only deeper, but more passionate than that of the boy. And this love is the great thing with me. All outside ups and downs are trivial compared with that."

March 30, 1876.

"Mills was saying the other night that if a man and woman kept up their love, they never grew old to each other, and I told him he was right. You are to me prettier, more loving and more tempting than when you were a little delicate slip of a girl. Do you know that it is a keen delight to me to think how you have improved. I always have felt towards you a good deal as Abelard must have felt towards Héloïse—as though you were my pupil as well as wife."

March 31, 1876.

"Did you ever notice one thing about the higher pleasures—they don't pall, as the grosser ones do. On the contrary, they become more exquisite. The very regularity of the letter gives it new delight. There is such a proud satisfaction in feeling you are not mistaken. I like even that boy[1] to know that 'my girl' thinks so much of me. And then they weave such links between us, and keep us together in spirit, even though we are separated in space. I once read a little story—I don't know where it was—of how a husband was beginning to wander in thought a little from his wife when he was away, and how her letters held him and brought him back to her, more her lover than before. And is there not something in this which goes even beyond the present life? Others may, but it is not for you and me, my darling, to doubt the goodness of God. The more I think of it, the more I feel that our present life will not bound our love."

Upon such a foundation of affection was reared a noble superstructure. One day as his wife sat close beside him in a low chair, the husband while lying on his sofa said: "What do you most admire in a man?"

"Courage," the wife answered.

---

[1] Reference to a hotel boy, who, bringing his letters, would say, " Another letter from your girl, Mr. George "

"Courage," he repeated, jumping up and walking the floor. "I thought you would say virtue."

"No, not virtue, because I have come to perceive that the world sets up separate standards for men and women, and that what would be a breach of virtue in the woman might not be considered as such in the man. I do not say that that is right, but I do recognise that the world so holds it."

"But why courage?" asked the husband.

"Because it is the manly quality."

"But courage might seem to go with physique—and I am a small man. How do you find this courage in me?"

"I do not mean physical courage," replied the wife, "but moral courage; the courage that impels a man who sees his duty to follow it, though it mean to make sacrifices—to stand up against the world."

The husband said that this strengthened as well as gratified him, and that some day he might have to ask her to support him when duty called him to stand up against the world.

CHAPTER VI.

FIRST SET POLITICAL SPEECH.

1876-1877.   AGE, 37-38.

WILLIAM S. IRWIN, Democrat, the new Governor of California, was sworn in at the State Capitol at Sacramento on Jannary 1, 1876, and one of his first acts was to appoint Henry George to what was regarded as among the most lucrative offices within the Executive gift —State Inspector of Gas Meters. He did this partly from a motive of assisting a man who had through the "Evening Post" and the "Morning Ledger" done much to help his election. But E. W. Maslin, who was the Governor's private secretary, says that another motive played an important part in the matter.

"Henry George was recognised as nominally a Democrat, but not a partisan. He had no political backing and was regarded to be without political claims upon the Governor. It was therefore a political surprise when he was appointed Gas-Meter Inspector. The appointment was more than anything else a tribute to intellect.

"I was the Governor's private secretary, and in the leisure hours of the office we were accustomed to discuss books, public men and measures. The Governor was chary of giving praise, yet not once but many times he expressed his strong admiration for Mr. George's intel-

262

lectual ability, and laid peculiar stress upon his logical mind, power of statement and clear and brilliant style. In one of those conversations he declared that George possessed the clearest and finest style of all English writers. I was not surprised that the Governor should speak of the logic and power of statement, for this arose from the character of his own mind. He had little imagination, but he was logical, well read and highly trained. I was not surprised that he should speak of similar qualities in George; but I was astonished that the latter's style should have attracted his attention. I myself had in 1871, when Secretary of the State Board of Equalisation, supplied George with some statistical matter which he used at the time in his pamphlet, 'Our Land and Land Policy,' and I had read a number of things, long and short, from his pen afterwards; but though I recognised his ability, I did not appreciate his mode of expression, as did the Governor. The fact that this cold, unimpassioned man should so often break into praise of George's 'elegant and brilliant style' made a profound impression on me."

Henry George took official charge on Jannary 13 and within a few days began to "test" the registry of meters by forcing a measured quantity of air through them in place of gas, fastening a brass seal on all that met the lawful requirements. A set fee was allowed on every meter so tested and sealed.

The office of inspector of gas meters had been established for the protection of gas consumers and did much to correct impositions. But a loop-hole had been left, perhaps inadvertently, by which the law did not reach some of the towns scattered over the State, where large numbers of meters, purchased from or through the San Francisco Gas Company or its officials, had without being inspected and sealed been put into use. George, or rather his friends who were most zealous for his interests, had an amendment introduced into the legislature which should compel companies to submit for inspection all unsealed meters in use or intended for immediate use. The gas companies, and particularly the San Francisco company through its president, raised hot opposition. After cutting off some features to which the companies particularly objected, the measure went through and the inspector during the next few months went to the chief cities throughout the State and demanded that all unsealed meters be brought to him to be tested, his brother, John V. George, going with him to assist in the work. Though at first by virtue of this amendment of the inspection law, Mr. George obtained what seemed to him like large sums of money from places like Marysville and Grass Valley where numbers of untested meters were in use, the office of inspector yielded only an intermittent revenue and on the whole only enough to live on comfortably and without extravagance. Mr. George for a while entertained the expectation of going East in the summer to visit the old folks and to see the international exposition then to be opened with great ceremony at Philadelphia in commemoration of the hundredth celebration of the nation's independence. This had to be given up, as for the time the receipts from the office fell off.

"Though my official duties were light," said Mr. George when reviewing this period,[1] "I never ate the bread of idleness, but was always very hard at work." Among the matters engaging him were a number of measures before the State legislature and chief of these were two bills introduced by William M. Pierson in the Senate, both relating to the publication of newspapers, one to compel the retraction of false or defamatory articles and the other

---

[1] Meeker notes.

requiring the signature of all original articles or corre-spondence.   Mr. George was particularly interested in the latter and wrote in support of it two bright, vivacious, signed articles for the "Sacramento Bee," which were afterwards printed in pamphlet form.   His contention was that the march of concentration was putting newspapers more and more into the hands of massed capital, making newspaper workers more and more dependent upon special interests and utterly helpless to get outside recognition so long as they should work anonymously.

"The effect of the present anonymous system is to make the newspaper everything, the writer nothing. The tendency of the personal system would be to transfer importance and power from the newspaper to the writers—to diffuse instead of to concentrate; to make the men who see for the people and think for the people independent of capital, instead of dependent on capital; and to facilitate the establishment of new papers whenever the old ones abandoned the popular cause."

He got some personal satisfaction from this article, for he wrote to his wife (March 14) : "I spent a good part of the afternoon listening to the debate in the Senate upon the signature bill.   Uncle Phil [Philip A. Roach. one of the editors and part proprietor of the "San Francisco Examiner"] threw himself in opposition, though he made a very handsome allusion to me, as all the principal speakers have done."   Both the signature and the retraction bill, while they passed the Senate, had the powerful opposition of the San Francisco papers and were killed in the House.

As helping to make his ideas known, the articles in support of the signature bill were probably worth the effort he made, but a few months later there was an occurrence of much greater importance to Mr. George personally—the first set speech. At various times, beginning as far back as 1865 when a member of the Sacramento Lyceum, he had got upon his feet for a few impromptu remarks. Now came a chance for a formal effort. The Presidential campaign was opening, with Governor Rutherford B. Hayes of Ohio, candidate of the Republican party, and Governor Samuel J. Tilden of New York, for the Democratic. Mr. George entered on the campaign with lively feelings, for Hayes, he considered, represented the reactionary policy of his party, while Tilden, he believed, was a free trader, and while demanding the remission of war-tax burdens, would take the side of the industrial masses, just now idle in thousands all over the country.

Animated by something akin to the admiration Governor Irwin had for George's abilities, a number of energetic young men of radical opinion in San Francisco, enrolled in what was known as the "Tilden and Hendricks Central Club," asked Mr. George to speak under its auspices, hoping, as one of them, Walter Gallagher, said, "to make this speech the keynote of the canvass in California." George was thereupon formally invited. He spoke before a big meeting in Dashaway Hall on the evening of August 15, on "The Question Before the People." He stood beside the reading desk on which he had his manuscript spread out, read by glances and spoke slowly and distinctly. He avoided the usual political declamation and struck a high tone at once.

> "Remember this, the political contest is lifted above the low plane of denunciation and demagogism, and becomes not a contest for spoils in which the people are simply permitted to choose which gang shall plunder them; but a solemn, momentous inquiry, demanding from each voter a conscientious judgment."

The kernel of the speech was this:

"The Federal tax-gatherer is everywhere. In each exchange by which labour is converted into commodities, there he is standing between buyer and seller to take his to'l. Whether it be a match or a locomotive, a dish-cloth or a dress, a new book or a glass of beer, the tax-gatherer steps in. He says to Labour as the day's toil begins: 'Ah! you want to do a little work for yourself and family. Well, first work an hour to pay the interest on the national debt and defray the necessary expenses of government; and then another hour for the national banks and subsidised corporations, and the expenses of governing the Southern States! Then an hour for the army and navy and the contractors thereof; then an hour for the manufacturers of New England, and an hour for the iron millionaires of Pennsylvania; half an hour for the Marine Corps and the various comfortable little bureaus; and then, after you have done a little work for your State Government, and a little work for your county and municipal government, and a little work for your landlord—then you can have the rest of the day to work for yourself and family.' . . .

"Fellow-citizens, negro slavery is dead! But cast your eyes over the North to-day and see a worse than negro slavery taking root under the pressure of the policy you are asked as Republicans to support by your votes. See seventy thousand men out of work in the Pennsylvania coal-fields; fifty thousand labourers asking for bread in the city of New York; the almshouses of Massachusetts crowded to repletion in the summertime; unemployed men roving over the West in great bands, stealing what they cannot earn. . . . It is an ominous thing that in this Centennial year, States that a century ago were covered by the primeval forest should be holding conventions to consider the 'tramp nuisance'—the sure symptom of that leprosy of nations, chronic pauperism. . . .

"Be not deceived! You might as well charge the bullet or the knife with being the cause of the death

of a murdered man as to think that all the things of
which you complain result from the accident of having
had bad men in office. What can any change of men
avail so long as the policy which is the primary cause
of these evils is unchanged?"

Ex-District Attorney Thomas P. Ryan was president of
the club. He presided at this meeting and says of the
speaker and the speech:

"At that time he looked to me to be about thirty
years of age. He impressed me then, as he always did,
as being a man of naturally nervous temperament, but
one who had so schooled himself as to give no expression
as a rule to that fact by his manner. In repose his
habit was calm, almost placid, and age sits lightly upon
those so blessed. In action there was no want of fire,
and when the situation required, it was fittingly displayed. If we rate his speech that night by the standard of eloquence of the great French orator, Bishop
Dupanloup—a thorough knowledge of one's subject—
he was indeed eloquent. That the address was extraordinarily able and convincing was the universal opinion
of those who heard it. The impression it left on me is
lasting and the best evidence of its force and effect is
to be found in the fact that at this late day I am, almost
without effort, able to recall in the main most of the
facts then presented and the circumstances surround-
ing the speech's delivery.

"At its conclusion, Mr. James G. Maguire, since so
devoted a disciple of Henry George, and distinguished
as an upright judge and Member of Congress, arose
and said that it was the ablest political address to which
he had ever listened, and moved that it be printed for
distribution as a campaign document, which was done.

"The audience was a large and most appreciative one,
Governor Irwin, among other distinguished men, being
present.

"Touching this speech, and indeed, of everything else
Henry George said and wrote subsequently, I have car-

ried in my mind the thought so happily expressed by Mommsen in speaking of Renan: 'He is a savant in spite of his fine style.' "

This Dashaway Hall speech was carefully prepared. Mr. Gallagher tells of an unprepared one that Henry George made very soon afterwards.

"Some days after the Dashaway Hall meeting Mr. George was present at a very large and enthusiastic meeting at the Mission in Humboldt Hall. I was expected to speak at that meeting and did not expect to see Henry George there. Cameron H. King, I think, presided. Mr. George, who was familiar to a large number in the audience, was vociferously called for. He was very backward about responding and hesitated quite a while before he was finally persuaded to go upon the rostrum. I think I can picture him now in my mind's eye as he appeared on that night. He was sitting close up to the front where he could easily see and hear all that was going on. He held a little old soft felt hat crumpled up tightly in his hand. When he finally made up his mind to respond to the cheers and calls he went with a rush. It seemed to me that he ran to the rostrum and immediately in a loud, full voice, at a very high pitch, entered into a discussion of the issues before the people—all the time holding his hat in his hand. The audience expected a different kind of speech from him than from the rest of us. The audience was not disappointed, for what he said was full of thought and force. But I remember that his elocution was not of the best. He was earnest and sincere, but his manner and gesticulation were not to be commended as accompaniments of oratory. He did not have the proper control of his voice, and there appeared to be in his manner an absolute disregard for those little arts of the orator which have so much effect upon a crowd."

But it was the speech on "The Question Before the People" that attracted chief attention and the Democratic

State Committee invited him to "stump" the State and deliver it in the principal cities and towns. From no speaking reputation whatever, he sprang through this one address to the place of a leading speaker in California, and was given the honour of making the final speech of the campaign in Platt's Hall, San Francisco. Dr. Shorb was chairman and knew George well, but amused himself by introducing him as "Colonel Henry D. George." Mr. George, somewhat disconcerted, protested that he had neither a title nor a middle initial, whereupon somebody in the audience shouted: "Oh, go ahead, Harry. We all know who you are."

So the campaign passed; election day came and went, and the decision was not yet clear when Mr. George wrote to his mother (November 13) touching his personal interests:

"Well, the campaign is over, though its result is as yet unsettled. I cannot say that I am glad that it is over, for although I think Tilden is President, the way this coast went is a great disappointment to me; but at any rate I shall now have a resting spell—a longer one and a better one than I have had before.

"I did my best, for my heart was in it, and that is a consolation. And personally what I accomplished was very gratifying. I have shown that I could make myself felt without a newspaper, and shown that I possessed other ability than that of the pen. I have always felt that I possessed the requisites for a first-class speaker, and that I would make one if I could get the practice; and I started into this campaign with the deliberate purpose of breaking myself in. It was like jumping overboard to learn to swim. But I succeeded. I think no man in the State made as much reputation as I have made. From not being known as a speaker I have come to the front. I wanted to do this, not as a matter of vanity or for the mere pleasure of the thing; but to increase my power and usefulness. Already well known as a writer, I knew that this kind of a reputation would aid me immensely in the future. And so it will—whether I go into politics, into the law or into the newspaper business again. I do not intend to rest here; but to go ahead step by step.

"You need not be afraid of politics doing me harm. I do not propose to mix in lower politics, nor do I propose to chase after nominations. I shall wait till they seek me. I propose to read and study, to write some things which will extend my reputation and perhaps to deliver some lectures with the same view. And if I live I shall make myself known even in Philadelphia. I aim high.

"So far as my personal interests are concerned, defeat is as good to me as a sweeping·victory—in fact, I think better, as a man of my kind has a chance of coming forward more rapidly in a minority than in a majority party. However, about all such things, I am disposed to think that whatever happens is for the best. Talent and energy can nearly always convert defeats into victories. I could easily have started a paper during the campaign, and could, I think, readily do so now. But I don't feel like going back into newspaper harness. The best thing for me, I think, is to keep out of newspapers for a while."

Thus he wrote of himself. What he meant by wanting to be a speaker "not as a matter of vanity or for the mere pleasure of the thing," but to increase his "power and usefulness," he could not bring himself to tell any one as yet. He must wait for time to show even his mother the exalted purpose he had in his heart of hearts.

When he wrote to his mother, Mr. George believed that Tilden had been elected President. It was conceded that the Democratic candidate had received the largest popular vote, and that from the States where the returns were undisputed he had received one hundred and eighty four electoral votes, so that he lacked just one vote of the number required to elect, while Hayes lacked twenty. The difficulty lay with the returns of Oregon and three Southern States—Louisiana, South Carolina and Florida—which were contested. This condition of things, involving such great consequences, could not fail to stir to the depths an active participant in public affairs like Henry George. As weeks passed without a settlement and the time fixed by the constitution for the inauguration of the new President approached, he became so aroused that in January he wrote a long presentation of the matter and put it in the form of an eight paged pamphlet entitled, "Who shall be President?—A Survey of the Political Situation," saying that the fact that who should be President should be treated as an open question was "both scandalous and dangerous"—scandalous because the uncertainty imimplied "a doubt of the efficacy of law"; and dangerous "because when law fails, force is the necessary resort." He made a careful analysis of the matter to show why he believed Tilden was entitled to the office, giving his explanation of the persistent contention by the Hayes partisans that "a coup d'état was contemplated."

It was Mr. George's intention to send this paper East, where he thought it would get consideration; but before he could carry out his plan news came that Tilden had given his consent to remand the question of returns to the decision of an electoral commission—a tribunal specially created by Congress. This commission, composed of eight Republicans and seven Democrats, by a party vote decided in favour of the Republican electors in every case, thus awarding 185 electoral votes to Hayes and 184 to Tilden, and placing Hayes in the Presidential chair.

Nine years after this, in the pages of his "Protection or

Free Trade," Henry George gave expression to a great change of feeling towards Mr. Tilden.[1]

"A wealthy citizen whom I once supported, and called on others to support, for the Presidential chair, under the impression that he was a Democrat of the school of Jefferson, has recently published a letter advising us to steel plate our coasts, lest foreign navies come over and bombard us. This counsel of timidity has for its hardly disguised object the inducing of such an enormous expenditure of public money as will prevent any demand for the reduction of taxation, and thus secure to the tariff rings a longer lease of plunder. It well illustrates the essential meanness of the protectionist spirit —a spirit that no more comprehends the true dignity of the American Republic and the grandeur of her possibilities than it cares for the material interests of the great masses of her citizens—'the poor people who have to work.' "

---

[1] Chap. XXX, (Memorial Edition, p. 327).

LECTURE AT THE UNIVERSITY OF CALIFORNIA.

1877.   AGE, 38.

AS by distinct stages, Henry George's mind showed development. In the first half of 1877 came the last two stages before it was to break into full flower. The first of these took the form of a lecture on political economy before the University of California; the second, of an oration on the Fourth of July.

Scarcely had the Presidential question ceased to absorb him when he was invited to deliver several lectures before the students and faculty of the University of California which now had been established permanently at Berkeley, adjacent to Oakland. He was to be one of a number of prominent men to give a course of addresses on various topics, and the first subject that it was agreed he should treat was "The Study of Political Economy."

There was no separate chair of political economy in the University and now came talk of establishing one, with George to fill it. His Chinese article; his pamphlet, "Our Land and Land Policy"; and many of his "Evening Post" editorials marked him as qualified to hold such a position. It was thought that the lectures he was about to deliver would make the ground of his appointment.

Touching this he never afterwards had much to say, in the family observing that there had been talk of a chair and of him to fill it. He never mentioned who of his friends were interested in the project. At the time, possibly from his old habit of secretiveness, but more probably from a feeling of modesty until the project should take definite form, he said nothing about the matter to his wife, except indirectly remarking that there was no title in the world he cared to have save that of "Professor."

At any rate, on March 9, accompanied by his friend, Assemblyman James V. Coffey, he lunched with Professor John Le Conte, the President of the University, after which the three men proceeded to the hall where the students and most of the faculty were gathered. The lecturer read from his manuscript and occupied about three quarters of an hour—probably three quarters of an hour of astonishment for regents and faculty.

He said that as his lecture was to be more suggestive than didactic, he would not attempt to outline the laws of political economy, nor even, where his own views were strong and definite, to touch upon unsettled questions. He wished to show the simplicity and certainty of a science too generally regarded as complex and indeterminate; to point out the ease with which it may be studied, and to suggest reasons which make that study worthy of attention.

"The science which investigates the laws of the production and distribution of wealth concerns itself with matters which among us occupy more than nine tenths of human effort, and perhaps nine tenths of human thought. In its province are included all that relates to the wages of labour and the earnings of capital; all regulations of trade; all questions of currency and finance; all taxes and public disbursements—in short, everything that can in any way affect the amount of wealth which a community can secure, or the proportion in which that wealth will be distributed between individuals. Though not the science of government, it is essential to the science of government. Though it takes direct cognisance only of what are termed the selfish instincts, yet in doing so it includes the basis of all higher qualities."

A hundred years had elapsed, the lecturer said, since Adam Smith published his "Wealth of Nations," yet political economy had made little progress. This he thought "referable partly to the nature of the science itself and partly to the manner in which it has been cultivated."

"In the first place, the very importance of the subjects with which political economy deals raises obstacles in its way. The discoveries of other sciences may challenge pernicious ideas, but the conclusions of political economy involve pecuniary interests, and thus thrill directly the sensitive pocket-nerve. For, as no social adjustment can exist without interesting a larger or smaller class in its maintenance, political economy at every point is apt to come in contact with some interest or other which regards it as the silversmiths of Ephesus did those who taught the uselessness of presenting shrines to Diana. . . . What, then, must be the opposition which inevitably meets a science that deals with tariffs and subsidies, with banking interests and bonded debts, with trades-unions and combinations of capital, with taxes and licenses and land tenures! It is not ignorance alone that offers opposition, but ignorance backed by interest, and made fierce by passions.

"Now, while the interests thus aroused furnish the incentive, the complexity of the phenomena with which political economy deals makes it comparatively easy to palm off on the unreasoning all sorts of absurdities as political economy. . . . But what is far worse than any amount of pretentious quackery is, that the science even as taught by the masters *is* in large measure disjointed and indeterminate. As laid down in the best text-books, political economy is like a shapely statue but half hewn from the rock—like a landscape, part of which stands out clear and distinct, but over the rest of which the mists still roll. . . . Strength and subtilty have been wasted in intellectual hair splitting and super-refinements, in verbal discussions and disputes, while the great high-roads have remained unexplored. And thus has been given to a simple and attractive science an air of repellent abstruseness and uncertainty."

And from the same fundamental cause had arisen an idea of political economy which had arrayed against it the feelings and prejudices of those who had most to gain by its cultivation.

"The name of political economy has been constantly invoked against every effort of the working classes to increase their wages or decrease their hours of labour. . . . Take the best and most extensively circulated text-books. While they insist upon freedom for capital, while they justify on the ground of utility the selfish greed that seeks to pile fortune on fortune, and the niggard spirit that steels the heart to the wail of distress, what sign of substantial promise do they hold out to the working man save that he should refrain from rearing children?

"What can we expect when hands that should offer bread thus hold out a stone? Is it in human nature that the masses of men, vaguely but keenly conscious of the injustice of existing social conditions, feeling that they are somehow cramped and hurt, without knowing what cramps and hurts them, should welcome truth in this partial form; that they should take to a science which, as it is presented to them, seems but to justify injustice, to canonise selfishness by throwing around it the halo of utility, and to present Herod rather than Vincent de Paul as the typical benefactor of humanity? Is it to be wondered at that they should turn in their

ignorance to the absurdities of protection and the crazy
theories generally designated by the name of socialism?"

What he wished to impress upon his hearers was the
"real simplicity of what is generally deemed an abstruse
science, and the exceeding ease with which it may be pursued."

"For the study of political economy you need no special knowledge, no extensive library, no costly labora-
tory. You do not even need text-books nor teachers, if
you will but think for yourselves. All that you need is
care in reducing complex phenomena to their elements,
in distinguishing the essential from the accidental, and
in applying the simple laws of human action with which
you are familiar. Take nobody's opinion for granted;
'try all things: hold fast that which is good.' In this
way, the opinions of others will help you by their suggestions, elucidations and corrections; otherwise they
will be to you but as words to a parrot. . . . All
this array of professors, all this paraphernalia of learning, cannot educate a man. They can but help him to
educate himself. Here you may obtain the tools; but
they will be useful only to him who can use them. A
monkey with a microscope, a mule packing a library,
are fit emblems of the men—and unfortunately, they
are plenty—who pass through the whole educational
machinery, and come out but learned fools, crammed
with knowledge which they cannot use—all the more
pitiable, all the more contemptible, all the more in the
way of real progress, because they pass, with themselves
and others, as educated men."

And then addressing himself directly to the students,
he said:

"I trust you have felt the promptings of that highest
of ambitions—the desire to be useful in your day and
generation; the hope that in something, even though

little, those that come after may be wiser, better, happier that you have lived. Or, if you have never felt this, I trust the feeling is only latent, ready to spring forth when you see the need.

"Gentlemen, if you but look you will see the need! You are of the favoured few, for the fact that you are here, students in a university of this character, bespeaks for you the happy accidents that fall only to the lot of the few, and you cannot yet realise, as you may by and by realise, how the hard struggle which is the lot of so many may cramp and bind and distort—how it may dull the noblest faculties and chill the warmest impulses, and grind out of men the joy and poetry of life; how it may turn into the lepers of society those who should be its adornment, and transmute, into vermin to prey upon it and into wild beasts to fly at its throat, the brain and muscle that should go to its enrichment! These things may never yet have forced themselves on your attention; but still, if you will think of it, you cannot fail to see enough want and wretchedness, even in our own country to-day, to move you to sadness and pity, to nerve you to high resolve; to arouse in you the sympathy that dares, and the indignation that burns to overthrow a wrong. . . .

"Political economy alone can give the answer. And if you trace out, in the way I have tried to outline, the laws of the production and exchange of wealth, you will see the causes of social weakness and disease in enactments which selfishness has imposed on ignorance, and in maladjustments entirely within our own control. . . .

"You will see that the true law of social life is the law of love, the law of liberty, the law of each for all and all for each; that the golden rule of morals is also the golden rule of the science of wealth; that the highest expressions of religious truth include the widest generalisations of political economy."

So much for the nature of the address. The lecturer read his audience correctly, for when he went home he

told his wife that his utterances had been well received
by the students, but by the authorities with a polite and
dignified quietness that made him think that he might not
be invited to lecture again.

What wonder! Was this a sample of what the man
was to preach? Perhaps much of what he said was as
plain and fair as common sense; but did he propose to go
wide of the beaten path—to set up a new scheme of
things? Were the faculty and regents to be committed to
new principles—principles that they had not yet even
considered; that wrenched at old things, that jarred to
their centre institutions which, right or wrong, had come
down through the generations? Was this Inspector of
Gas Meters, this warring newspaper editor, this political
speech-maker, who had never given an hour's study inside
a university to continue to proclaim among them that
"all this array of professors, all this paraphernalia of
learning, cannot educate a man," and prate of "a monkey
with a microscope" and "a mule packing a library" as
emblems of men "passing through the educational machinery"? And then were they—the professors and the
regents—to find themselves *willy-nilly* bumping against
new problems at every turn? Starting in this way, where
was the thing to stop?

This fear of heresy and revolutionary utterance seemed
to govern some. Others had a more material reason for
opposing the San Francisco man. Through a charge by
George in the columns of the "Evening Post" in 1874 of
peculation in connection with the building of North Hall
or the College of Letters, and a legislative investigation
that followed, the Chairman of the Building Committee
of the Board of Regents, was requested by the Governor
of California to resign, which he did. But he left behind
him for the "Post's" editor the resentment of his friends

and of those on or connected with the Board whose lax attention to duty had permitted the scandal to occur.

Thus for perhaps personal and impersonal reasons Mr. George was quietly forgotten. Nothing was said about a chair by those who had the power to confer it. He was not even invited to speak again, although brief notes in his diary lead to the inference that he had commenced work on a second lecture. Yet whatever disappointment arose from this could not have been lasting, as there was uninterrupted interchange of social visits with Professor John Le Conte and his brother, Professor Joseph Le Conte, the physicist, and with other friends at Berkeley.[1] And his high regard for universities as institutions of progressive thought could not have been much, if any, diminished by this incident. Indeed, two years later, when about to launch "Progress and Poverty," it was his expectation that at least some of the professed teachers of political economy would take up the truths he endeavoured to make clear and "fit them in with what of truth was already understood and thought." It was not until subsequently that a change came "o'er the spirit of his dream."

---

[1] His friend Prof. William Swinton had resigned three years before, and going to New York, had entered upon a remarkably successful career of text-book writing.

CHAPTER VIII.

A FOURTH OF JULY ORATION.

1877.   AGE, 38.

NOW came the last stage before the writing of "Progress and Poverty."

The oration on the Fourth of July, 1877, like the lecture before the University of California, showed the broad sweep that Mr. George's mind was taking. "Our Land and Land Policy" regarded politico-economical conditions primarily from the standpoint of the Californian; his mind now enveloped the world. Not the progress of California, but human progress, was what engaged him; not particulars, but generals; not a question of policy, but the enunciation of the eternal law of "each for all and all for each."

And as the lecture was the exordium, the Fourth of July speech became the peroration. One pointed to the simplicity of the natural order, the other to the necessity of following it. One turned to the fundamentals of the science relating to the social conditions under which civilised men should get their daily bread; the other sounded the war clarions and gave the battle cry of "liberty and equality." One came from the solitary—the man of the closet; the other from the man of the practical world of struggle and conflict. Each was the complement of the

other—the two primary elements in "Progress and Poverty"—the reflections of the thinker who hands down the
law; the call of the leader who marshals the hosts.

A season of depression having set in, and the income
of the Inspector of Gas Meters having diminished very
considerably, husband and wife decided to reduce domestic
expenses. They gave up the San Francisco house, and
storing part of the furniture, moved the remainder to
Saucelito, a pretty little village on the north side of the
bay. There they took a six-roomed cottage, where they
lived comfortably during the summer months, the wife
doing the domestic work herself. During these Saucelito days Mr. George did a good deal of reading and thinking. He also spent much time with his wife, frequently
taking little walks or rides; and with his children, taking them swimming or sailing, or helping to make or
float toy boats. Moreover, there was the frequent interruption of friends from San Francisco. But the matter
of chief importance was the Fourth of July speech.

It was the custom for the city of San Francisco to have
a military parade and civic exercises in celebration of
the nation's birthday, and towards the middle of June
Henry George was notified that he had been chosen to be
"the Orator of the Day" for that year. He had been expecting this; had, in fact, begun work on his oration—
"The American Republic."

The afternoon of the Fourth was sultry, but the old
California Theatre where the exercises were held was
crowded. First came the reading of the Declaration of
Independence and the poem of the day, and then the oration. There had been a miscalculation as to length, and
the speech was long for the exercises. Nevertheless the
effort—the greatest that Henry George had yet made—was
well sustained.

It did not take him long to come to the consuming thought that would not give him rest.

"We are yet laying the foundations of empire, while stronger run the currents of change and mightier are the forces that marshal and meet. . . . For let us not disguise it—republican government is yet but an experiment. That it has worked well so far, determines nothing. That republican institutions would work well under the social conditions of the youth of the Republic —cheap land, high wages and little distinction between rich and poor—there was never any doubt, for they were working well before. . . . The doubt about republican institutions is as to whether they will work when population becomes dense, wages low, and a great gulf separates rich and poor. Can we speak of it as a doubt? Nothing in political philosophy can be clearer than that under such conditions republican government must break down. . . .

"Six hundred liveried retainers followed the great Earl of Warwick to Parliament; but in this young State there is already a simple citizen[1] who could discharge any one of thousands of men from their employment, who controls 2,200 miles of railroad and telegraph, and millions of acres of land; and has the power of levying toll on traffic and travel over an area twice that of the original thirteen States. Warwick was a king-maker. Would it add to the real power of our simple citizen were we to dub him an earl? . . .

"Here is the test: whatever conduces to the equal and inalienable rights of men is good—let us preserve it. Whatever denies or interferes with those equal rights is bad—let us sweep it away. . . .

"Wealth in itself is a good, not an evil; but wealth concentrated in the hands of a few, corrupts on one side, and degrades on the other. No chain is stronger than its weakest link, and the ultimate condition of any people must be the condition of its lowest class. If the

---

[1] Leland Stanford.

low are not brought up, the high must be brought down.
In the long run, no nation can be freer than its most
oppressed, richer than its poorest, wiser than its most
ignorant.   This is the fiat of the eternal justice that
rules the world.   It stands forth on every page of history.   It is what the Sphinx says to us as she sitteth
in desert sand, while the winged bulls of Nineveh bear
her witness!"

The oration closed with a majestic apostrophe to Liberty, that became the key-note, indeed, with but few
changes, the very language of "Progress and Poverty."[1]

"They who look upon Liberty as having accomplished
her mission, when she has abolished hereditary privileges and given men the ballot, who think of her as having no further relations to the every-day affairs of life,
have not seen her real grandeur—to them the poets who
have sung of her must seem rhapsodists, and her martyrs fools!   As the sun is the lord of life, as well as
of light; as his beams not merely pierce the clouds, but
support all growth, supply all motion, and call forth
from what would otherwise be a cold and inert mass,
all the infinite diversities of being and beauty, so is
Liberty to mankind.   It is not for an abstraction that
men have toiled and died; that in every age the witnesses of Liberty have stood forth, and the martyrs of
Liberty have suffered.   It was for more than this that
matrons handed the Queen Anne musket from its rest,
and that maids bid their lovers go to death!
"We speak of Liberty as one thing, and of virtue,
wealth, knowledge, invention, national strength and national independence as other things.   But, of all these,
Liberty is the source, the mother, the necessary condition.   She is to virtue what light is to colour, to wealth
what sunshine is to grain; to knowledge what eyes are
to the sight.   She is the genius of invention, the brawn

---

[1] "Progress and Poverty," Book X, Chap. v
(Memorial Edition, pp. 543-545).

of national strength, the spirit of national independence! Where Liberty rises, there virtue grows, wealth increases, knowledge expands, invention multiplies human powers, and in strength and spirit the freer nation rises among her neighbours as Saul amid his brethren—taller and fairer. Where Liberty sinks, there virtue fades, wealth diminishes, knowledge is forgotten, invention ceases, and empires once mighty in arms and arts become a helpless prey to freer barbarians!

"Only in broken gleams and partial light has the sun of Liberty yet beamed among men, yet all progress hath she called forth.

"Liberty came to a race of slaves crouching under Egyptian whips, and led them forth from the House of Bondage. She hardened them in the desert and made of them a race of conquerors. The free spirit of the Mosaic law took their thinkers up to heights where they beheld the unity of God, and inspired their poets with strains that yet phrase the highest exaltations of thought. Liberty dawned on the Phœnician Coast, and ships passed the Pillars of Hercules to plough the unknown sea. She broke in partial light on Greece, and marble grew to shapes of ideal beauty, words became the instruments of subtlest thought, and against the scanty militia of free cities the countless hosts of the Great King broke like surges against a rock. She cast her beams on the four-acre farms of Italian husbandmen, and born of her strength a power came forth that conquered the world! She glinted from shields of German warriors, and Augustus wept his legions. Out of the night that followed her eclipse, her slanting rays fell again on free cities, and a lost learning revived, modern civilisation began, a new world was unveiled; and as Liberty grew so grew art, wealth, power, knowledge and refinement. In the history of every nation we may read the same truth. It was the strength born of Magna Charta that won Crecy and Agincourt. It was the revival of Liberty from the despotism of the Tudors that glorified the Elizabethan age. It was the spirit that brought a crowned tyrant to the block that planted here

the seed of a mighty tree. It was the energy of
ancient freedom that, the moment it had gained unity,
made Spain the mightiest power of the world, only to
fall to the lowest depth of weakness when tyranny succeeded Liberty. See, in France, all intellectual vigour
dying under the tyranny of the seventeenth century
to revive in splendour as Liberty awoke in the eighteenth, and on the enfranchisement of the French
peasants in the Great Revolution, basing the wonderful strength that has in our time laughed at disaster. . . .

"Who is Liberty that we should doubt her; that we
should set bounds to her, and say, 'Thus far shall thou
come and no further!' Is she not peace? is she not
prosperity? is she not progress? nay, is she not the goal
towards which all progress strives?

"Not here; but yet she cometh! Saints have seen
her in their visions; seers have seen her in their trance.
To heroes has she spoken, and their hearts were strong;
to martyrs, and the flames were cool!

"She is not here, but yet she cometh. Lo! her feet
are on the mountains—the call of her clarion rings on
every breeze; the banners of her dawning fret the sky!
Who will hear her as she calleth; who will bid her come
and welcome? Who will turn to her? who will speak for
her? who will stand for her while she yet hath need?"

Who would stand for liberty, indeed! *his* kind of Liberty? There was general wonderment at the orator's fine
imagery and eloquent periods, but who comprehended his
philosophy? The stage was crowded with men distinguished in the city and the State. Some of these were
conspicuous representatives of the institutions which Mr.
George more than vaguely threatened, though they made
no sign. The great audience applauded the flowing and
lofty language, but who save the personal friends scattered about understood that the speaker was striking at
the castle of vested rights—private property in land? As

for the press, its attitude was not very encouraging, the friendliest paper, the "Examiner," saying faintly that "the oration was good throughout and full of food for thought," while the most hostile, the "News Letter," observed that the "gas measurer . . . kindly spoke for several hours on the Goddess of Liberty and other school-reader topics." Privately the newspaper men expressed surprise that "Harry George" could write so well.

Shortly following this event the family moved back to San Francisco, taking a house on Second Street, Rincon Hill, just around the corner from the former Harrison Street residence. The new house was dusty in the dry season from the heavy travel through the street to and from the wharves, but it was comfortable withal, and the rent low—an important consideration in that period of general depression.

Mr. George was in the troubles of moving when suddenly he found himself pitchforked into politics. In his diary he noted on August 20, "Found I had been nominated for the State Senate at Charter Oak Hall," an independent political organisation. Five days later the diary showed that he was "nominated last night by Anti-Coolies," a workingmen's anti-Chinese movement. But he was not to be drawn from his seclusion just then, and on Sunday, August 26, he made this entry: "John M. Days at house in morning. Went to office and wrote declination to Anti-Coolies. Home and wrote declination to Charter Oak, and sent it to Days by Harry."

And so for the first time in a number of years, Henry George was a spectator of political affairs, and there is little to note up to election day early in September other than that he stayed at home and read, among the books being German history, Code of Civil Procedure and Knight's "History of England."

CHAPTER IX.

"PROGRESS AND POVERTY" BEGUN.

1877-1878.   AGE, 38-39.

UNDER date of September 18, 1877, the pocket diary bears the simple entry: "Commenced 'Progress and Poverty.' "[1]

Another child was expected soon to be added to the family circle. In the period preceding and following its advent the husband was tenderly attentive. He spent his time chiefly with his wife, for a whole month not leaving the house more than half an hour each day. He conversed on all manner of cheering subjects and read much aloud— newspapers in the mornings, and magazines or books later. George Eliot's "Daniel Deronda" had just reached the Pacific Coast. Mr. George was not much of a novel reader, yet he read this to his wife, and afterwards "Middlemarch," which he liked better. He regarded George Eliot as a woman of great powers.

---

[1] Although the work was begun on Sept. 18, the diary entry was not made until later, as the title, "Progress and Poverty," selected from among several, as one of his note books shows, was not decided upon until the writing had begun to take form. In a speech in 1893 (on "the Single Tax," Art Institute, Chicago, Aug. 29) Mr. George said: "I remember how much the name of 'Progress and Poverty' bothered me when it first suggested itself to my mind, for when I talked to my friends about it some thought it was too alliterative, while others thought that with what followed, it was too much like Benjamin Franklin's sign."

But in the parts of the day when he was by himself in his workroom, and he had taken his favourite thinking position—stretched out on his lounge, smoking—his mind reverted to the old problem that "appalled and tormented" and would not let him rest. The whole country was suffering an industrial depression. In many of the larger centres were social disorders. Great railroad strikes occurred in the East, and in six States troops were under arms. A riot broke out in Baltimore, and in Chicago artillery was used; while at Pittsburg more than two hundred lives were lost and wealth aggregating $12,000,000 destroyed.

In California the depression was deepened by a drought during the preceding winter months and by a heavy decline in the output of the silver mines on the Comstock Lode, which brought down all the stocks on the California exchanges and for the time stopped the speculation of the outside world through this market. At this period when workmen all over the State were idle, the Central Pacific Railroad, controlling practically every mile of track in the State, proposed to reduce wages. In San Francisco workmen held mass meetings, to denounce on the one side the great monopolies, and particularly the railroad, as oppressing the masses of labouring men; and on the other, Chinese immigration, as subjecting them to starvation competition. But there was no disorder. The railroad magnates—Stanford, Crocker, Huntington and Hopkins—were by name stigmatised, and in some few instances Chinese laundries were stoned by boys. But there was no head or form to the discontent until timid Privilege, under pretext of restraining anarchy, organised under the leadership of William T. Coleman five thousand men in what was called a Committee of Public Safety, armed them with pick handles; obtained a reserve of 1,700 rifles and

500 carbines from the United States War Department, and supported them with United States vessels, which were sent down to the metropolis from the Navy Yard at Mare Island with Gatling guns and other arms.

The uprising among the society savers tended to bring to a head discontent among the disorganised working classes. All that was needed was a voice to ring out, and the voice that came—in clear, though harsh tones—was that of a drayman named Dennis Kearney, an uncouth, illiterate young man who had a facility for rough, profane speech. He had denounced working men and had carried a club in the Committee of Public Safety, but now jumping to the other side, he arraigned the aristocrats and monopolists, and Chinese immigration, and in the tide of passion that was flowing expressed for the moment the strong feeling of his hearers. The hungry and discontented flocked to his standard and in August of 1877 he organised the "Working men's Party of California," which, strengthening in organisation and numbers, by the commencement of 1878 threw general politics into chaos. The social discontent had changed into a political upheaval.

It was amid these circumstances inspiring serious thought that Henry George sat down on the 18th of September, 1877, to commence what resulted in a momentous work. The question that engaged his mind was the phenomena of industrial depressions. One had thrown him out of employment when a boy in Philadelphia in 1858 and sent him forth to seek his fortune in the new country. Others had overtaken him while he was a struggling young man. Now came a greater than all the others; manifesting itself all over the United States in discontent, turmoil and suffering.

Mr. George's purpose was to write a magazine article on the subject of progress and poverty. It was to be, more than anything else, an inquiry into the cause of industrial depressions and of increase of want with increase of wealth, and was to indicate a remedy. Using all opportunities, he pursued the writing, and when the article was in form he read it to his close friend, Dr. Edward R. Taylor, who had formerly been Governor Haight's private secretary and was now his law partner in San Francisco. Taylor was much impressed; so much so that he urged George to reserve publication of the article and to give the subject a more extended treatment. After consideration, Mr. George decided to yield to the suggestion, concluding at length to make this the more extended politico-economic work, which, soon after the publication of "Our Land and Land Policy" in 1871, he realised would be necessary if he were to present his views properly. Those views had cleared and strengthened during the years of debate in his newspaper work, by his speeches, and through private conversations among his friends and acquaintances; while much, if intermittent, reading had made his mind a very arsenal of information; so that with quickened and sharpened powers of perception, statement and argument, and a new driving force in the widespread turmoil and distress, the elements were set in action to produce from the acorn of "Our Land and Land Policy" the oak of "Progress and Poverty." He realised that this would require elaborate and difficult work; that from his point of view so much confusion enshrouded political economy that he would have to clear away before he could build up; and that he would also have to write at once for those who had made no previous study of such subjects and for those who were familiar with economic reasonings.[1]   In accordance with this decision to expand the

1 Preface to fourth edition and all subsequent editions
of "Progress and Poverty."

writing, we find in the diary on November 5 an entry: "Started on 'Rent.' "

Meanwhile had come an important interruption. On October 2 the fourth child had been born—a girl. The other children—Harry, Dick and Jennie—were now fifteen, thirteen, and ten years old, respectively. The baby was named Anna Angela—Anna, after her mother, and Angela, as suggested by her aunt Sister Theresa Fox, because her birth came on the Feast of the Angels. The husband was all tenderness during this time of trial and he went to market daily for some dainty that might tempt his sick wife. From the pleasure he showed in providing these and other small luxuries, it was evident that his mind kept reverting to the terrible time when baby Dick was born and there was not a mouthful of food in the house to give to the mother.

Yet even now Old Adversity once in a while made his presence known. The year 1877 closed in hard times for the family, and memoranda among his papers show that Mr. George was personally $450 in debt. The meter inspector's office which was thought to be so lucrative was at the time yielding next to nothing. It was perhaps the necessity of eking out his livelihood during the work of writing on his book that caused him to turn to the idea of lecturing.

This idea held out some hope for him, for there was now an organisation composed of his friends and based upon his principles to support him. In the latter part of 1877 a few men, among them William M. Hinton, James G. Maguire, John M. Days, John Swett, Joseph Leggett, Patrick J. Murphy and A. L. Mann, met a few times with Henry George and his brother, John V. George, in Maguire's law office on Clay Street, above Montgomery, to discuss the economic parts of "Our Land and Land

Policy." These discussions resulted one Sunday afternoon early in 1878 in a meeting in the City Criminal
Court room, in which on other days of the week, Robert
Ferral, formerly on the editorial staff of the "Evening Post,"
sat as judge. At this meeting, perhaps thirty persons attending, "The Land Reform League of California" was
organised. It had for its purpose "the abolition of land
monopoly," and it was the first organisation of any kind
in the world to propagate Henry George's ideas. Joseph
Leggett, a lawyer, who was born in the county of Dublin,
Ireland, and who came to California in 1868, was elected
president; and Patrick J. Murphy, a newspaper writer
trained on the "Evening Post," became secretary.

About the first thing the League did was to invite
Henry George to deliver a pay lecture under its auspices
in one of the large halls of the city, and to take for his
text the prevailing industrial depression and labour troubles. Accordingly he laid aside work on his book to lecture at Metropolitan Temple, on March 26, under the title
of "Why Work is Scarce, Wages Low and Labour Restless." He was very nervous about his manner and voice,
and in the afternoon went to the hall for practice, inviting his wife to go with him. He went upon the platform
and made a few trials, reading from the manuscript of his
intended lecture. Mrs. George sat midway in the audi-
torium, and their old friend, George Wilbur, who had also
come, sat up in the gallery. Rev. Isaac S. Kalloch, who
delivered Sunday discourses in the hall, came in while
Mr. George was practising and said that if those were
the sentiments he intended to utter that night he would
talk over the heads of the workingmen whom he expected
mainly to compose his audience, since their selfish instincts
must be appealed to. Mr. George drew himself up and
replied: "Working men are men and are susceptible of lofty

aspirations. I never will consent to appeal to them on any but high grounds."

By eight o'clock that night the lecturer was seized by "stage fright"; though for that matter he never in the rest of his life, even after his long election campaigns and lecturing trips, was free from high nervous tension before speaking. There was reason enough that night for nervousness. He told no one, yet he was about to prove the ends for which he had desired to be a speaker. As the book on which he was at work was to contain his written message to the world, so now he intended to commence with this lecture his spoken word—to set forth his perceptions, thoughts, convictions, philosophy; to proclaim the equal rights of all men to the land as one potent means of ridding civilisation of involuntary poverty.

His expectations of a big audience were badly disappointed. All his friends had been interested in the lecture, and advertisements and notices had appeared in the daily papers, but the house, the largest and finest of the kind in the city, was only partly filled. Yet though his audience was small, his words were the words of hope, in this way closing his lecture:

"Only a little while ago nations were bought and sold, traded off by treaty and bequeathed by will. Where now is the right divine of kings? Only a little while ago, and human flesh and blood were legal property. Where are now the vested rights of chattel slavery?

"And shall this wrong that involves monarchy and involves slavery—this injustice from which both spring —long continue? Shall the ploughers forever plough the backs of a class condemned to toil? Shall the millstones of greed forever grind the faces of the poor?

"Ladies and gentlemen, it is not in the order of the universe! As one who for years has watched and waited, I tell you the glow of dawn is in the sky.

Whether it come with the carol of larks or the roll of
the war-drums, it is coming—it will come!

"The standard that I have tried to raise to-night may
be torn by prejudice and blackened by calumny; it may
now move forward, and again be forced back. But once
loosed, it can never again be furled!

"To beat down and cover up the truth that I have
tried to-night to make clear to you, selfishness will call
on ignorance. But it has in it the germinative force
of truth, and the times are ripe for it. If the flint
oppose it, the flint must split or crumble!

"Paul planteth, and Apollos watereth, but God giveth
the increase. The ground is ploughed; the seed is set;
the good tree will grow.

"So little now, only the eye of faith can see it. So
little now; so tender and so weak. But sometime, the
birds of heaven shall sing in its branches; sometime,
the weary shall find rest beneath its shade!"

A gleam was in the speaker's eye, hope shone in his
face; his shoulders were squared, his head was up. Intense earnestness and intense conviction were in his manner. It was as if he spoke with his soul. Yet when his
voice sank to the deep tones and he uttered the words,
"So little now, only the eye of faith can see it," it seemed
as though he spoke in an empty hall. He had started
out to preach his word to the world. His voice was like
a "cry in the wilderness."

Mr. George drew little money from this lecture, as the
expense very nearly equalled the receipts. Moreover, the
city newspapers dismissed it with few words. But as some
of the State papers noticed it favourably, he delivered it
in Sacramento and several of the other cities, under the
short title of "The Coming Struggle." But he nowhere
attracted large or even moderate sized audiences.

Measured in material results, the return from this lecturing effort was meagre, but he had made a start to

preach that faith which came from his heart's core; and that counted for more than all else to him.

Nor did he let this effort stand alone. He delivered another lecture a few months later, in June; one that must be considered to be in many respects the most fin-ished address he ever gave. The Young Men's Hebrew Association of San Francisco, had just then been organ-ised. It was composed of a number of bright, intelligent young men. They invited Mr. George to deliver their opening address. He accepted, but surprise and some-thing like embarrassment seized the progressive members when he announced "Moses" as his text, as they had looked for some live topic of the day. Their feelings changed when they heard the discourse. The leader of the Exodus was held up as the colossal ancient figure of the Hebrew nation. More than that, he was hailed as "one of those star souls that dwindle not with distance, but, glowing with the radiance of essential truth, hold their light while institutions and languages and creeds change and pass"; a "lawgiver and benefactor of the ages," who pointed the way for the new exodus—the exodus of the people of this modern age out of the bondage of poverty, and laid down a code for the observation of common rights in the soil and the establishment of a commonwealth, "whose ideal was that every man should sit under his own vine and fig-tree, with none to vex and make him afraid." The discourse abounded in vivid passages and exquisite imagery, so that at its close Dr. Elkan Cohen, Rabbi of the Temple Emanuel, turned to Max Popper, chairman of the lecture committee, and said with deep feeling, "Where did you find that man?"

Nevertheless Dr. Edward Taylor, who also had heard the address, observed to Mrs. George as they walked to a car on the way home: "Considered in itself, that lecture was a fine effort, but Mr. George is writing a book that is so much superior in importance that to stop for matters like this is like wasting time."

But if just now he gave no more time to lectures, he did give it to other things. Besides contributing an article entitled "Each and All" to a volume of miscellaneous essays published for the benefit of the Youth's Directory, a benevolent institution of the city, he gave much thought and labour to the organisation and establishment of the Free Public Library of San Francisco. As early as 1872 he had talked with State Senator Donovan in advocacy of this means of popular amusement and education, and in 1878 with other public-spirited citizens worked for the passage of a State law providing for the establishment of a number of public libraries in California. He became a member and the first secretary of the original Board of Trustees of the San Francisco library, the records showing the minutes in his handwriting and the same blue ink which he was using at the time in writing "Progress and Poverty."[1]

But the chief interruption to the work on the book grew out of politics. In obedience to a popular demand, the legislature had passed an act providing for the holding of a convention for the general amendment of the State constitution, delegates to which were to be elected in June. Seeing in this convention a possible opportunity to graft into the organic law of California his principles touching the taxation of land values, Mr. George issued early in May an address to the citizens of San Francisco, announcing himself as a candidate "for the support of such voters, or bodies of voters," as might deem that as a delegate he would fitly represent them. After declaring his general

---

[1] This library, with its several city branches, is the most complete west of the Rocky Mountains.

principles, he told in what particulars he would endeavour, so far as he had power, to amend the constitution, giving chief place to this:

> "That the weight of taxation may be shifted from those who have little to those who have much, from those who produce wealth to those who merely appropriate it, so that the monopoly of land and water may be destroyed, that wealth may be diffused among the many, instead of stagnating in the hands of a few; and an end put to the shameful state of things which compels men to beg who are willing to work."

The Land Reform League, of course, became active in support of George and of his principles, and it moreover issued a list of questions to be put to all candidates for the convention. Mr. George was nominated by the Democratic party and afterwards by the new Working men's party, which, rising from the discontent with social and political conditions, and drawing from both of the two old parties, had a strength that no one pretended to ignore.

With the double nomination, Mr. George seemed sure of election. All that remained was for him to go before the Working men's ratification meeting, and acknowledging the leadership of Kearney, subscribe to their party platform. But there the difficulty lay. He went before the meeting where others had gone before him, and was asked the questions in which others had smoothly and quietly acquiesced. His reply was almost a shout, "No!" He said he would acknowledge no man leader to do his thinking for him; that moreover there were some planks in their platform that he did not believe in and must oppose. He would receive their nomination as a free man or not at all. Hisses greeted his speech and the nomination was revoked.

This left him with the single nomination of the Democratic party, and with small prospects of election, for that party was known to be greatly weakened by the political upheaval. The whole Democratic ticket was beaten at the polls, but George received more votes than any other Democrat. His friend, Assemblyman Coffey, who had run on the same ticket, on the following morning called at the meter inspector's offiee. Not fiuding him in, he pinned a card on the door bearing the message: "Accept congratulations on leading the Democratic party to the devil!"

Thus, for the second time standing for the suffrages of the people, Mr. George had been beaten; but he had the consolation now, as in 1871 when he ran for the Assembly, of knowing that he had kept faith with himself.

He turned once more to work on his book and did not again suffer any important interruption.

CHAPTER X

"PROGRESS AND POVERTY" FINISHED.

1878-1879. AGE, 39-40.

ENTERING his library, one might witness the author, slightly inclined over an ample table in the centre of the room, writing on his book. Perhaps wearing a little house jacket, he sat, one hand holding the paper, the other moving a soft gold pen over it. And as he roused at sound of your entrance and turned and sank back, with one arm still on the table, the other thrown over the back of his chair, he raised a countenance not to be forgotten—a slight smile on the lips, a glow in the cheeks, tense thought in the brow and a gleam in the deep-blue eyes that looked straight through and beyond you, as if to rest on the world of visions of the pure in heart.

It was in a house on First Street,[1] near Harrison, to which the restless family now moved, that the main work on "Progress and Poverty" took place and the book was finished. For a while there was no parlour carpet, because the family could not afford to buy one, but the library, which was the workroom, was sufficiently furnished and was large and light and comfortable, and had three windows looking out on the bay.

Mr. George by gradual accumulation had acquired a

---

[1] No. 417 First Street.

library of nearly eight hundred volumes. They were his chief possessions in the world. They related to political economy, history and biography, poetry, philosophy, the sciences in popular form, and travels and discovery, with but few works of fiction. But these were only a few of the books he used, for he drew from the four public libraries of the city—the Odd Fellows, Mercantile, Mechanics and Free—and from the State Library at Sacramento; while he also had access to the books of his friends and acquaintances. Dating from the time of his leaving the "Evening Post," he had applied himself assiduously to reading, adding to a natural taste the sense of duty of storing his mind. His method or order of reading suited the needs of his work or the bent of his fancy, though he most frequently read poetry in the mornings before beginning labour, and after the midday and evening meals. He had not what would be called a musical taste or "ear," yet he said that all poetry that appealed to him—and it took a wide range—set itself to music in his mind.

He read mostly reclining, a pile of books drawn up beside him. He devoted himself with care to the reading of the standard works of political economy, yet freely confessed that of all books, these gave him the greatest labour. At night, if wakeful, he would ask his wife to, or would himself, take up some solid work, preferably some law treatise, which would invariably send him to sleep. He would frequently mark passages, and at times make notes; but he could generally with little difficulty turn to whatever in his past reading would serve an argument, fit as an illustration or adorn his diction. To most of his friends he seemed a browser rather than a deep reader, because he spent so little time on a book: and in truth, to use his own expression, he read "at" most books, not through them. Yet in this dipping he had the art of culling the particular parts that were useful to the purposes of his mind.

He needed eight hours sleep nightly, and what he lost at one time he would make up at another. He arose about seven, took a cold bath and dressed, careless about his outer clothes but invariably donning fresh linen. After breakfast he smoked a cigar and looked over the newspaper, then he stretched out on his lounge and read poetry for perhaps half an hour. And lying on his back he would do most of his thinking; but he also thought as he walked and smoked. He seldom sat in his chair except to write.

As he wrote much by inspiration, especially on the more elevated parts of his book, he could not always work at a set time or continuously. When his mind would not act to his suiting he would lie down and read, or go sailing or visit friends. To the casual observer his brain must have seemed intermittent in its operation; whereas, there really was an unconscious, or half conscious, cerebration when all the faculties seemed wholly occupied with outward trifles, for after such diversion he could write freely on the point that before was confused.

His writing, therefore, he did at any hour—early or late—suiting the state of his mind. Sometimes it fell in the middle of the night, when sleep was coy and thought surged. Brilliant passages of his book came in these hours, as by voluntary gift, and his pen ran rapidly over the paper. The analytical sections he wrote slowly and with labour, since this could not be dashed off, but required thought in conception, thought in construction, thought in the use of every word. Throughout the work he applied himself without saving, and if genius is the art of taking pains, his application bespoke consummate genius.

First came the rough drafting, in which he used a sys-

tem of simple marks to represent the smaller common
words. Numerous revisions and re-writings followed for
sense, arrangement and diction, the requirements of the
latter being clearness and simplicity, with a preference
for short, Saxon words. Over and over again he wrote,
arranged, expanded, contracted, smoothed and polished,
for his motto was, "What makes easy reading is hard
writing." When finished, the matter was submitted to
the criticism of his friends, and strengthened wherever, to
his view, they could find weak spots, so that eventually—
in the preface to the fourth edition of the book—he was
enabled to say that he "had yet to see an objection not
answered in advance in the book itself." Indeed, so un-
remitting was his toil that it might almost be said that the
labour of writing was with him finished only when the book
was printed and beyond further work.

Careless about his personal appearance, the greatest
neatness distinguished his manuscript. He wrote on sermon paper, for the most part in dark blue ink, with a
straight margin on the left-hand side. The words, in
large, clear letters, were separated by wide, even spaces.
The manuscript when finished was inviting and easy to
read. The influence of his father's plain, clear, direct
manner of thinking and speaking and of his mother's fine
nature and lofty language showed in his style so early that
he may be said to have been a born writer. And when
he sat down to write his book, common sense and melody
mingled harmoniously as the events of his restless life
rolled before him like a varied panorama—a panorama to
which books brought the parallels and contrasts of shade
and colour. As without knowledge of the schools, he
had read the suggestions of scenes about him, drawn his
own deductions and constructed his own philosophy; so
without training in the rules of style, he followed the

quick, nervous action, and force and cadence of his own mind. And type and illustration came as a natural consequence from life around—no man too common, no incident too trivial, to make a picture or grace an argument.

Points to treat and forms of speech to use were frequently set down, mostly on loose sheets, though two small blank books exist containing such notes, among them being two early ideas for a title—one of them, "Must Progress Bring Poverty?" another "Wealth and Want."

The eldest son had reached the top grade in the grammar school, which was thought to be enough schooling, so that he was taken away and became amanuensis to his father, at the same time studying shorthand with the view of taking dictations and in other ways becoming more helpful. Mrs. George gave every encouragement in her power and verified fair with marked copies of the manuscript. It was perhaps with this period taking chief place in his memory that Dr. Taylor, after his friend's death, said:

"Surely, never were man and woman closer to each other in affection and sympathy than were Mr. and Mrs. George—companions ever till death stepped between them; companions, too, of the noble sort that breasted together not only their own sufferings, but the sufferings of the world around them."

And so, too, the relations between Henry George and his friends were extremely warm; perhaps singular. As if in pursuance of his father's early injunction, to "make friends and use them," few men with close friends ever drew more from them. No matter how they differed among themselves, to him each offered earnest devotion. None of them was what could be called a political economist; yet for that matter George held that political economy is the one science that cannot be safely left to specialists, the one science which the ordinary man, without tools, apparatus or special learning, may most easily study.[1] At the beginning, at least, it was not so much the principles he proclaimed as it was two personal qualities he possessed that drew his chosen friends closely about him and commanded their strong support. One of these qualities was courage—described as "his sublime courage in attacking the most gigantic vested right in the world." The other quality was sympathy.

This quality of sympathy was, perhaps, Henry George's predominant trait of character. It had made him heartsick at sight of the want and suffering in the great city; it had impelled him to search for the cause and the cure. In the bonds of friendship it carried him into the other's thoughts and feelings. Intuitively he put himself into the other man's place and looked at the world through those other eyes. Rarely demonstrative in such circumstances, he did not speak of his sympathy, but it was as plain as if the word was written on his face. He had not studied man from the closet. He had all his rugged life been at school with humanity, and to him the type of humanity was the common man. Civilisation built up from the common man, flourished as the common man flourished, decayed and fell with the common man's loss of independence. He himself had climbed out on swaying yards like the commonest man, carried his blankets as a prospector and common miner, felt something of the hardships of farming, tramped dusty roads as a pedlar, had every experience as a printer, and suffered the physical and mental tortures of hunger. Learning and pride and power and

---

[1] This idea is expressed in all of his books, but most explicitly and fully in "The Science of Political Economy," General Introduction, p. xxxv.

tradition and precedent went for little with him; the human heart, the moral purpose, became the core thing. Towards him, from this very quality of sympathy, each friend—blacksmith or lawyer, man of little reading or lover of *belles-lettres*—had a singular consciousness of nearness—a feeling that this man could see *what* he himself saw and *as* he saw—could understand *his* labours, *his* sufferings, *his* aspirations. Nor was this condition peculiar to the "Progress and Poverty" period. It developed at that time and continued to Henry George's death. On the part of most of the men with whom he came in close contact, in California and in other parts of the world, there were feelings of attachment which if unspoken, were deep, solemn and lasting.

Among the friends closest to him during the writing of "Progress and Poverty" and whose criticism or counsel he asked in one particular or another were Assemblyman James V. Coffey, Ex-Assemblyman James G. Maguire, William Hinton and his oldest son, Charles; State Senator P. J. Donovan and Ex-State Senator John M. Days, John Swett, Principal of the Girl's High School; A. S. Hallidie, Regent of the University of California and Trustee of the Free Public Library; James McClatchy of the "Sacramento Bee"; H. H. Moore, the bookseller; and Dr. Edward R. Taylor. Two of them were Englishmen born, the others came from various parts of the United States. Not one of them had received a finished education in the European sense. All were positive, aggressive, independent men, representing distinct opinions, tastes and habits of life. Each had made his way in the community chiefly by the force of his own nature. George made requisition upon these different men for different purposes. But Taylor was the mainstay—the only man who read all of the manuscript and subsequently all of the proofs.

Edward R. Taylor had worked as purser on a Sacramento steamboat, set type and written for a newspaper,
studied and practised medicine, served as private secretary to Governor Haight, and afterwards studied law and
entered on a profitable practice in partnership with him.
With it all he had found time to attain many of the re-
finements of life, had read carefully and widely, made
himself master of polished verse and a competent judge
of the fine arts.   To him George made constant reference,
and he responded with tireless zeal.   After his friend's
death, Taylor said:[1]

"When 'Progress and Poverty' was in process, as on
its completion, it occurred to me that here was one of
those books that every now and again spring forth to
show men what man can do when his noblest emotions
combine with his highest mentality to produce something
for the permanent betterment of our common humanity;
that here was a burning message that would call the
attention of men to the land question as it had never
been called before; and that whether the message was

---

[1] The following lines were written by Mr. George in a copy of the
original edition of "Progress and Poverty" that he gave to Dr. Taylor:
TO
E. R. Taylor
this copy of a book which he knows from the first
and in the production of which
he has aided not only as compositor, proof-reader, critic and poet,
but still more
by the clearness of his judgment, the warmth of his sympathy, the
support of his friendship and the stimulation of his faith
is
on the day when the long, hard struggle breaks into the first success,
presented by Henry George
in token of feelings which it could but poorly
symbolise were it covered with gold and crusted with
diamonds.
San Francisco, Oct. 20, 1879.

embodied in an argument of absolute irrefragability or not, it was yet one that would stir the hearts of millions.

"And similarly, the author of the book never for a moment doubted that his travail had resulted in a great deliverance; and he firmly believed (this faith never once faltering up to the moment of his death) that he had pointed out the one true road for burdened humanity to follow."

During the work on "Progress and Poverty" the author gave many proofs of his preoccupation. This appeared mostly at table. He was impatient of service and was willing to commence and finish with anything, so long as he did not have to wait. One day at lunch he sat down in a dreamy way, drew a dish of cold stewed tomatoes towards him and helped himself bountifully, for he was very fond of them. By the time he had eaten them the other edibles were served. Presently his eyes fell upon the tomatoes at the farther end of the table. "Well," he said with some asperity, "am I not to have any tomatoes? Don't you know I like them?" At another time one of the boys on a Sunday evening went to the cupboard and took out a cake with the intention of eating some, for the family was accustomed on that day to take an early dinner. He had the knife in hand and was about to cut a slice, when he was caught in the act, so to speak, by his father's entrance. Instead of reproving him, as the boy half expected, the father took the knife, cut himself a slice and sat down to eat it, all the time in a reverie, holding the knife and forgetful of the boy. When that was eaten, he cut himself another and afterwards a third slice, still holding the knife. It was only then that he noticed that his son was not eating. "Here, have a piece," he said. "It is good."

As he was in these respects, so was he in others. While

contending with the loftiest problems possible for the human mind and writing a book that should verily stir the hearts of millions, there was no more personal show or pretence in or out of his workroom than if he were engaged daily in filling out government weather reports. Thoughtless of dress, and often abstracted, he was unconventional in speech, at times even to lapses in syntax. There was an utter absence of anything that was stiff or pompous. He could work with his boys over a toy boat in the yard and then go and help sail it; unbend to his older girl and talk doll and party until her eyes shone; sing and coo to the new baby and call her "sunshine"; discuss lighter literature with his wife as if it shaped his daily course; defer to a visitor who came to break bread as with an absorbed purpose to learn; lead in the merriment of a mild practical joke among his friends and laugh with the ring and cheer of boyhood over a comical story. There were times in the family when the strain of following the long examination and argument and of watching the multitude of details told on the strong, quick, high-strung nature with bursts of impatience; but they passed as April showers.

Though writing a book that was quickly to become famous, he could not absolutely foresee this. He believed he was writing the truth and this urged him on, yet constantly came the disheartening thought, how hopeless the effort, how futile the sacrifice; for what could avail against such stupendous odds? And while waged this inner conflict, there was outward stress and struggle, debts and difficulties. At one time just for a little ready money he pawned his watch. But despite all, he pressed on, until by the middle of March, 1879, almost a year and a half after he first sat down to it, the task was done. "On the night in which I finished the final chapter of 'Progress and Poverty,'" he subsequently wrote,[1] "I felt that the talent intrusted to me had been accounted for—felt more fully satisfied, more deeply grateful than if all the kingdoms of the earth had been laid at my feet."

The full meaning of these words, and what reveals the living fire that burned in the breast of him who uttered them and the religious zeal that possessed and drove him on, is to be found in a postscript to a letter he wrote four years later (February 1, 1883) to Rev. Thomas Dawson of Glencree, Ireland—a letter which in a former chapter we have quoted in part.[2] Written in his own hand, it was attached to a letter he had dictated to his eldest son and was never seen by any eye but Father Dawson's until after death had claimed its author.

"There is something else I wanted to say to you that I can only write with my own hand. Don't be disturbed because I am not a Catholic. In some things your Church is very attractive to me; in others it is repellent. But I care nothing for creeds. It seems to me that in any church or out of them one may serve the Master, and this also that faith that is the soul of your Church holds. And in my way, in the line that duty has seemed to call me, that I have tried to do. Because you are not only my friend, but a priest and a religious, I shall say something that I don't like to speak of— that I never before have told to any one. Once, in daylight, and in a city street, there came to me a thought, a vision, a call—give it what name you please. But every nerve quivered. And there and then I made a vow. Through evil and through good, whatever I have done and whatever I have left undone, to that I have been true. It was that that impelled me to write 'Progress and Poverty' and that sustained me when else I should have failed. And when I had finished the last page, in the dead of night, when I was entirely

---

1 Preface to "The Science of Political Economy."	2 Page 193.

alone, I flung myself on my knees and wept like a child. The rest, was in the Master's hands. That is a feeling that has never left me; that is constantly with me. And it has led me up and up. It has made me a better and a purer man. It has been to me a religion, strong and deep, though vague—a religion of which I never like to speak, or make any outward manifestation, but yet that I try to follow. Believe this, my dear father, that if it be God's will I should be a Catholic, he will call me to it. But in many different forms and in many different ways men may serve Him.

"Please consider this letter to *yourself alone*. I have only said this much to you because you wrote my wife hoping I would become a Catholic. Do not disturb yourself about that. I do not wish you not to be a Catholic. Inside of the Catholic Church and out of it; inside of all denominations and creeds and outside of them all there is work to do. Each in the station to which he has been called, let us do what is set us, and we shall not clash. From various instruments, set to different keys, comes the grand harmony. And when you remember me in your prayers, which I trust you sometimes will, do not ask that I shall be this or that, but only for grace, and guidance, and strength to the end."

CPSIA information can be obtained
at www.ICGtesting.com
Printed in the USA
BVHW09*1317160818
524721BV00015B/1045/P